623.4      Bishop, Chris
ENC        The encyclopedia of
           weapons of World War
           II
                    SEP     2008


                    DATE DUE

OCT 0 2 2008
NOV 1 9 2008

# The Rise and Fall of
# IMPERIAL
# JAPAN

# The Rise and Fall of IMPERIAL JAPAN

Millis Public Library
Auburn Road
Millis, Mass. 02054

36462

NOV 10 1987

**THE MILITARY PRESS**

New York

A BISON BOOK

This edition is published by
The Military Press, distributed by
Crown Publishers Inc.

Produced by
Bison Books Corp
17 Sherwood Place
Greenwich CT 06830
USA

First published in 1976 as
*The Japanese War Machine* by
Bison Books Limited

Copyright © 1976 Bison Books
Limited

Copyright © 1984 Bison Books
Corp.

All rights reserved. No part of
this publication may be
reproduced, stored in a retrieval
system or transmitted in any
form by any means, electronic,
mechanical, photocopying or
otherwise, without first obtaining
written permission of the
copyright owner.

Printed in Hong Kong

ISBN 0-517-423138

H G F E D C B

Reprinted 1984

A.J. BARKER graduated from the Staff College, Quetta in India and the Royal Military College of Science in Shrivenham, England. Colonel Barker campaigned in Somaliland, Ethiopia, the Middle East, Burma and Malaya and has written, among his many works, *Pearl Harbor, Midway, Rape of Ethiopia, The March on Delhi* and *Behind Barbed Wire*, the highly praised study of prisoners of war. He is presently living and writing in Capetown, South Africa.

**Chapter 11.**

RONALD HEIFERMAN was educated at Brooklyn College, Yale University and New York University and has specialized in modern Chinese and Japanese history. Author of *Flying Tigers* and *World War II* and co-author of *Wars of the 20th Century*, he is working on a study of Philippine politics immediately prior to World War II. He is an Associate Professor of History and Assistant to the President of Quinnipiac College, Connecticut.

**Chapters 1, 5, 7, 9 and 12.**

IAN V. HOGG served in the British Army for 27 years, completing his career with the rank of Master Gunner. Among his many works are *Armies of the American Revolution, The Guns: 1939–45, The Guns of World War II, German Secret Weapons, Artillery, The Guns: 1914–18, German Pistols and Revolvers* and his forthcoming *Infantry Weapons of World War II*. He is one of the world's leading specialists in the study of artillery and small arms.

**Chapters 2 and 3.**

# CONTENTS

JOHN GRAYSON KIRK was educated at Harvard University and Columbia University. A former US naval intelligence officer, he has written extensively on the battles and weaponry of World War II. He is at present editor-in-chief in a large American publishing firm.

**Chapter 6.**

WILLIAM J. KOENIG was educated at Yale University and the London School of Oriental and African Studies. He has specialized in Southeast Asian history and has written *Over the Hump, Epic Sea Battles.* He co-edited *European Manuscript Sources of the American Revolution* and *The World Wars: Manuscript Sources in the United Kingdom.* An author of numerous articles on Southeast Asia in World War II, he is presently working on a study of Burmese politics in the late 18th and early 19th centuries.

**Chapters 8 and 10.**

ANTONY PRESTON was educated at the University of Witwatersrand, South Africa and served on the staff of the National Maritime Museum, Greenwich. Among his many works are *Navies of the American Revolution, Battleships of World War I, Submarines, V and W Destroyers* and his most recent work, *An Illustrated History of the Navies of World War II.* An editor of *Navy International* he is one of the world's foremost specialists in modern naval history.

**Chapter 4.**

兵徴募
海軍志願

# INTRODUCTION BY S.L.MAYER

BELOW LEFT: Japanese naval troops march through Osaka on their way to the China campaign in 1941.

RIGHT: General Hideki Tojo, Prime Minister of Japan 1941–44, on the cover of a wartime picture magazine *Photo Weekly*.

FAR RIGHT: Members of the Kwantung Army Pioneers in Manchuria. The Kwantung Army was feared because of its successes against the Soviets in the 1930s, but it was never used in World War II. It was estimated to have had over a million men in the early stages of the war.

BOTTOM RIGHT: A Japanese naval squadron with its aerial escort in the early days of the Pacific war.

Japan's popular image in the Western World has been colored, not to say damaged, by the propaganda of World War II. The comic strips and bizarre films produced during the war and immediately after which portrayed the Japanese as something less than human, buck-teethed, grinning demons who liked nothing better than to torture and kill Anglo-Saxons was not enhanced by the genuinely terrifying zeal of the *kamikazes* toward the end of the war and the rather apologetic attempts by Hollywood to rectify racist-inspired, wartime errors, as in Marlon Brando's screen versions of *Sayonara* and *The Teahouse of the August Moon*. Once the madman prepared to justify any act to serve his Emperor, the Japanese was now seen as the civilized creator of ornamental flower-arrangements, the appreciator of the moribund delicacy of the geisha or the contemplator of falling cherry blossoms. More recently, in the light of Japan's dramatic economic recovery since the war, the Japanese have been popularly viewed through the bifocals of admiration and jealousy as the super-efficient, globetrotting businessmen purveying Japanese-built television sets and automobiles with the missionary zeal of atonement for war crimes both real and imagined.

While all of these caricatures are as pathetic as they are absurd, like all cartoon figures, they contain more than a small measure of recognizable truth. As contradictory as each definition of the Japanese character may be, they almost disguise the fact that the Japanese people themselves are equally contradictory. The Japanese are a people wedded to the past as they chart and create the future. This dichotomy of alienation with the present as they test and surpass its boundaries has been a characteristic of the Japanese people ever since the decision was taken in the 1860s to absorb Western technology and folkways into the nation in order to prevent the destruction of the essence of the Japanese national character (*kokutai*) through colonization, which appeared more than possible just over a hundred years ago. The heart of the problem lies in the fact that in becoming superficially Westernized the *kokutai* may be destroyed or permanently altered by the Japanese themselves. This contradiction, as important to understanding Japan today as it is to understanding the history of the past century, was never more present during the years before and during the Second World War.

The Japanese warrior tradition was a thousand years old when a group of *samurai* from the Provinces (*han*) of Satsuma, Choshu, Hizen and Tosa conspired to overthrow the Tokugawa shogunate (*Bakufu*) and establish the Emperor Meiji as *de facto* ruler of Japan in 1868. These *samurai* took this step when it became clear that under the *Bakufu*, modernization which could stave off Western invasion would never take place. In the generation which followed the Meiji Restoration of 1868 Japan sought to create a modern industrial machine as well as a defense force which could ward off invasion from the West. Japan had seen how other oriental nations had been humiliated by Western arms – China, India, and the countries of Southeast Asia – and was unwilling to be dealt with in such a cursory manner. The first test of the nascent Japanese War Machine came in the Sino-Japanese War of 1894–95. Although Japan won a stunning victory against a poorly-equipped and badly-organized Chinese Army and Navy, two facts became readily apparent to Japan's new masters: first, all the spoils of war could be stripped from them by a mere piece of paper, what William Langer called the Far Eastern Triplice, when Russia, France and Germany ordered Japan to remove her troops from territory recently won in the war, the strategically located Liaotung Peninsula in southern Manchuria. Secondly, Japan's military might could handle an Asian enemy, but was no match for a combination of Western forces which might be ranged against her. Japan had no choice but to renew her efforts to build a modern army and navy and to look for a Western ally in order to accomplish this end.

Japan found her ally in Great Britain, which at the turn of this century was without diplomatic friends in Europe and which was shown to be vulnerable to the actions of a few thousand Dutch-speaking South Africans in the attenuated Boer War. With Germany rearming Britain wanted to withdraw forces from the Far East and elsewhere to strengthen her position closer to home, and signed the Anglo-Japanese alliance in 1902. This document protected Japan against a renewal of the Triplice and permitted her, as an ally, to purchase military equipment of a high standard which at the time she was unable to produce in quantity herself. Although Japan had already placed orders for ships in British yards, the alliance placed her in a more favorable

position to acquire weapons of war virtually on demand. When Japan avenged the humiliation of 1895 in the attack on Russian Port Arthur in the Liaotung Peninsula early in 1904, Japan took her first step on the road to world recognition as a major military power. It was the first step toward her involvement in World War II. While her victory over Russia stunned the world, Japan found herself at the end of the conflict with only one significant rival for hegemony in the Pacific: the United States. Japan as well had become the champion of Asian nationalism, since it was Japan which was the first country in Asia to defeat a Western power in modern times. Asian nationalists in China, Indonesia and India took heart at what had happened at Port Arthur and Tsushima. Japan's victory proved the West was not invulnerable.

Racist claims of white superiority were disproved, and Japan saw herself as not only the leader of a pan-Asian attempt to rid the area of the Westerners; she saw herself as a world power ready to take her place as a world-class decision-maker equal to all and second to none.

The Western powers did not view Japan's victory in the same light. Britain tried unsuccessfully to dissuade Japan from entering World War I and was subjected to heavy criticism from her Antipodean Dominions, Australia and New Zealand, for allowing Japan to seize so much territory from Germany in 1914–15. The capture of Shantung Province placed Japan in a dominant position in North China, but the acquisition of the Marshalls, Marianas and Carolines gave Japan dominance in the Western Pacific which threatened Australia's

north coast. Her rapid victory did not escape the notice of the United States either, whose Philippine colony lay exposed to possible Japanese attack from two sides. But there was little the Anglophone nations could do. Japan was determined to create a sphere of influence in the Pacific and continued to build and rebuild a war machine to maintain and expand it.

Although the Western victors in World War I could not deny Japan the spoils of her easy conquests at the Paris Peace Conference in 1919, they did try to limit Japanese naval expansion at the Washington Conference of 1921–22. On balance the terms were not unreasonable, but within a Japanese context it was difficult to justify either to the voters or to the growing military machine the fact that Japan was still being treated as an in-

BELOW: Admiral Soemu
Toyoda, C-in-C Combined
Fleet.

ferior. While this was not of primary importance during the 1920s when business, particularly with the US, was good, it quickly became of vital importance when the Depression began in 1930. Japan, as a recently industrialized state, was hit first and hardest by the slump in America which soon became worldwide. Since Chiang's China was already encroaching on Japan's sphere of influence in Manchuria, it was inevitable that someone would take action. In the event, it was the Japanese Army which acted alone in seizing the whole of Manchuria in 1931. From this point on the position of civilian government in Japan began to crumble. The Army and the Navy vied for influence with the government, the industrial barons and the Emperor. Greater incursions were made in China and government by assassination became the rule of the day.

Was there any way for the West to mitigate these steps which can now be seen to have led Japan down the road to authoritarian government, war with the West, and inevitable defeat? Certainly the West could have been less hypocritical in allowing Japan a tangible sphere of influence in China. But even this would not have appeased the leaders of an ever-powerful Japanese War Machine to achieve hegemony at home and dominance abroad. Japan was diplomatically isolated in an increasingly dangerous world in the 1930s. Her industrial development, still in a formative stage, demanded a secure market and source of raw materials in a world economic crisis. Led by men whose training and upbringing echoed the warrior code of *Bushido* transmitted to them from scores of generations of *samurai* administrators, Japan, in her search for security, could not fail to turn to those who were prepared to find international security in a decisive way. It was the only way they knew: the way of the warrior.

Yet, because of her still slender industrial base, Japan could not hope to wage war and win it on her own. Japan's conquest of China was as easy as it was brutal in its early stages, but in order to achieve final victory, if final victory over a nation like China was ever possible, Japan needed raw materials which still lay in Western hands. The choice was retreat and humiliation, or bold attack and certain defeat. To a warrior defeat with honor was preferable, and to them, defeat was by no means certain. If victory was attainable, the opportunity of a

millenium had to be taken. When the Japanese War Machine took on the West at Pearl Harbor, the honorable, heroic and disastrous decision was made.

The contradictions of Japan's rapid rise to world power became all too evident in the four years of World War II in the Pacific. In China the Japanese War Machine was already stretched to its limits; after Pearl Harbor it reached the breaking point. The amazing resilience of the Japanese people and their continual inventiveness kept the machine going. The courage and tenacity of her fighting men compensated for the lack of pilots, planes and ships when Japan's industrial capacity broke down under the dual pressures of Allied bombing and fundamental weakness. Nevertheless Japan held off the most powerful industrial nation for four years. She dominated Southeast Asia and China as no modern nation has ever done. Her ferocity in battle and courage in the face of disaster was second to none in the greatest war the world has ever known.

The Japanese War Machine had many

BELOW: Japanese Army Ki-21 Sally bombers over Corregidor Island in the Philippines in May 1942. Corregidor's fall represented the collapse of the last vestiges of American power in the western Pacific and complete victory for Japan in their 100-day offensive which began with Pearl Harbor.

RIGHT: Admiral Chuichi Nagumo, C-in-C First Air Fleet.

BOTTOM: Pilots of the Naval Air Force play with their mascot in the heady days of victory for the Japanese War Machine.

facets. Tanks, small arms, ships, planes and artillery were its tools. The warrior spirit of medieval Japan was its engine. Placed in the hands of Japanese men imbued with nationalistic fervor, it was a formidable weapon. The authors of this study of the Japanese War Machine analyze every aspect from both a technical and historical point of view, from the origins of the modern Japanese state to the battles in which this war machine took part, from the jungles of Burma and the great carrier battles of Coral Sea and Midway to the greatest naval battle ever fought, Leyte Gulf. Through their eyes the myths of wartime propaganda and postwar apologia are swept aside. What emerges from their work are the fundamental contradictions in the character of the Japanese people, contradictions which still remain in Japan's *kokutai*. Westerners ignored them to their discredit in the prewar years, and the price we paid to learn was far too high. They must still be examined today, because in one respect the situation is different. Japan is now the third largest industrial nation in the world.

兵徴募
海軍志願

# THE RISING SUN

BOTTOM: The *Chen Yuen*, a Chinese battleship built in 1882, shortly after her capture by the Japanese. She was taken into the Japanese Navy and renamed *Chin Yen*.

RIGHT: The Battle of the Yalu River during the Sino-Japanese War of 1894–95 destroyed the nascent Chinese fleet and established the Japanese Navy as a significant factor in the power struggle for the partition of China. The Japanese battleship *Saikyomaru* under the command of Admiral Kashiyama attacks the Chinese flagship and other vessels in the Yellow Sea.

On 3 January 1868, samurai from Satsuma, Choshu, and other domains forced the abdication of the Tokugawa shogun, Keiki, and proclaimed an imperial restoration, ending a period of two and one-half centuries of Tokugawa rule during which time real power was exercised by a military regime (*bakufu*) in Edo (Tokyo) while the Imperial Court in Kyoto retained only symbolic and ceremonial power. Thus began the Meiji Restoration, one of the most unusual events in modern history.

The decline of the Tokugawa shogunate, which had begun decades before 1868, was hastened by the American and subsequent European efforts to 'open' Japan to Western commercial and religious entrepreneurs. Coming at a time when the Tokugawa system was threat-ened by political dissension and economic decline, Commodore Perry's arrival in Tokyo Bay in 1853 precipitated an external crisis and opened up a Pandora's box which the shogunate could not close, leaving the Tokugawa regime further weakened and exposed and paving the way for its demise some fifteen years later.

To be sure, Tokugawa authorities had little choice but to accept Western overtures and end the policy of seclusion which they had instituted some two hundred years earlier. To have done otherwise would have been to invite an extension of gunboat diplomacy from the China coast into Japan. Being aware of the disastrous consequences of the Opium War in China and other military incursions by Europeans elsewhere in Asia, Tokugawa authorities were anxious to

12

BOTTOM: The Chinese cruiser *Chen Yuen* was sunk by the Japanese after its capture in the harbor of Weihaiwei in February 1895. This tactic, common to the Japanese Navy during that period, prevented the Chinese from using their Shantung port during the final stages of the Sino-Japanese War.

RIGHT: The Japanese cruiser *Matsushima* in the Tategami drydock in Nagasaki during its construction in the 1890s.

preclude a similar disaster in their country and acceded to Perry's ultimatum as well as similar demands from other European powers. Although such concessions spared the Japanese a Western occupation, Tokugawa authorities were hardly lauded for their efforts. On the contrary, they were criticized for failing to prepare the country to withstand foreign pressures and for having allowed Japan's defenses to fall behind those of the West.

In a futile effort to silence the considerable criticism of their policy of accomodation with the West which poured forth from friends and foes alike, the Tokugawa house turned toward the Imperial Court in Kyoto to provide sanction and legitimacy for the policy of opening up the country. Not only did this effort fail but it further exposed the weakness of the shogunate, making it possible for opposing lords (daimyo) and samurai to step up their efforts to influence the court and oppose the *bakufu*. When such opposing forces joined hands in the late 1860's, the fate of the Tokugawa shogunate was sealed. With their new Western weapons and superiority in numbers of samurai, the anti-Tokugawa coalition had little trouble in executing their *coup d'état* in 1868. Their real problem was not the physical overthrow of the old order but, rather, the substitution of new institutions capable of providing a unified and strong government for the country in a perilous new age.

The men who engineered the Imperial restoration did not have a program for creating a new state. They did, however, share certain values and perceptions which ultimately allowed them to fashion a viable new regime. Foremost among these was the view that only a strong, unified, and centrally administered political system could succeed in protecting the country from further foreign incursions. Rallying behind the Meiji Emperor and taking advantage of his vast symbolic and sacedotal powers, the men who were to lead the government inaugurated a series of programs designed to strengthen the state and evolve a new governance system immediately after the restoration in January 1868.

The first obstacle to realizing effective central administration of the country was the continued existence of the some 250 odd semi-autonomous domains (*han*) of the daimyo. As long as these remained independent of the new regime in Tokyo, there could be no significant political reform nor could the government raise the funds necessary for the modernization of Japan's armed forces. Realizing this fact, Meiji leaders took quick action, first redefining the relationship between the domains and the new government in 1869 and then abolishing the han altogether by the end of 1871, pensioning off the daimyo and samurai in return for their passive acceptance of the new order and to compensate them for the loss of their former economic and political power which inevitably followed from the abolition of the domains. In place of the han, the Meiji government established new administrative units (*ken*) and appointed administrative heads for each of these units.

The abolition of the daimyo domains brought all territory under the control of the central government and provided the new regime with tax revenues far greater than any the Tokugawa house might have drawn from its own estates. This new tax base would permit the Meiji leaders to undertake a rapid improvement of Japan's defenses, including the creation of a central army based on conscription in place of the han armies based on samurai privilege, thus further strengthening the state and placing it on a par with the European states. The new army and navy would be trained by European officers and equipped with the most modern weaponry that could be purchased abroad. Furthermore, Meiji leaders also sought to found modern arsenals and shipyards in Japan so that self-sufficiency in munitions production might quickly be achieved. Unlike their reluctant counterparts in China, Japanese leaders had little hesitation about adopting Western technology to serve the nation's needs. Above all, it was their intention to strengthen the country and preclude foreign invasion or incursion.

In the process of abolishing the daimyo

OVERLEAF: The *Matsushima* in action during the Battle of the Yalu River against the Chinese. She is flanked by typical uniforms of Japanese soldiers during the Sino-Japanese War copying European uniforms of the period. On the left is a corporal, on the right is a general of the Army. Both uniforms indicate the influence of Prussia on the Japanese Army.

the Hermit Kingdom was still minimal as was Chinese control over the Korean monarchy despite the traditional tributary relationship which had linked China and Korea for centuries. Indeed, the new Meiji government had made overtures to 'open-up' Korea as early as 1868 only to be rebuffed, thus providing the rationale for some kind of an armed incursion which might provide temporary employment for the ex-samurai as well as a relatively cheap victory. In short, had the Meiji regime wished to press the matter, it would not have had to look far for support. The fact that the Meiji leaders eventually chose not to take advantage of this opportunity, even after preliminary preparations for such an invasion were launched in 1873, reflected no lack of popular support but, rather, indicates that other considerations were considered of greater weight than public opinion.

The abortion of the Korean expedition in 1874 was based upon two fundamental assumptions. First, Meiji leaders feared that the cost of a war in Korea might quickly deplete the meager resources of the new regime. Second and perhaps more important, preoccupation with the Korean venture would divert attention and resources from necessary domestic programs of reform and economic development. These arguments were sufficient to persuade some Meiji leaders to sacrifice expansion into Korea, at least for the time being, in favor of modernization. Others, e.g. Saigo, Itagaki, and Ito, did not accept this view and resigned from the government, creating the first major crisis of the post-restoration period.

Advocates of the Korean expedition did not limit their protests to resignation from their government posts. Some of them, like Saigo Takamori of Satsuma, continued to press for such a campaign

domains and creating a new conscript army, Meiji leaders advertently destroyed the samurai as an elite class by abolishing their former privileges. This fact was formally recognized in 1873 when the Meiji government abolished samurai status as such, forbidding the former samurai to wear the traditional trappings of their class including the famous short and long swords. Although many of the Meiji leaders were themselves of samurai origin, they recognized the need for certain egalitarian measures in order to fashion the new society they wished to create and took them without hesitation, although considerable problems were created in doing so.

As the Meiji period progressed, the plight of the ex-samurai worsened. Stripped of their elite status and pensioned off on frugal annual stipends which were eventually commuted into a single lump sum payment, part in cash and part in government notes, the former samurai found themselves floating in a strange new world, a world in which many of them could not survive. Increasingly they looked toward the new regime to provide some outlet and opportunity for their talents and energies. Among the remedies for their ills most often suggested was an expansion of Japanese interests into Korea, a proposal which had support in other quarters as well.

For leaders of the ex-samurai, Korea seemed a fertile and ready opportunity for the expansion of Japanese interests on the Asian mainland. European interest in

while organizing former samurai of his domain into an opposition military force which would soon challenge the authority of the Meiji regime. In 1877 Saigo and 20,000 of his followers launched a full-scale rebellion against the government. Although Saigo's forces were eventually defeated by the new conscript army of 40,000, thus proving the superiority of the new army over traditional samurai forces, the idea of Japanese expansion onto the Asian mainland did not die with the suppression of the Satsuma Rebellion. On the contrary, patriotic societies and conservative political critics nurtured the idea and kept it very much alive.

The decade which followed the suppression of the Satsuma Rebellion saw a major expansion of Japanese military and naval forces which would eventually facilitate the expansion of Japanese interests that Saigo and his supporters had so earnestly advocated. In 1878 Yamagata Aritomo reorganized the Imperial Army along German lines, expanding its numbers to approximately 75,000 men on active service with another 200,000 in reserve status. This whole force was equipped with modern weaponry, much of which was by this time of Japanese manufacture. Not to be outdone, the Imperial Navy also underwent an important reorganization and expansion which brought its strength from 17 ships of 14,000 gross tons in 1872 to 28 ships, all ironclad, of some 57,000 gross tons by 1894. That the Meiji government took the matter of defense seriously can also be seen in the fact that by the end of the nineteenth century approximately one-third of the national budget was being appropriated for the Army and Navy.

The decade of the 1880s not only saw the rapid modernization of Japan's armed forces; it was also marked by an increase in the activities of nationalist groups and patriotic societies, several of which revived the idea of expanding Japanese interests into Korea. Thanks to the efforts of groups like the Genyosha which had been formed in 1881 by supporters of Saigo's Satsuma Rebellion, large numbers of Japanese became convinced of the need for some kind of continental expansion. The Meiji government could not long ignore such pressures. Furthermore, Chinese reluctance to recognize Japanese interests in Korea forced the hand of the government, leading to a negotiated settlement of Sino–Japanese interests in Korea in 1885.

The Sino–Japanese Accord of 1885,

although unsatisfactory from the point of view of patriotic societies in Japan, remained in force until 1894 at which time a crisis in Korea precipitated an armed clash between China and Japan. Although it was an internal political crisis in Korea which triggered the Sino–Japanese War, it is clear that larger considerations dictated the decisions of Peking and Tokyo to risk war in order to establish which power would dominate the Korean peninsula. The Chinese, threatened by Anglo–French expansion in Burma and Indochina, determined to take a stand against further enchroachment on the tribute system in Korea, believing the Japanese to be much less formidable adversaries than the British or French. The Japanese, having completed the modernization of their armed forces by 1894 and under intense domestic pressure for some action on the continent, were now willing to risk war to establish their supremacy in Korea. With both parties holding fast to such incompatible positions, war was inevitable.

Formal declarations of war were issued by both China and Japan in August 1894. Soon thereafter, in a series of relatively easy but nevertheless stunning victories, Japanese forces quickly overran the Korean peninsula. Much to the surprise of European observers and the Japanese themselves, the Imperial Army swept through Korea in less than two months time, crossing into Manchuria early in October 1894 by which time the Imperial Navy already controlled the Yellow Sea. By the beginning of 1895, Japanese forces had moved through the Liaotung Peninsula and were poised to advance south toward Peking. Given this situation, the Chinese sued for peace, sending Li Hungchang to Japan to arrange terms for the cessation of hostilities.

In April 1895 the Chinese and Japanese came to terms and signed the peace treaty ending the Sino–Japanese War. The Treaty of Shimonoseki eliminated Chinese claims to suzerainty in Korea, ceded Formosa and the Liaotung Peninsula to Japan, recognized Japan as a 'most-favored nation' in China, and provided for a large cash indemnity to be paid to Japan. The Japanese had won a psychological as well as a military victory, emerging from the Sino–Japanese War as a Pacific power to be reckoned with. But by so doing, the Meiji government soon found itself embroiled in a new struggle with other interested parties.

The ink was hardly dry on the Treaty

BELOW: Tasuka Sereta as a midshipman at the US Naval Academy, Annapolis, Class of 1881. He attained the rank of Rear Admiral in the Japanese Navy at the time of his death in 1900.

of Shimonoseki when the European powers intervened to voice concern over Japanese expansion on the Asian mainland. On 23 April 1895 Russian, French, and German diplomats expressed the displeasure of their governments over Japanese annexation of the Liaotung Peninsula, threatening a possible tripartite intervention if the Meiji government did not return this area to Chinese control. Faced by such a real threat, Meiji leaders reluctantly agreed to return the Liaotung Peninsula to China. In so doing, they avoided another war but the return of the territory was seen in Japan as a national humiliation and cost the Meiji leaders dearly in terms of public opinion. Furthermore, this humiliation gave impetus to new calls for self-strengthening so that further concessions to the Europeans might be avoided even at the risk of war.

In 1896 the Meiji government embarked on its second major expansion of the Imperial Army, nearly doubling its strength. In 1897 a comparable naval construction program was started. By 1903 the Imperial Navy had added four battleships, sixteen cruisers, 23 destroyers, and countless smaller vessels to its already impressive fleet. As might be imagined, the cost of these programs was staggering but one that was born of necessity by Japan's leaders.

In addition to strengthening Japan's armed forces to preclude another foreign intrusion into Japanese foreign policy, Meiji leaders also sought allies among the powers, finding one in the British government as early as 1902. The Anglo-Japanese Alliance of that year was based upon common British and Japanese concern over Russian interests in

Manchuria. For the British, Russian dominance in Manchuria posed a threat to their interests in China. For the Japanese, Russia's presence in Manchuria presented a similar threat to their interests in Korea.

From Japan's point of view, the Anglo–Japanese Alliance was a diplomatic triumph. Although the treaty did not obligate the British to come to the aid of the Japanese in the event of a conflict with Russia or vice versa, it did recognize Japan's interests in China and Korea and put the Japanese in a better position to deal with Russia should there be any further disagreements about respective spheres of influence. Furthermore, because the Anglo-Japanese Alliance promised aid to Japan in the event of an attack by two or more parties, a second tripartite intervention would prove less attractive to the powers.

Encouraged by the new alliance with England, Japanese leaders proposed a diplomatic settlement of the Manchurian question to the Tsarist government in June 1903. When this initiative failed, Japanese leaders prepared for war, sending a final ultimatum to the Russians in January 1904. The Russians refused to accede to Japan's demand for the withdrawal of all forces from Manchuria. Furthermore, they sent troops across the Korean border at the beginning of February, inviting Japanese reprisal in the process. On 10 February 1904 Japan declared war on Russia.

RIGHT: A Japanese soldier during the Russo-Japanese War 1904–05. They were equipped with Type 30 rifles, the first modern Japanese anti-personnel weapon, a five-shot rifle with 6.5mm ammunition.

BOTTOM: The Japanese battleship *Hatsuse*, built by the British, on the Tyne in 1903. She was sunk by a mine off Port Arthur by Russia in 1904.

Japan's first goal in the Russo–Japanese War was to win control of the straits between Japan and Korea so that Japanese forces could be safely dispatched to reinforce troops already stationed in Korea. This was accomplished on 13 April 1904 when the Russian fleet was defeated outside of Port Arthur. With this done, Japanese troops were rushed into Korea. By 1 May the Imperial Army crossed into Manchuria, laying siege to Port Arthur and forcing the Russian army to retreat north to Mukden which was also placed under siege. Port Arthur was not taken until January 1905 and not without significant casualties and losses on both sides. Mukden fell to the Japanese at the end of March under similar circumstances. The last great battle of the war was decided in May when Admiral Togo's fleet decimated the Russian Baltic fleet in the Tsushima Straits on the 27th of the month.

Although the Japanese had won a stunning psychological victory over the Russians, their resources had been strained to the limit by the war. As a consequence, Japanese leaders were eager to arrange an end to the hostilities and asked the United States to mediate a settlement with the Romanov government. The Russians, for their part, were also anxious to be done with the war. Faced with domestic unrest and rebellion, a renewal of hostilities with the Japanese made little sense. Thus, when Theodore Roosevelt agreed to host a peace conference in

LEFT: Japanese troops landing in Korea in the early stages of the Russo-Japanese War, February 1904.

CENTER: Admiral Count Heihachiro Togo, Commander-in-Chief of the Japanese Navy during the Russo-Japanese War, the hero of the Battles of Port Arthur and Tsushima.

RIGHT: Japanese howitzer battery before Port Arthur during the long siege which reduced the Russian-held fortress-port.

FAR RIGHT: Russian gun batteries defend Port Arthur during the siege.

BOTTOM RIGHT: The capitulation of Port Arthur. The Russians depart as the Japanese enter the city.

the United States, both the Russians and Japanese promptly dispatched delegations to the conference.

Japanese and Russian diplomats arrived in Portsmouth, New Hampshire, the site eventually selected by Roosevelt for the talks in August 1905. Within a month a draft treaty was ready for ratification. In its final form the Treaty of Portsmouth recognized Japanese interests in Korea and southern Manchuria. It did not, on the other hand, provide for an indemnity to Japan, nor did the Russians agree to other territorial concessions demanded by the Japanese. Since their resources were depleted and the Russians seemed willing to break off the talks if the Japanese persisted in all of their demands, the Japanese government gave way on the question of the indemnity and certain territorial questions, paving the way for the signing of the treaty on 5 September 1905.

The Treaty of Portsmouth was not well received in Japan where the public had assumed that the peace settlement would be more favorable to Japan. On the other hand, the Japanese were able to take comfort and pride in the fact that for the first time in modern history, an Asian nation had defeated a European power. If the Anglo-Japanese Alliance had resulted in Japan's entry into the family of nations as a full-fledged power, her victory over Russia was of even greater significance, paving the way for further expansion on the Asian mainland and providing her with a leadership role among the Asian peoples.

Within two months after the signing of the Treaty of Portsmouth, Korea became a Japanese protectorate. Five years later Korea was annexed. During the same period, the Japanese also expanded their control and interests in Manchuria, forming the South Manchuria Railway Company and investing heavily in mining, public utilities, and commercial activities. Manchuria had become an economic colony of Japan by the time of the death of the Meiji Emperor in 1912.

The outbreak of the European War in August 1914 provided the Japanese with yet another opportunity to expand their interests on the Asian mainland. Although the Anglo-Japanese Alliance did not specifically apply to European hostilities, the Okuma Cabinet was quick to declare war on Germany, seeing an immediate opportunity to gain a foothold in China proper by annexing German leaseholds and concessions in China.

The Japanese lost no time in attacking German bases in China. Within two weeks after their declaration of war against Germany of 23 August, Japanese forces were landed on the Shantung Peninsula and immediatly moved toward Tsingtao and Kiaochow Bay. By the middle of November, Tsingtao and Kiaochow Bay were taken. It should also be noted that the Japanese likewise occupied Germany's island colonies in the Pacific. By the beginning of 1915, the Japanese were firmly ensconced in China and ready to further press their aims. Surely no participant in the First World War won so much with so little effort.

Given the preoccupation of the powers with the European war, a power vacuum was created in China allowing the Japanese an unprecedented opportunity to expand their influence in China. And the Japanese government lost no time in taking advantage of this opportunity. In February 1915 the Twenty-One Demands were presented to Yuan Shih-kai's government in Peking. If accepted by the Chinese, the Twenty-One Demands would have made China a virtual protectorate of Japan. That being the case, even a government as corrupt as Yuan's had little choice but to attempt resistance. Unfortunately, the efficacy of such resistance was rather limited due to the preoccupation of the powers with the war and the internal political divisions which plagued the Chinese. In the end, the Chinese had to agree to most of the terms included in the Demands. A formal Sino-Japanese Accord to this effect was signed on 25 May 1915. By virtue of this agreement, Japan's position in China became preponderant and the balance of power in East Asia was critically altered. Whatever their reservations about this state of affairs, the European powers could do nothing to stop the Japanese nor did the Americans do more to stop the Japanese from cementing their position in China. Neither Bryan's diplomatic warning of 1915 nor the Lansing-Ishii Agreement of 1917 effectively limited Japan's role on the continent.

It was only after the war that an effort

BELOW: Japanese ships complete the work of Tsushima by capturing or sinking the remaining Russian ships in the Sea of Japan.

CENTER: Japanese cavalryman during the Russo-Japanese War.

RIGHT: Admiral Viscount Yukyo Ito, President of the Japanese Naval Staff during the Russo-Japanese War.

FAR RIGHT: Japanese 7cm mounted cannon in action in Manchuria in 1904.

was made to restore the *status quo ante* in China and this occurred at the Paris Peace Conference. This effort was spearheaded by the Chinese delegation to the conference and strongly seconded by the United States, which championed the call for redress of Sino-Japanese differences. The Japanese, for their part, had no intention of returning the former German lease-holds and concessions to the Chinese nor did they want to give up other gains they had made during the war. Armed with copies of secret agreements and treaties which the Chinese government had signed as late as November 1918, the Japanese delegation at the peace conference was able to neutralize the Sino-American effort to force Japan to return to its prewar position in China. Although the conferees did not recognize the validity of Japan's annexation of German leaseholds or concessions or the Twenty-One Demands, Japan remained in *de facto* control

of these areas, including Shantung province, and her economic gains were left intact. About all the Chinese could do was to refuse to sign the treaty.

Although the new balance of power in East Asia was not altered as a consequence of the Treaty of Versailles, the powers remained concerned about the situation in the area and convened a special conference in 1921 to deal with a whole range of Pacific and East Asian questions. The Washington Conference opened in 1921 with a triple agenda. Of primary interest to the major participants, England, France, Japan, and the United States, was the question of guaranteeing a stable balance of power in East Asia which, at the same time, recognized the various interests of those powers. Of almost equal import was the question of naval arms limitation. Last, the powers were concerned about China and the Shantung problem.

Of all the major participants at the Washington Conference, the Japanese had the most at stake. Having established a position of primacy on the Asia mainland at great cost and sacrifice, the Japanese government could not risk the alienation of their public by hard won gains in Korea, Manchuria, and China too easily. Furthermore, as a major Pacific power, the Japanese were concerned about maintaining parity if not superiority of naval arms with their rivals, particularly the Americans and the British. On the other hand, the Japanese understood the need for some concessions and came to the conference in a conciliatory mood.

The Washington Conference proved to be more successful than might have been anticipated. By 13 December 1921 the powers reached tentative agreement on a system for maintaining the power balance in East Asia and signed the Four Power

LEFT: Russian sailors abandon ship as the *Borodino* meets a watery end at Tsushima.

LEFT: Vice Admiral Baron Yamamoto, Minister of Marine during the Russo-Japanese War, wearing the French Legion of Honor and the Prussian Black Eagle among his many decorations. He adopted the illustrious Admiral Yamamoto of Pearl Harbor and Midway to give him an opportunity for advancement, since the young Yamamoto was born into an area which was considered untrustworthy by the Japanese High Command.

BELOW: The Battleship *Mikasa*, flagship of Admiral Togo's fleet. Displacement: 15,200 tons; Speed: 18.6 knots. She was built in Barrow-in-Furness in northern England in 1900.

RIGHT: Garden party given in honor of the US Navy by the Mayor of Yokohama. Front row, from left to right: Vice Admiral Baron Iriu, graduate of the US Naval Academy in 1881; the Mayor of Tokyo; Rear Admiral Joseph B. Murdock; Vice Admiral Baron Saito, Minister of Marine; Rear Admiral John Huggard; Admiral Iginu, Chief of the Naval Staff.

BOTTOM RIGHT: The Japanese cruiser *Asama* which, under the command of Vice Admiral Iriu, sank the *Variag* at Tsushima.

Pact which provided that each of the signatories would recognize and respect the rights of the other signatories and that in the event of a crisis, consultations would take place before unilateral action was taken. It should be noted that the Four Power Pact took the place of the Anglo-Japanese Alliance which was allowed to lapse in August 1923.

In addition to defining the relationship between the powers in East Asia and the Pacific, the Four Power Pact also included an agreement relative to naval arms limitation. According to this agreement, Japan would be permitted to maintain a fleet 3/5 the size of the American and British fleets. While this 5:5:3 ratio did not coincide with the initial Japanese proposal of a 10:10:7 ratio, it still gave Japan naval dominance in the Western Pacific and along the China coast. Furthermore, the Japanese were able to force their rivals into accepting a moratorium on the construction of fortifications in

Guam, Hong Kong, and Manila in return for agreeing to the 5:5:3 ratio proposed by the British and Americans.

The question of China was taken up separately from the consideration of other issues at the Washington Conference, with the governments of Portugal, Holland, Italy, Belgium, and China invited to join the four powers in discussing the matter. The Nine Power Treaty was the end result of these deliberations. This treaty provided for the recognition of the independence and integrity of the Republic of China and gave the Chinese greater control over the collection of custom's revenues. Although no mention

was made in the treaty of the Shantung question, an atmosphere conducive to conciliatory discussions between China and Japan was created. Indeed, shortly after the end of the Washington Conference, the Chinese and Japanese signed a bilateral agreement which restored Shantung to Chinese rule but recognized Japan's economic interests in the area.

Japan's conciliatory position at the Washington Conference and her subsequent negotiation of a bilateral pact with China marked the beginning of a brief interregnum during which time further military incursions on the Asia mainland were postponed in favor of con-

BOTTOM: The sinking of the Russian cruiser *Variag* in 1905. Men of the French cruiser *Pascal* try to save Russian sailors who have abandoned ship.

BELOW: The Treaty of Portsmouth ended the Russo-Japanese War. The United States offered its 'good offices' to end the conflict, and the negotiations took place at the American naval base in New Hampshire. From left to right: Count Witte, Baron Rosen, President Theodore Roosevelt, Baron Komura and Ambassador Takahira.

solidation of previous economic gains and interests. To an extent, this shift in Japan's foreign policy reflected the political milieu at home which found proponents of aggressive expansion outnumbered in the Diet by supporters of a new internationalism which rested on peaceful gain and not force. On the other hand it should be noted that the conciliatory policies pursued by Foreign Minister Shidehara during this period did not, in any way, compromise or contract Japan's position on the continent. On the contrary, that position remained intact throughout the 1920s.

In many ways, the 'liberal twenties' in Japan represented an aberration, a temporary break in an otherwise conservative and expansionist path. Moreover, the liberal and internationalist tendencies of the time were not characteristic of the majority of the Japanese, particularly the rural folk, who were alienated and isolated from such developments. Indeed, patriotic societies continued to flourish throughout the period. Characterized by anti-Western and anti-capitalistic platforms, such groups found adherents in the military as well as among the rural population. Although frequently dismissed by politicians in the Diet, such groups as the Sakurakai (Cherry Blossom Society)

BELOW LEFT: Emperor Hirohito at his coronation, 10 November 1928.

BELOW CENTER: Empress Nagako at the Coronation in her twelve-robe *juni-hitoe* court costume

BELOW: Japanese citizens line the street to witness a military parade led by the Emperor in 1934. Japanese people were expected to bow low when the Emperor passed, making it extremely difficult to see the man they had been waiting for.

BOTTOM: Emperor Hirohito at a military exercise near Tokyo in 1929. As Head of State and considered Divine by his subjects, he was titular Commander-in-Chief of all Japanese military forces.

were taken seriously by millions of Japanese. Their call for moral rejuvenation and attacks on the *zaibatsu* found much support and this support increased as economic conditions, particularly in the rural areas, declined. Given this situation, the slightest provocation might ignite a volatile situation. Such a situation developed in 1930 as a result of the London Naval Conference.

The London Conference represented yet another effort to limit the naval arms race among the powers. It was held at a time when the Japanese government, headed by Premier Yuko Hamaguchi, was ready to reduce appropriations for the Imperial Navy just as the Kato government had done with appropriations for the Imperial Army several years before. Thus, the call of the powers at London for an extension of the 5:5:3 ratio to non-capital ships of war was welcomed by the Japanese government. On the other hand, such limitations were bitterly opposed by the Chief of Staff of the Imperial Navy and all senior naval officers. Disregarding their objection that the London Treaty would limit Japan's freedom of action, Hamaguchi forced the treaty's ratification in the Privy Council and secured the resignation of the Chief of Staff of the Imperial Navy as well. This action precipitated a vitriolic and violent debate culminating in the attempted assassination of the Premier by a young member of one of the patriotic societies in November 1930. Hamaguchi died of wounds sustained in this attack several months later. Although his death did not result in an abrupt change of policy, it was symptomatic of more to come. As the military lost confidence in the ability and integrity of the government and parliamentary system, they would take matters into their own hands. More important, such actions would be applauded rather than condemned by the majority of Japanese.

兵徴募
海軍志願

# THE ARMY AND THE THE STATE

BOTTOM: General Sadao Araki (left in uniform) joins the Inukai Cabinet as War Minister in 1931. Prime Minister Inukai is sixth from the left, and on his right is Finance Minister Korekiyo Takahashi, who was killed during the 1936 Army coup. Araki's presence in the Cabinet marked the beginning of the military's take-over of Japan.

The peculiar position of the Japanese Army within the organization of the Japanese State can be traced back, with some justification, to the Middle Ages, but such a long digression is unnecessary for our purposes here. Its modern rise to prominence began, as did every other modern Japanese institution, with the national resurgence which followed the famous visit of Commodore Perry. Having thus been presented with ample evidence of the superiority of other nations in material matters, the Japanese Army, formed virtually overnight from the private armies of the daimyo, set out to become as proficient as any Western army and to do this at high speed. It was helped in this aim by the fortunate accident of history that the very period in which the Japanese set out to build up their forces was the period in which new ideas in armament and military technology were coming along almost every day.

In the 1850s Armstrong had introduced the rifled and built-up gun to replace the old cast smooth-bore cannon; rifled small-arms were replacing smooth-bore muskets and breech-loading weapons were being designed. The American Civil War stimulated this development and acted as a proving ground for numerous designs of artillery and small arms, shells, mines and every other munition of war. The same war explored new tactical ideas, brought out by the new weapons. During the 1860s the ironclad warship was developed and improved, another stimulus to the improvement of artillery. Then came the Franco-Prussian War, another field in which new weapons and new tactics were brought together with results which were as far-reaching as they were astounding to the military pundits of the day.

All these took place on the eve of Japan's emergence, and since all these events gave the same stimulus to every nation, so every nation was as well or ill-placed as Japan to assimilate them. Britain changed her system of artillery three times in fifteen years as new methods came hot on the heels of old. Germany, Austria and France were all compelled to buy their experience in the same fashion, and the newspapers of the day were always well-filled with reports of new inventions of weapons. As a result, though Japan came late to the field of tech-

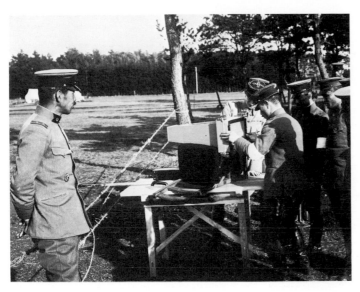

LEFT: A French military adviser in Japan in the late 1920s. French artillery and small arms formed the models on which some Japanese arms were built. In many cases World War I equipment was purchased from various European states.

BELOW LEFT: The Emperor Hirohito rides in an open car in Tokyo with the Prince of Wales during the future King Edward VIII's and Duke of Windsor's visit to Japan in the years when Britain's relations with Japan were still tolerably good.

BELOW: Japanese naval troops in an exercise in Manchuria shortly after its seizure by Japan.

nology, she came at a time which placed her on almost an equal footing with other nations, and given the national urge to excel, there can be no surprise at the result. The world's best military ideas were being paraded for all comers in the 1870s and 1880s; the only problem lay in selecting the best system of those offered, and by careful observation of events in the west, Japan was able to adopt sound military systems and weapons, basing her choice on actual performances rather than upon theoretical advantages.

The first guides to the new Japanese Army were the French, since the Japanese, like most other people, took the French Army at its own assessment and believed it to be the most technically and tactically advanced in the world. The events of 1870 soon disproved this contention, and the Japanese forthwith switched their allegiance to the Germans, their opinion being that the victors were more likely to provide sound teaching and weapons than the vanquished.

The fruits of this early period of education and expansion were seen in the Sino-Japanese War of 1894–95, a war in which the newly-equipped and highly-motivated Japanese forces rapidly overcame the poorly organized and equipped Chinese to secure a foothold on the mainland.

Unfortunately, while the Japanese had assimilated much of the Western technology and military teachings, they had failed to assess the political consequences correctly, and the resulting actions of the Western powers stripped away much of the advantages gained by the war. If it

did nothing else, this sudden reaction strengthened the Japanese suspicions of foreign nations, making them aware that whatever they achieved there would always be a powerful array of forces on the outside ready to whittle away any advantage gained. And one of the most prominent of these was Russia, which had astutely managed to reap more benefit from the Sino-Japanese War than Japan.

The result of this, of course, was the Russo–Japanese War of 1904–5, which placed the Japanese firmly in control of Korea, severely embarrassed the Tsarist regime, demonstrated that the Japanese could take on a first-rank power and win, and brought Japan into prominence as a major world power.

Japanese intervention in the First World War enabled them to gain a small foothold in mainland China Proper, and the pre-occupation of the great powers with the war in Europe presented Japan with an opportunity to put forward the famous 'Twenty-One Demands' to China, demands which would have almost turned China into a Japanese colony had they been met. But the Chinese were sufficiently astute to realize that the publication of the 'Demands' would be an embarrassment to Japan; so the text was 'leaked' to the world and, sure enough, the Japanese again realized that the world powers were never so pre-occupied with other things that they couldn't keep an eye on their trade prospects.

The partial failure of the demands, together with the relatively small part played by the Japanese Army and Navy in the war and the powerful boost to trade

brought about by war contracts, turned the natural order of things upside down in the postwar years. For the first time the industrialists and merchants of Japan had a powerful voice, and for the first time in history the Army found itself in low esteem. In the 1920s the Japanese Army was described by one of its officers as being 'in the doldrums'; its equipment was rapidly becoming obsolete, its leaders were ignored, its soldiers despised. Something had to be done to win back public esteem.

As the Army saw it, their only hope of salvation lay in Manchuria. After the Russo–Japanese War the Japanese had taken over the South Manchurian Railroad Company, running from Port Arthur through Mukden to Harbin to connect with the Chinese Eastern line, which crossed the country and formed a link between the Trans-Siberian Railroad and the Russian port of Vladivostok. In 1917 the SMRR took control of all the Korean Railroad Company lines and formed connections with them, and, by various treaty obligations and agreements, controlled a strip of land on either side of the railroad tracks throughout Manchuria. Moreover the company was empowered to station troops along this strip in order to protect Japanese property and interests. In fact this line-of-communications army virtually became an army of occupation, since very little went on in the railroad enclave which was not approved by the Army. The Army, in fact if not in name, controlled the railroad and not, as was intended, the other way around. The railroad company exec-

LEFT: Japanese field gun opens fire in September 1931 during the take-over of Manchuria.

BELOW RIGHT: A naval demonstration in Osaka Bay on 26 October 1936 after the results of the London Naval Conference became known. The Conference left Japanese naval planners dissatisfied, and from this point on Japan's military leaders thought in terms of taking foreign policy out of the hands of the government.

utives acquiesced in this, so that soon the whole Japanese presence in Manchuria revolved around the Army's decisions. Hence, the Manchurian Army became a power in the land and, as is the way of such powers, gradually amassed more and more authority and took less and less notice of what the High Command or the Government in Tokyo said to it.

In the late 1920s the Japanese government, led by Count Hamaguchi, pursued a policy of friendship to the Chinese, a policy which was looked upon with distaste by much of the Army and by many of the patriotic secret societies of the day, who actively campaigned against this policy, pushed for expansion into Manchuria and looked longingly to the day when Japanese forces would occupy China. At the same time the world financial crisis rumbled to its climax in 1929, the world went into a slump, and of all the nations which suffered, none suffered so much as Japan. The loss of markets, exacerbated by tariff barriers which sprang up overnight, led to massive unemployment and poverty in Japan and this, in turn, led to a change of heart in the country. No longer was the world Japan's friend; the activities of the financiers and politicians showed conclusively that Japan was without friends. Why talk of friendship with China when China now refused to buy goods from Japan? Had China been under Japanese domination there would have been a captive market and a bountiful provider ready to hand to deflect the worst blows of the financial and trade collapse. Hamaguchi was assassinated by members of one of the 'patriotic' societies in 1930 and with him went the last hope of friendship with China – or anyone else.

Before this, though, the first steps had been taken to plan the moves to be taken in Manchuria and other places. In July 1927 a conference was held in Mukden, convened by the then Prime Minister, Baron Tanaka, at which all the civil and military officials in Manchuria attended. The conference lasted eleven days and was ostensibly to determine Japanese policies in East Asia. However, shortly afterwards a remarkable document was published by the Chinese, the 'Tanaka Memorial', which claimed to be the secret minutes and report of this conference. Ever since the appearance of this paper there has been speculation as to its authenticity; even now, almost fifty years later, there is still argument, some experts claiming it to be spurious, others insisting

it to be true. Leaving these considerations aside, the fact remains that it was a detailed blueprint of how Manchuria, Mongolia and China were to be brought under Japanese domination by a mixture of military and economic steps. Financial and trade pressures were to be brought to bear on Chinese concerns to drive them out of business; railroads were to be built to open up Manchuria and take advantage of the raw materials in the country; and the Army was to gradually assert its control over more and more territory. And, true or false as the document may have been, its basic lines of action were to be faithfully followed by the Army in the ensuing years.

The Army, at that time, consisted of seventeen divisions, a force sufficiently large to garrison the railroad enclaves in Korea and Manchuria and provide a home defense force for the Japanese mainland. If expansion were to take place, then the Army had to become stronger, and at the same time the defense of Japan had to be assured. This latter feature took first place in the planning of the High Command, and in 1928 they began a program of strengthening the coastal defenses of Japan by building some of the most sophisticated artillery installations ever seen. At the same time, the Army in Manchuria began trying to extend its sphere of influence by covert moves. The Chinese warlord Chang Tso-lin, whose writ ran more or less through-

out Manchuria and part of North China, was approached – not to say bribed – to allow Japanese 'advisers' to move into his area. But Chang vacillated so much, changing his mind and intriguing first with Japan and then with Chiang Kai-shek's Nationalist Army in China, that Japanese patience ran out. If Chang was unwilling or unable to see reason, perhaps his successor might be more pliable, and so Chang Tso-lin was removed from the scene by a charge of dynamite under his personal railroad train.

His son, Chang Hsueh-liang, succeeded him, and he turned out to be even less amenable to Japanese influence. He was ready to do a deal with Chiang Kai-shek to allow the Chinese Army to move into Manchuria, the very thing which the Japanese were desperate to avoid. Since the High Command in Tokyo were not being very helpful, the Manchurian Army of Japan decided to make its own plans to move as soon as a suitable pretext arose.

By 1931 events in Manchuria were fast approaching a climax. The Chinese wanted to build new railroads parallel to the South Manchurian company's lines, a step which the Japanese quite rightly interpreted as economic warfare. The Japanese were, at this time, pursuing a policy of settling immigrant Japanese and Korean families on land adjacent to the railroad, backing them with generous loans and grants, but the local inhabitants resented the newcomers and frequently ran them off their new lands. The Chinese merchants of Shanghai organized a boycott of Japanese goods, making Japan's economic condition even worse. And finally, in the summer of 1931, a Captain Nakamura of the Japanese Army was shot by Chinese troops in a mysterious affair near Mukden.

At this time too came the first fundamental split between the Army and the civil government in Japan. The government proposed to support the forthcoming Disarmament Conference in Geneva and to make some sweeping commitments regarding Japanese military strength. The military, for their part, protested against any reduction in armament expenditure, which was just beginning to increase and produce the weapons the Army desperately needed and, in various public statements, violently opposed the whole idea of disarmament. Japan's future, as they saw it, lay in Japanese dominance throughout East Asia, and a disarmed army was no way to dominate anybody.

Another specter now loomed over the horizon. Soviet Russia, in the throes of its first Five Year Plan to improve the Red Army, suddenly become a tangible presence on the far borders of Manchuria and Mongolia and began infiltrating

ABOVE RIGHT: The headquarters of Major General Tojo at Hsinking, Manchukuo, from which he commanded the Kempeitai (a Japanese Military Police) in 1935.

RIGHT: Senior officers of the naval powers aboard a Japanese flagship in Chinese waters in 1932. Among them are Admiral M. M. Taylor USN, Commander of the US Asiatic Fleet (fourth from right, front row), Vice Admiral Kichisaburo Nomura (front row center, and officers of the British, French and Italian navies).

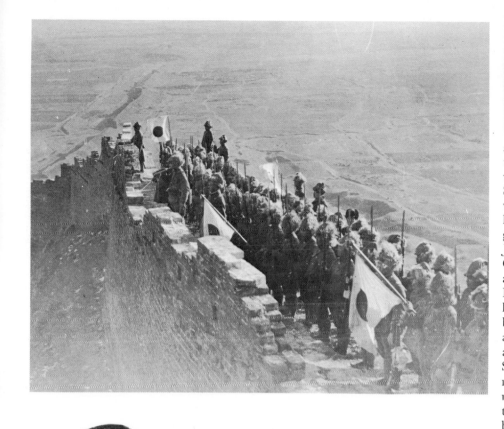

agents into both areas. So long as vast tracts of Manchuria remained open there was always the danger that a strong Soviet force might move first and turn the whole area into a Soviet colony, which had already happened in Outer Mongolia, and this threat was another spur to Japanese Army activity. The Japanese General Staff were anti-Soviet to a man, and they viewed the possibility of another Russo–Japanese War as being extremely likely; and if this had to happen it would be better to have it happen after the Japanese Army had occupied Manchuria and was better positioned to throw the Soviets back, rather than have the Soviets move first and gather momentum as they rolled across the country to crash into the thin Japanese railroad army and drive it back into Korea.

The Japanese Army had modelled itself on the German, and one of the features copied had been the formation of a General Staff. As within the German Army, the Japanese General Staff had considerable autonomy; while the High Command in Tokyo laid down broad strategic concepts, the Staff Officers with field armies were left to their own devices as to how those concepts were implemented in their theater. The basic premise was that the man on the ground could do this more surely than could a desk-bound

TOP LEFT: Japanese soldiers arrive at the Great Wall of China after the occupation of Manchuria, December 1931.

TOP CENTER: Premier Baron Hiranuma, who sanctioned the conquest of China and who was sentenced to life imprisonment by the War Crimes Commission after the war.

TOP RIGHT: General Sadao Araki, leader of the 'Imperial Way' faction and War Minister in two Cabinets in 1931 and 1932.

BELOW: Japanese civilians join forces with the military to defend the Japanese enclave in Tientsin against rioting Chinese civilians, incensed about the capture of Manchuria.

BELOW RIGHT: Naval guard troops in Tientsin during the riots of November 1931. The Great Powers maintained extra-territorial areas within each city which Chinese citizens could enter only by special permission.

BOTTOM: Japanese cavalry enter a Manchurian village during the last week of September 1931.

warrior in Tokyo, thousands of miles away. Furthermore, the General Staff was responsible to the Emperor not the Diet. Without strict Imperial control, the Staff had a virtually free hand.

The 'Kwantung Army', that is the Japanese field army in Manchuria, had its role defined by the High Command as the protection of Japanese life and property in South Manchuria. But this, under the system outlined above, did not preclude the Staff of the Kwantung Army from making plans to cover any threat which they might possibly envisage or to provide for any course of action which they thought probable. As far as that went

they were in the same position as staff officers of any army who pass their time away in peace by planning for every possible contingency in war. But two Staff Officers of the Kwantung Army, Colonels Itagaki and Ishiwara, took this a stage further; after carefully studying the size and potential of the Chinese forces in Manchuria they drew up carefully detailed operational plans for taking control of the whole country and disposing of the Chinese Army. Ishiwara, at a conference of Staff Officers in Tokyo, produced his plans to the General Staff, offering them purely as contingency plans; they were approved on that basis. He then returned

to Manchuria and showed the plans to General Honjo, commanding the Kwantung Army, again pointing out that they were only contingency plans and that they had the approval of the General Staff in Tokyo. Again on this basis, Honjo approved the plan, on the condition that, of course, it was only to be brought into use in the event of some major crisis.

All that now remained was to have the crisis, and there is little doubt that Ishiwara and Itagaki were well able to attend to this small detail. There is equally little doubt that the crisis was in the process of being manufactured. Colonel Doihara, the 'Special Service Section' commander, one of the most astute intelligence officers of his day and frequently called the 'Lawrence of Manchuria', (he was to be hanged as a war criminal in 1945) obviously had his tongue firmly in his cheek when he said, in a public statement in early September 1931, 'There is no telling what might happen in Manchuria.'

Doihara was, at that time, acting as a negotiator with the Chinese Marshal Chang Hsueh-liang over the matter of the murder of the unfortunate Captain Nakamura. The Army Headquarters demanded a personal apology from Marshal Chang, his acceptance of personal responsibility, and an assurance that nothing of the sort would happen again. Needless to say, the chances of receiving that sort of abject apology from a Chinese warlord were microscopic, and it seems probable that Doihara and the Kwantung Army were hoping for a suitably rude reply which would give them the chance to act. But the Government in Tokyo were tired of the affair and ordered it brought to a speedy and diplomatic conclusion; Doihara was recalled to

33

BELOW: Henry Pu-Yi, Emperor of the new Japanese puppet state of Manchukuo, after his installation in office. Flanked by surviving members of the Chinese Imperial Household, Pu-Yi, the last Emperor of China who was deposed as a child in 1911, found a new role as a Japanese collaborator. On the far right is Major General Togo, head of the Kempeitai.

BOTTOM: Soldier of the Manchurian campaign returns home on leave and is greeted by his wife as a hero.

Tokyo and given instructions to negotiate for some less onerous terms. Doihara gave this news to Ishiwara and Itagaki who were less than delighted to see the chances of their plan receding into the distance. In their turn, they suggested that the Kwantung Army might as well go ahead with the operation without waiting for approval from Tokyo, but their Chief of Staff, General Miyaka, doubted whether Tokyo would approve of such a course. In order to try and take the wind out of the plotter's sails he cabled Tokyo and asked the Chiefs of Staff to come over to Manchuria and discuss the whole question. Tokyo decided to send General Tatekawa of the General Staff to speak with General Honjo and advise him to be 'prudent and patient' while the negotiations took place. This move, however, was secretly signaled to the Special Service Section in Mukden, advising them of the time of arrival of the General in two days time; in effect giving the conspirators in Manchuria 48 hours in which to put up or shut up.

General Tatekawa duly arrived in Mukden, was formally welcomed, and escorted to a geisha house where entertainment had been provided for him. At 11 pm that night a mysterious bomb explosion occurred just outside Mukden, on the line of the South Manchurian Railroad and close to the barracks of the Chinese Army. In the confusion which followed, a Japanese patrol which happened, providentially, to be close to the scene, exchanged shots with a Chinese patrol which came out from the barracks to see what was going on. In accordance with the usual chain of command the matter was reported to the senior Staff Officer on duty in the Military District which, again providentially, happened to be Colonel Itagaki. He immediately ordered an attack on the Chinese barracks and the capture of the entire city of Mukden. The Staff Officers then roused General Honjo, pointed out that a crisis had arisen, and obtained his approval to implement the operational plan. The conquest of Manchuria had begun, and with it the long path to Japan's dominance in East Asia.

We have dealt at some length with this incident since it formed the starting point of Japan's wars and also illustrates, in a nutshell, much of the operational systems of the Japanese Army. There was, primarily, the difference of aim between the civil government and the military chiefs. The civil government was intent upon

LEFT: Japanese naval troops search for spies among the native Chinese population during the Shanghai Incident of 1932. Japanese forces overran large parts of the city before they consented to withdraw.

BELOW: Chinese killed during the violence in Shanghai in 1932. Serious reprisals were instituted against those Chinese who resisted the naval forces of Japan.

peaceful expansion by trade and commercial means; the Army, apprehensive of Soviet and Chinese intentions, was reluctant to wait on events and preferred to gamble on direct military intervention. But even though it felt this course to be desirable, it was sensible enough not to push things too far until the Army had reached a strength and a standard of training and equipment that the Chiefs of Staff felt desirable. On the other hand lay the Kwantung Army, a state within a state, confident of its own ability, quite incapable of looking beyond Manchuria to the large stage of the world and appreciating what the world might have to say about its activities. And due to the independence of this army, both in location and in operational planning, it was able to go its own way without much reference to anyone else.

With the Manchurian affair under way the Army began to polarize into two groups, the *Kodo-ha* and the *Tosei-ha*. The *Kodo-ha* or 'Imperial Way' group were largely young firebrands, though leavened with older officers, who regarded the Manchurian intervention as merely the beginning of greater things; their avowed aim was that of a one-party state under army control and run on a war economy for the army's benefit, and they were in no mood to wait for this Utopia to appear. To assist in their aims they enlisted the aid of various secret societies and brotherhoods which flourished in Japanese political circles at that time, though it is still open to debate as to which was using which.

The *Tosei-ha* or 'Control Group' was largely composed of senior officers and the General Staff; their aim was the preservation of the existing administrative systems but with the removal of fractious party politics, a return to the ancient virtues of discipline and martial spirit, and an end to the corruption of politics by big business interests. They had no particular quarrel with capitalism provided the manufacturers did as the Army told them. In the words of one foreign observer the *Tosei-ha* 'laced their faith in divine inspiration'. Insofar as both of these groups were anxious to see the Army's power increase and the power of Japan spread

RIGHT AND BELOW RIGHT:
Japanese forces move into the
province of Jehol in Inner
Mongolia in 1933. The seizure
of Jehol placed Japanese forces
along the Great Wall for
hundreds of miles in a position
to invade northern China at
will.

wider, they were in some form of agreement, but they tended to disagree on the pace of change and how it was to be brought about.

Eventually the *Kodo-ha* tired of delay and procrastination and decided to give events a prod. During the years 1931–35 they had, with the aid of the Societies, promoted a variety of assassinations of leading political figures who appeared to stand in their way, a course of action which led to the coining of the phrase 'Government by Assassination', but, by and large, the *Tosei-ha* had acquiesced in this activity, since the late lamented were inimical to both groups anyway. But in 1935 dispute arose between the two; the *Kodo-ha* began to feel that they were, in some ways, being used by the *Tosei-ha*, and the *Tosei-ha*, in their turn, felt that the *Kodo-ha* were getting above themselves and began to take steps to curtail their influence. This could be done by

RIGHT: Japanese soldiers who participated in the coup of February 1936, which tried to place the military in charge of the civilian government. Their officer in charge issues the orders for attacks on government buildings on the morning of 26 February.

FAR RIGHT: Sentry loyal to the government guards the Imperial Palace.

BOTTOM: Barricade erected in a Tokyo street by soldiers and civilians who supported the uprising. Although the coup was unsuccessful, public support of the civil government was badly shaken, and both the Army and Navy were encouraged to launch further adventures on the Asian mainland.

normal military processes; thus, General Mazaki, one of the more vociferous heads of the *Kodo-ha*, was removed from his post as Inspector-General of Military Training and 'kicked upstairs' to a relatively innocuous post on the Supreme War Council. Although this move was instigated by the War Minister and the Chief of Staff, it was implemented by General Nagata, head of the Military Affairs Bureau and responsible for officer careers and movements, and this brought Nagata into conflict with Mazaki and the *Kodo-ha*. Nagata followed up Mazaki's removal with a wholesale 'general post' of *Kodo-ha* officers, assigning them to remote outposts where they would have little influence. One of these officers was a Colonel Aizaka, posted to Formosa; Aizaka, however, turned up in Tokyo and murdered Nagata instead, a response frequently contemplated by soldiers in receipt of unpleasant assignments, but never actually carried out, before or since.

Aizawa went on trial, a trial which threatened to become a public laundering of the army's dirty linen, with accusations and counter-claims flying thick and fast. But while this was dragging on the *Kodo-ha* took action; in February 1936 they engineered a revolt of the 1st Infantry Division which, ordered to Manchuria, instead rose and seized parts of Tokyo. Several members of the government were murdered, though an attempt upon the Prime Minister failed. The mutineers were then confronted with strong military and naval forces and, in obedience to an Imperial order, surrendered. Courts-martial were convened and the ringleaders (including Aizawa) were executed.

The February revolt and its place in Japanese political history has been hotly debated ever since, but it can be seen to have had two major results. In the first place it effectively broke the back of the *Kodo-ha* and placed the *Tosei-ha* firmly in the saddle; and in the second place it acted as the wedge which enabled the Army to take control of the government. In the course of the rebellion the Cabinet resigned, and in the discussions leading to the formation of a new Cabinet the military groups pushed through one vital reform, the manner of nominating the service ministers. Up to about 1905 the posts of War Minister and Navy Minister had been filled by serving generals and admirals, a policy which gave the services considerable power. After the

Russo–Japanese War, this arrangement had been changed, the posts then being filled by retired officers; this, however, was not felt to be in the best interests of the services. Retired officers were no longer under military control, whereas serving officers could be ordered what to do or say, were familiar with current service thinking, and could be removed if they failed to toe the line. Since removal of a minister automatically dissolved the Cabinet, and since a cabinet could only be formed if a service minister were appointed, it followed that by having serving officers in these posts the Army and the Navy had a stranglehold on the government. It could force a course of action by threatening to remove the ministers, and it could prevent formation of a cabinet of the 'wrong' political shade by refusing to supply a minister. With these thoughts prominent in their minds, the service chiefs now obtained Imperial agreement to revert to the old system of appointing serving officers to the ministerial posts.

The first appointment soon showed just how the system was going to work. General Terauchi became the War Minister, and he treated the rest of the Cabinet with scarcely-disguised contempt. He flatly refused to co-operate with any 'liberal' politican and, virtually, the new cabinet was one which had been approved by Terauchi and the Chiefs of Staff beforehand; one result of this 'packed' cabinet

FAR LEFT: General Jinsaburo Mazaki, leading member of the clique which engineered the 1936 coup.

LEFT: Emperor Henry Pu-Yi of Manchukuo greets Prince Takamatsu on a state visit.

BELOW: The atmosphere of prewar Japan: a cafeteria near the Ginza which featured the presence of famous models and records of the 1930s.

RIGHT: Japanese ladies' swimming team at the Berlin Olympics in 1936 are protected by SS troops.

FAR RIGHT: A guard loyal to the civilian government stands before the anti-coup (martial law) headquarters.

BOTTOM RIGHT: Troops supporting the coup defend Police Headquarters.

was the allocation of over half the national budget on armaments.

In November 1936 Japan signed the Anti-Comintern Pact with Germany, a move designed to secure Japan against the possibility of Russian intervention. This pact was engineered not by the normal diplomatic channels, but largely by the Japanese Military Attaché in Berlin, the Japanese Ambassador being excluded from the discussions. In the following month General Terauchi once again demonstrated the Army's political leverage; he confronted the Cabinet with his resignation, demanding that the gov-

ernment be dissolved and a one-party national government be set up. By his resignation the cabinet automatically dissolved, since under the Japanese constitution it could not remain in office without a War Minister. A fresh Prime Minister was selected, but he achieved nothing since the Army refused to provide his chosen cabinet. Eventually a Prime Minister acceptable to the Army was found and a new government formed.

In the spring of 1937 the General Staff held a conference to settle their policy. They came to the conclusion that the omens in Europe pointed to a war of

major proportions breaking out there sooner or later. When it came, their view was that Japan should stay clear of it and concentrate on building up her position in the Far East. Since Soviet power in the Far East was also beginning to build up, and as there was also a rising tide of Chinese nationalism, activity in these areas should be circumspect and stirring up trouble avoided; so strongly was this felt that a special emissary was sent from Tokyo to Mukden to impress the point upon the Kwantung Army.

The analysis was sound, but the Kwantung Army was in no mood to agree with it. The one thing they feared above all was the prospect of China and Russia coming to some sort of agreement to divide Manchuria between them, to the detriment of Japanese ambitions. The commanding general in Manchuria at that time was General Hideki Tojo, and he informed Tokyo of his fears, suggesting that it might not be a bad idea to get in first with some sort of pre-emptive strike. His arguments were strengthened by reports coming out of Russia of the massive

purge of the Red Army, a blood-letting which, it seemed, was leaving the patient weak and dizzy and in no condition to stand up to Japan.

Tojo's suggestion was not accepted in Tokyo, but it was certainly applauded in the lower echelons of the Army. The junior officers were intent on establishing their own ideas of a buffer state to keep the Chinese and Soviets away from Japan and each other. The government, on the other hand, was again trying to promote friendship with China, and the Chinese, seeing advantages in Tokyo's attitude, began demanding the withdrawal of Japanese troops from the Chinese border areas.

It was against this background that the incident at Loukouchiao, which has gone down in history as the 'Marco Polo Bridge Incident', erupted in July 1937. Once again the Manchurian Army took the bit between its teeth, provoked an 'incident' (though the exact authorship of the incident is still in doubt) and proceeded to make the best of it, the result of which was the Sino-Japanese War. National feeling ran high as a result of the Army's action against China. Newspapers and cinema newsreels promoted a euphoric feeling of national destiny and victory, and the government, though privately doubting the wisdom of the Army's move, had perforce to support it, both in answer to the national martial feeling and, simply, as a matter of 'face'.

By this time, however, there was growing estrangement between the Army and the Navy over matters of national policy. While the Army were becoming more and more involved on the mainland of China, the Navy liked the idea less and less; they were alarmed at the prospect of Japan becoming mired in a war of attrition with two nations, China and Russia, whose manpower reserve appeared to be inexhaustable. In the Navy's view it would be more sensible to be satisfied with holding Manchuria, avoid upsetting Russia, leave North China

alone, and look to the south for their territorial gains. Rather more conservative in outlook than the Army's generals, the admirals viewed Japan's role in the Far East much as that of Britain's in the West, a small nation who, by use of naval power, could expand their interests without getting too involved in continental warfare. The Navy's 'Southward Advance' policy envisaged gradual expansion by naval power, with the eventual aim of assuming control over the valuable Dutch oilfields in Java. This fundamental disagreement on policy was not improved by the belief (common to both services) that the other was receiving far too much of the national defense budget and spending it on the wrong things.

In 1938 the Army forced the government's hand once again; General Sugiyama, the War Minister, informed the Prime Minister that a government 'more

fitted to deal with the national emergency' was needed, and resigned, thus ending the cabinet's term of office. The Prime Minister had no option but to reform his cabinet in a manner acceptable to the Army, and the new body was almost entirely military in structure – even the Minister of Education was a serving General of the Army.

The Navy, alarmed at this new turn, decided that unless some move was made to turn the army's face from Manchuria and North China, there would sooner or later be a dangerous clash with Russia, and they began their 'Southward Advance' by taking the Chinese island of Hainan, thus placing themselves in a good position to move on French Indo-China. They also engineered a small incident with a naval landing party in Shanghai, forcing the Army to come to their aid, and from this small beginning

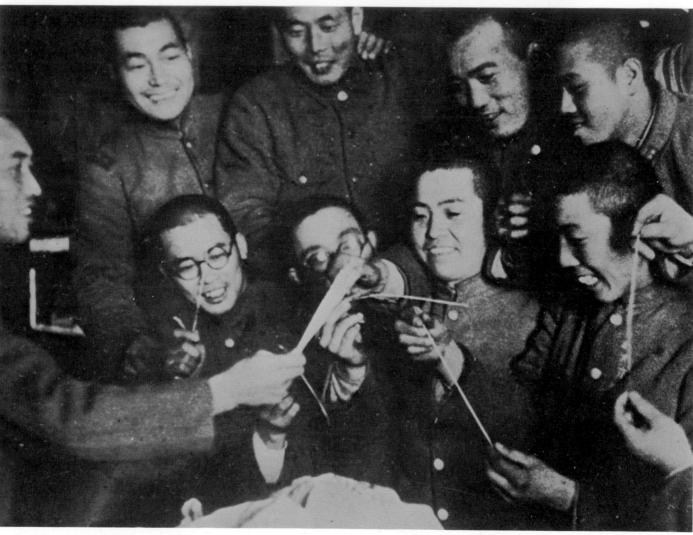

LEFT: The Cabinet of Prince Konoye (center) in 1937. Konoye tried to appease the military by giving them a relatively free hand in China while hoping to avoid a general conflict involving the West.

BELOW: Japanese soldiers draw straws for an assignment in Manchuria.

RIGHT: Japanese soldiers on the Russian border in 1938 during their summer skirmish with the Soviet Union. Russian troops appear in the background seemingly less than 50 yards away.

FAR RIGHT: Russian officers confer with the Japanese after the Nomonhan Incident on the Soviet frontier with Manchukuo in 1939.

CENTER RIGHT: Cavalry units of the Manchurian military academy charge near the Russian border.

BOTTOM RIGHT: Captured Russian soldier during the Nomonhan Incident in 1939.

the Army found themselves more and more involved in combined operations with the Navy on the China coast, gradually creeping southwards.

That the Navy's fears were well-founded was proved in late 1938 and the summer of 1939 with the occurrence of 'border incidents' in Manchuria. The Kwantung Army, over-confident of its own ability and under-estimating the opposition, provoked incidents with Soviet troops. In both cases, at Changkufeng in 1938 and Nomonhan in 1939, the Soviet response was a lightning counter-stroke heavily supported by armor and air forces, which gave the Japanese a severe mauling and considerable loss of face, the Nomonhan affair costing some 50,000 Japanese casualties. This boded ill for any ideas of continental expansion, and while the Nomonhan battle was in progress, news came of the German-Soviet Non-Aggression Pact of August 1939. This cut right across the assurances given by Germany in the Anti-Comintern Pact and left Russia free to act as it wished in Man-churia. The prospect of Soviet action, together with the evidence of Soviet strength which the border incidents had provoked, was enough to convince even the hardest Army head that the 'Southward Advance' policy made sense.

When war broke out in Europe in September 1939, the Japanese Army watched and waited; the more extreme nationalist elements argued for war, but the lightning German campaign in Poland was over before any decisions could be reached on the best way to act. While

Europe settled into the period of the 'Phoney War' there was a further pause while the Japanese Army studied the situation; perhaps the dictatorship had shot its bolt. But the German campaigns of 1940, with Denmark, Norway, Belgium, Holland and France falling like ninepins and Britain obviously next on the list, revived the jingoists in Japan. Using their familiar lever, the War Minister informed the Prime Minister that the Army 'desired a renovation of the internal structure in order to cope with the international situation' and resigned. A new government was formed with Tojo as the War Minister and Matsuoka, a notorious firebrand, as Foreign Minister.

With Germany gobbling up Europe and Britain about to be engulfed it was apparent that unless Japan moved rapidly she would finish up empty-handed; the colonies of France and Holland in the Far East were there for the taking, while the British colonies could be expected to follow suit at any time. The army expanded and made plans, while Matsuoka hurried to Berlin to ratify the 'Triple Alliance' with Germany and Italy and, on the way back, stopped in Moscow to sign a non-aggression pact with Russia. This, in theory, now left Japan with a free hand in the Far East, while ensuring that Russia would leave Manchuria alone in return for Japan keeping her fingers out of Mongolia.

With this uneasy agreement secured, the Navy once more put forward their 'Southern Advance' plans, and while these were being debated Germany invaded Russia. Now there was a danger that Japan would miss the bus unless it moved rapidly. The Navy policy was settled upon and the first move came with the completion of the occupation of French Indo–China. The world reaction to this startled the Japanese; trade embargos were placed on Japan; financial assets overseas were frozen; and the USA and Holland cut off oil supplies. Now it was the Navy's turn to become alarmed;

without oil there could be no 'Southward Advance'. The Army were equally worried, and now the two services saw eye to eye that the only solution was to be war. Plans were laid for action; a naval attack on the US fleet, Army attacks on Hong Kong, Singapore and the Philippines. But in order to give at least a nod to conventional diplomacy, the government were given until October 15th to reach an acceptable diplomatic solution.

Any hopes of such a solution were soon seen to be futile, since such a solution would have demanded the withdrawal of Japanese troops from Indo–China and parts of China itself, neither of which Tojo and the Army were prepared to countenance. As a result of this impasse, the Prime Minister resigned; General Tojo became Prime Minister in his stead. The Army was now in complete control of the government, and Japan's course to war was irrevocably fixed.

RIGHT: Colonel Masanobu Tsuji, former staff officer of the Kwantung Army and later chief of operations in the invasion of Malaya under General Yamashita.

BELOW: Armaments factory constructed in Manchukuo during the 1930s. Planes manufactured under Japanese supervision in Manchuria using Chinese labor were used against the US and her Allies after 7 December 1941.

BOTTOM: Members of the Hitler Youth pay a visit to Japan in 1938 as enthusiastic Japanese wave the swastika flag of the Third Reich.

兵徵募
海軍志願

# WEAPONS OF THE JAPANESE ARMY

TOP RIGHT: Type 44 cavalry carbine, which was introduced in the 44th year of the reign of the Emperor Meiji (1911). It had a hinged bayonet attached, and is pictured here with its bayonet extended. Below the Type 44 is a Type 38 rifle, one of the most widely used weapons in the Japanese Army, introduced in the 38th year of Meiji (1905). It had a manually operated bolt action. Caliber: 6.5mm; Length: 128cm; Weight: 3.95 kg; and barrel length 79.7cm.

BELOW LEFT: A column of Japanese infantry advances during the China campaign.

In spite of the vast sums of money absorbed by the Japanese Army over the years between 1930 and 1945, one is inclined to wonder at the weapons used by the Army. The unspoken question is 'Where did all the money go?', for it seems incomprehensible that such obsolete and obsolescent weapons could have been contemplated by a major power in the 1930s if funds were available for something better. Moreover the years of combat in Manchuria and China should have brought to light some of the shortcomings of the weapons and caused them to be rectified, but in fact the nature of that war lulled much of the weapons research staff into a false sense of security, and it was only appraised of the serious defects in some weapons when the war had been joined with the US and Britain, by which time it was too late to do anything about them.

The infantryman's basic weapon – and this meant the Army's basic weapon, since every Japanese soldier was primarily trained as an infantryman before he went on to some other speciality – was the Arisaka rifle. This venerable weapon had been developed in 1897 by a commission led by Colonel Arisaka and was a bolt action rifle largely based on the Mauser design, using a 6.5mm cartridge. As such things went it was as good as any of its contemporaries such as the Mauser, Mannlicher and Springfield, and it was improved in 1905 and called the 'Model 38'. The modifications made by Arisaka to the Mauser design turned the Model 38 into a crude (by Western standards) but immensely strong (by anybody's standards) rifle which would stand up to the hammering of service life with little or no maintenance. It was accompanied into service by the Model 38 Carbine; this was originally intended for cavalry, artillery and engineers who found the standard rifle, at 50 inches overall, too cumbersome. The carbine was only 38 inches long and in fact, in subsequent years, it gradually superseded the rifle in many infantry formations, since it was easier to handle in jungle conditions. A later model was the 'Model 44' cavalry carbine, which resembled the Model 38 but had a bayonet permanently attached beneath the fore-end, hinged back out of the way when not required.

It might be as well, at this point, to

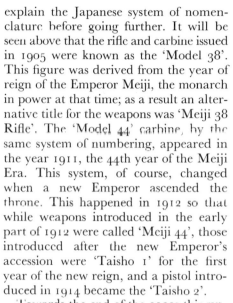

explain the Japanese system of nomenclature before going further. It will be seen above that the rifle and carbine issued in 1905 were known as the 'Model 38'. This figure was derived from the year of reign of the Emperor Meiji, the monarch in power at that time; as a result an alternative title for the weapons was 'Meiji 38 Rifle'. The 'Model 44' carbine, by the same system of numbering, appeared in the year 1911, the 44th year of the Meiji Era. This system, of course, changed when a new Emperor ascended the throne. This happened in 1912 so that while weapons introduced in the early part of 1912 were called 'Meiji 44', those introduced after the new Emperor's accession were 'Taisho 1' for the first year of the new reign, and a pistol introduced in 1914 became the 'Taisho 2'.

Towards the end of the 1920s this system became awkward; it was reaching the point where there were old weapons of the Meiji era in service which had model numbers similar to those which could soon be expected under the Taisho era numbering system, and so the system was changed. The identifying number of a piece of equipment would now be derived from the year of the Japanese calendar. This was considerably different from the Christian calendar used by the rest of the world but, fortunately for our purposes, the final digit is the same and thus once the system is understood a conversion can quickly be done. Thus the Japanese year 2597 was the Christian 1937, and any equipment called 'Type 97' would have been introduced in 1937.

Having explained all this, however, we must add that sometimes the nomenclature of a piece of equipment does not agree with either of the foregoing systems and seems to have been given quite arbitrarily; in this respect the Japanese were no better or worse than some Western armies.

As for the infantry rifle, while the 6.5mm cartridge had served well, by the end of the 1920s the War Department were beginning to have second thoughts about it. It had been designed during the 1890s when such small calibers seemed to be the coming thing, but subsequent experience had shown them to be a mistake. No other major nation, except Italy, had taken to this caliber, most having chosen something between 7 and 8mm. While the 6.5mm cartridge gave a low recoil, it also had a low striking energy, and after considerable discussion it was decided to change to a 7.7mm bullet, almost the same as the British service .303, which gave a better effect at the target end. This new cartridge was introduced for machine guns in 1932 in semi-rimless form; that is, the cartridge case had an extraction groove at the base and a rim which was very slightly wider than the body of the case. It was followed shortly after by a rimmed version, identical to the British .303, which was used in aircraft machine guns. And finally, in 1939, it was introduced in rimless form for the infantry rifle. Just what possessed the Japanese design authority to produce three totally different but easily confused cartridges in this manner has defied rational explanation ever since.

The rimless 'Type 99' cartridge was allied to the 'Type 99' rifle, which was little more than the Model 38 reworked to suit the new larger caliber and with a few small changes to make the design better suited to mass-production methods. It was, by and large, a better rifle than the Model 38 if only because it fired a better cartridge, but since its introduction came so late, relatively few of them were ever made and it never replaced the Model 38 in service. An interesting variant of the 'Type 99' was the 'Type O' (for 1940), which was a Type 99 modified so as to be taken apart for easier carriage by paratroopers. An interrupted thread collar in front of the chamber allowed the barrel to be removed from the rest of the action. It was ingenious but not particularly serviceable or easy to make, and a fresh design, the 'Type 2', replaced it; this used a horizontal wedge to lock the push-fit barrel into the receiver. It was a slightly better mechanical proposition, but few were made and they were rarely seen in combat.

A surprising blind spot in Japanese weapon procurement is the failure to provide a serviceable submachine gun; this,

LEFT: Type 14 pistol, the most widely used hand gun by the Japanese in World War II. Introduced in the 14th year of the Taisho Emperor (1925), it had a caliber of 8mm and a capacity of seven rounds.

RIGHT: General Hideki Tojo leaves Tokyo for a round of inspections of military defenses in Japan after he became Premier in 1941.

RIGHT: Type 14 pistol, an improved model used in the China campaign. The trigger guard was enlarged so it could be used while wearing heavy winter gloves.

FAR RIGHT: Hideki Tojo when he was Commandant of the Japanese Military Academy in 1934.

it might be thought, would have been the ideal weapon for the aggressive spirit of the Japanese soldier, as well as being one well-suited to jungle warfare, and the reluctance of the Japanese High Command to develop this weapon is inexplicable. Submachine guns were certainly tried at various times; small numbers of Swiss Solothurn guns were bought in the 1920s by the Japanese Navy for arming Marine landing parties, and some of these were tried out by the Army. Work then began, on low priority, on a design of submachine gun for Army use, and it was not until 1936 that prototypes appeared. This was chambered for an odd 6.5mm short

cartridge, bearing no resemblance to the service rifle cartridge, and tests of the weapon showed that further development was necessary. The designers went back to try again, but when the design reappeared in July 1937 it proved so poor in its tests that the whole project was cancelled.

In April 1939 the Nambu Armaments Company set about re-designing the original 'Prototype 1' and in the summer of 1940 this finally entered service as the 'Type 100' (which is, by the way, an example of a weapon's nomenclature bearing no resemblance to the approved systems previously outlined). By this time the caliber had been changed so that the weapon fired the standard 8mm Japanese automatic pistol cartridge. Since the design was based largely on the Swiss So-

lothurn, which had been chambered for the powerful 7.63mm Mauser cartridge, it is not surprising to find that the weak 8mm Japanese round produced a weapon which occasionally failed to function properly. Nevertheless, it was considered suitable for service and was allotted to paratroop units, though from what accounts remain it seems that production did not begin seriously until early in 1942, at the Naval Arsenal in Nagoya.

The Nagoya design staff then sat down to improve the design and in 1944 they produced a modified version; the main alterations were matters of short-cuts in production, but this later model had a higher rate of fire and also had a simple muzzle compensator which corrected the earlier model's tendency to climb off to the right when fired. This second model was not given a new nomenclature by the Japanese, still being the 'Model 100', but Western agencies differentiate between them by calling the earlier model the '100/1940' and the later the '100/1944'. In total, it is estimated that about 20,000 of both were produced before the war ended; by comparison it might be noted that in the same time the US produced 646,000 M3 submachine guns, while the Germans were turning out 225,000 MP40 models every year. The excuse given is that there was a lack of production facilities, but one cannot help feeling that there was also a lack of push behind the whole program.

The next infantry weapon is the machine gun, and here the Japanese selection was diverse and largely poor. Which is strange, since they were one of the first people to use the machine gun in warfare and, to boot, one of the first to get its tactical application right. In the Russo–Japanese War they had used French Hotchkiss guns to good effect, accompanying the infantry and giving covering fire, while the Russians, using heavy Maxim guns, rather tended to use

LEFT: Type 3 heavy machine gun was used as an anti-aircraft machine gun against low flying aircraft and was introduced in 1914.

OPPOSITE RIGHT: The ceremonial drinking of water (mizu sakazuki) was customary among soldiers immediately prior to a battle. This old samurai custom was a means of praying to the gods for good luck.

## Japanese Mortars

| Model | Caliber | Length | Total Weight (lbs) | Range (yards) | Ammunition | Remarks |
|---|---|---|---|---|---|---|
| "98" (1938)* | 50mm (1.97 in) | 2 ft 1 in | 48 | 450 approx (Stick bomb) 320 approx (Demolition tube) | (a) HE stick 14 lb (b) Demolition tube 18½ lb | Smooth bore. Range slide att to muzzle |
| "Taisho 11" | 70mm (2.75 in) | 2 ft 6 in | 133¾ | 1700 max | HE 4.7 lb Propellant in base. Operation similar to Model "98". HE shell. | Rifled barrel. Obsolescent in 1940 |
| "Barrage" | 70mm (2.75 in) | 4 ft (approx) | 25 (approx) | 4000 ft vertical | Projectile contains 7 bombs each with a parachute. | Smooth bore. Chiefly for use against low-flying aircraft. |
| "97" (1937)* | 81mm (3.18 in) | 4 ft 1½ in | 145 | 3100 max 550 (approx) min ‡ 1300 max† 210 min† | 6.93 lb 14 lb | Smooth bore. ‡ Light shell  † Heavy shell  Interchangeable with US M43 81mm ammunition. |
| "99" (1939)* "small" | 81mm (3.18 in) | 2 ft 1¼ in (barrel) | 52 | 2000 max | HE smoke 6.93 lb | Smooth bore. Trigger firing mechanism.  Can fire US M43 81mm bombs with range of 2500 yds. |
| "94" (1934)* | 90mm (3.54 in) | 4 ft 4 in (barrel) | 342 | 4150 max 600 min (approx) | HE Incendiary 11.5 lb | Smooth bore U-shaped recoil system  Obsolescent in 1940. |
| "97" (1937)* "Light" | 90mm (3.54 in) | 4 ft 3⅜ in (barrel) | 233 | 4150 max | HE Incendiary 11.5 lb | Replaced by Model "94". |
| "93" (1933) | 150mm (5.9 in) | 4 ft 11 in (barrel) | 220 (barrel) Total 558 | Sighted to 2100 meters (2296 yds) | 56 lb | Smooth bore. |
| "97" (1937) | 150mm (5.9 in) | 4 ft 11 in (barrel) | Total 778 | Sighted to 2100 meters (2296 yds) | HE | Smooth bore. |
| "98" (1938) | 250mm (9.8 in) | 2 ft 10 in (spigot) | 900 | 1000 max (estimated) | Model "98" HE shell 674 lb. 320mm (12.5 in) diam. | Spigot mortar. *These are the infantry mortars described on page 56. |

**1.** ►

**2.** ►

**3.** ▼

**4.** ▼

**5.** ▼

昭15.3
10854

**1.** Type 94 pistol, introduced in the Japanese calendar year 2594 (1934) for the protection of tank crews and airmen. It was used more widely by the Army and Navy later in the war because it was cheaper to produce than the more common Type 14 pistol. Its quality was poor and was more dangerous to its owner than to his opponents.

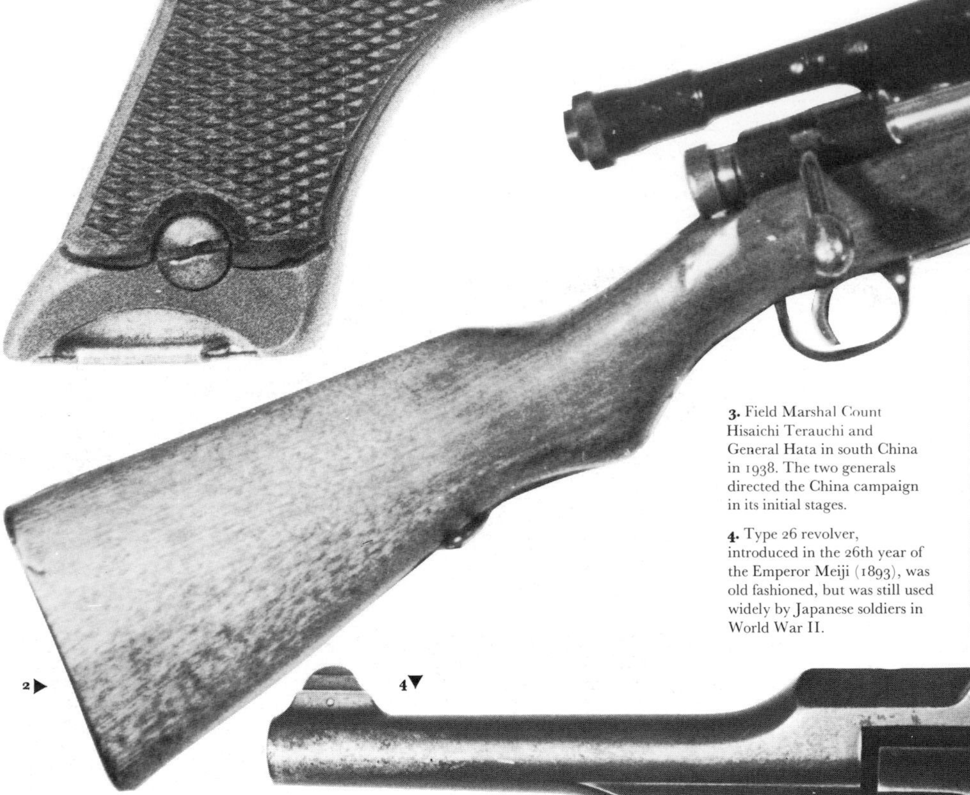

**2.** Type 97 sniper's rifle was a version of the Type 38. Introduced in 1937 it was equipped with a telescope which enlarged to 2.5 times. Its monopad was fired on its forearm. Caliber: 6.5mm; Weight: 4.45kg; Length: 127.5cm.

**3.** Field Marshal Count Hisaichi Terauchi and General Hata in south China in 1938. The two generals directed the China campaign in its initial stages.

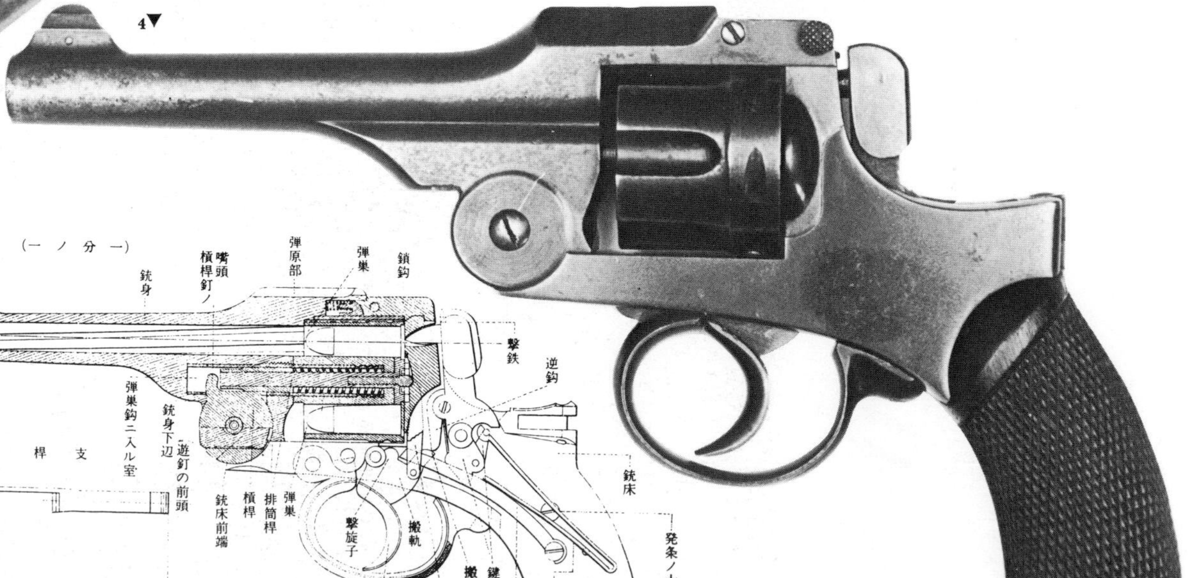

**4.** Type 26 revolver, introduced in the 26th year of the Emperor Meiji (1893), was old fashioned, but was still used widely by Japanese soldiers in World War II.

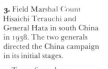

鈑桿横
鈑遊
筒薬弾
軸巣弾

照星
(一ノ分一)
銃身
槓桿頭ノ
槓桿釘ノ
弾原部
弾巣
鎖鈎
撃鉄
逆鈎
弾巣鈎二入ル室
遊釘ノ前頭
桿支
銃身前端
撃旋子
槓桿
弾巣排筒桿
搬軌
銃床
鍵
搬軌ノ嘴端
支桿
旋回子
引金
巣
発条の小枝
弾
発条ノ大枝
銃床

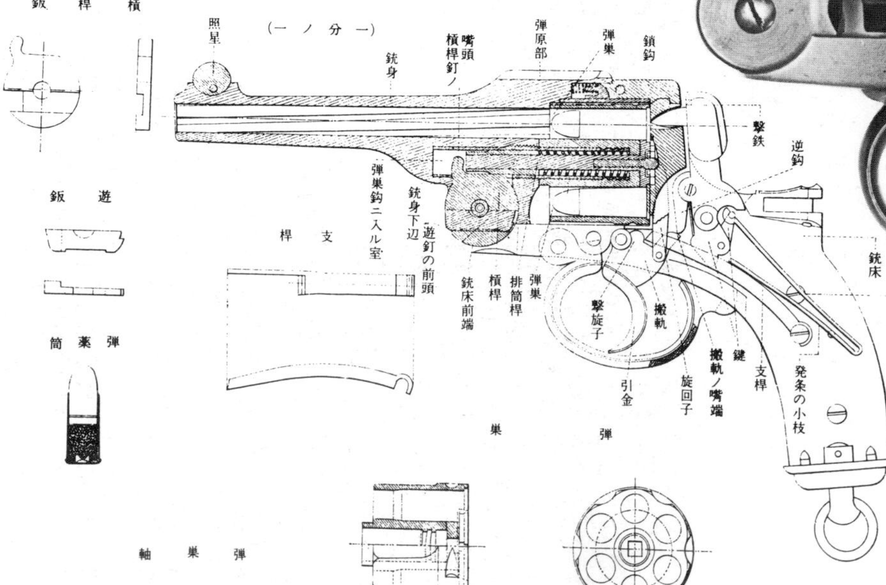

**5.** Type 26 revolver mechanism, taken from a Japanese manual.

**6.** Type 14 pistol, the standard Japanese infantry handgun in World War II.

**7.** Type 14 mechanism.

**8.** Examples of Japanese collar insignia. Left, from top to bottom: sergeant, corporal, 2nd lieutenant cadet, and 1st year cadet (plebe); right, from top to bottom: colonel, first lieutenant of a tank corps, 2nd lieutenant, and private first class from the 3rd battalion.

**9.** Field Marshal Terauchi was responsible for the indiscipline of Japanese troops during their progress through China.

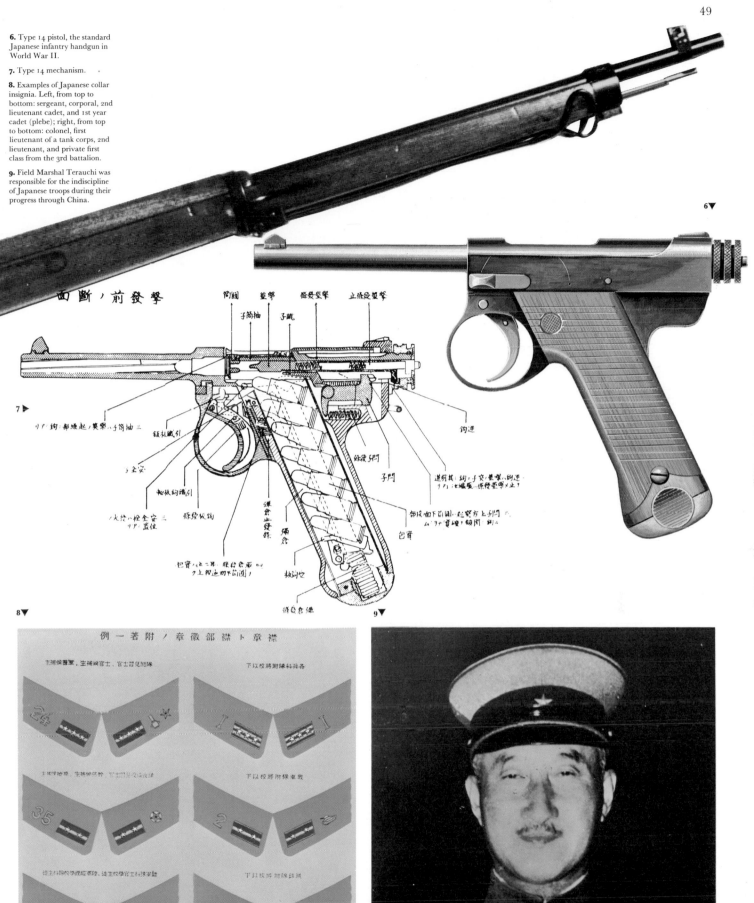

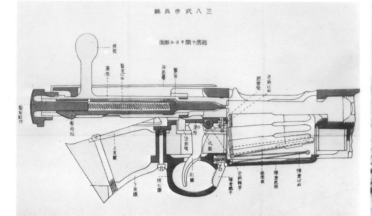

1. Type 97 anti-tank rifle was introduced in 1937. It was gas-operated, semi-automatic, with a 20mm caliber and was capable of penetrating 30mm of steel at a range of 250 yards.

2. Mechanism of a Type 38 rifle.

3. Type 3 heavy machine gun, introduced in the 3rd year of Taisho (1914), was a modified version of the French Hotchkiss machine gun.

4. The Type 93 heavy machine gun in action. Introduced as an anti-tank and anti-aircraft gun in 1933, it was used by naval troops as a twin-mounted anti-aircraft gun.

5. Nambu pistol, or the Rikushiki pistol, was widely used by Japanese naval troops in Shanghai and in the early stages of the Chinese campaign.

6. Type 92 heavy machine gun was a modified version of the Type 3, and was introduced in 1932. A gas-operated weapon also used as an anti-aircraft gun, it is shown here on a tripod with its carrying handle fixed.

7. Nambu pistol Otsu, sometimes known as a 'baby Nambu', a smaller version of the ordinary Nambu. It was used by high ranking officers for self-protection.

## Japanese Military Terms and Characters
### Important military characters

| 歩兵 | 騎兵 | 砲兵 | 師團 | 旅團 | 聯隊 | 大隊 | 中隊 | 小隊 |
|---|---|---|---|---|---|---|---|---|
| Infantry Hohei | Cavalry Kihei | Artillery Hohei | Division Shidan | Brigade Ryodan | Regiment Rentai | Battalion Daitai | Company Chutai | Platoon Shotai |

### Characters used in the nomenclature of army stores

**Date**

年號 =Nongo  年 =Year

明治 =Meiji  年内 =Within the year

大正 =Taisho  月 =Month

昭和 =Shōwa  日 =Day

紀元節 =Anniversary of Jimmu  式 =Pattern

**Numbers**

〇 =0
一 =1
二 =2
三 =3
四 =4
五 =5
六 =6
七 =7
八 =8
九 =9

十 =10
十一 =11
十二 =12
二〇 =20
二一 =21
二二 =22

三〇 =30
三一 =31
三二 =32

**Examples**

昭和一〇八式一〇〇式三年式
九 =9
八 =8
式 =Pattern
一 =1
〇 =0
〇 =0
式 =Pattern
三 =3
年 =Year
式 =Pattern

**Date**

昭和16.4.15 or 昭和十六年四月十五日
昭和 =Shōwa
十 =10
六 =6
年 =Year
四 =4
月 =Month
十 =10
五 =5
日 =Day

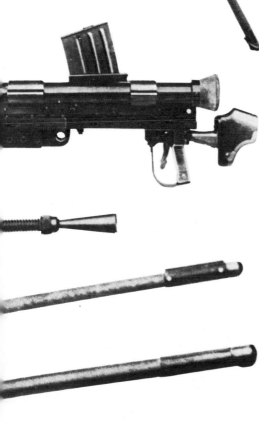

**8.** Type 96 light machine gun, introduced in 1936. It was gas-operated and equipped with a box type 30 round magazine on its top. On a tripod it was used as an anti-aircraft gun.

**9.** Type 92 machine cannon, used on tanks and armored cars, was also utilized as an anti-aircraft weapon.

**10.** Japanese military terms and characters.

them as weapons of position. Since the Hotchkiss had served Japan well, they decided to stick with the design in the future, but, as happened with the rifle, it was impossible for them to simply adopt the design as it stood; they had to 'improve' it. The modifications were done by General Kirijo Nambu, and his changes largely applied to a re-design of the extractor and chambering the weapon to fire the 6.5mm Japanese cartridge instead of the 8mm French Lebel round. This apparently innocuous change was the root of troubles which pursued the Japanese machine guns for years. The 8mm Lebel cartridge was tapered; the 6.5mm was almost parallel-sided, and this, combined with the extractor design which gave poor 'primary extraction' – the actual unsticking of the case from the chamber and the apparent inability of Japanese designers and machinists to get the clearance between bolt and barrel right, led to extremely difficult extraction of the fired cases. To remedy this, Nambu fell back on the bad designer's last resource – oiling the cartridge before loading so that it could be extracted easily. This trick, while solving the problem in laboratory conditions, always leads to trouble in the field, since the oily rounds invariably collect dust and carry it into the gun. Nevertheless, the 'Taisho 3' gun was put into service and some of them remained in use until 1945.

In 1922, reading the lessons of the First World War correctly, the Japanese Army decided on a light machine gun for the infantry squad, and Nambu now produced the 'Taisho 11'. The mechanism was still basically Hotchkiss, a gas-operated weapon, air cooled, but the remarkable thing about it was the feed system. Instead of using a removable magazine or a belt, Nambu designed a peculiar hopper system alongside the gun, into which six five-shot rifle clips were dropped, to be secured there by a spring arm. As the gun operated so the rounds were stripped from the lowest clip one at a time; the empty clip was then thrown clear and the stack of clips dropped down, the next clip starting to feed. The virtue of the system was that any infantry squad member could be tapped as a source of ammunition supply, while the hopper could be topped up at any pause in firing. On the debit side the open hopper allowed dust to get in and settle on the cartridges and the rounds were well-coated with grit by the time they were loaded, which didn't improve the extraction problem.

General Nambu then retired from the Army and set up the Nambu Armament Company of Tokyo, and here he designed the next Army machine gun, the 'Type 92' of 1932. This was designed for the new 7.7mm cartridge mentioned above; originally for the semi-rimmed cartridge, it turned out (probably by accident) that it would function equally well with the rimless rifle round, a useful feature in the field. In fact it was nothing more than the old 'Model 3' re-chambered for the new cartridge, and there was little about it that was original. It even retained the cartridge oiling system, which suggests that Nambu had learned little in the intervening years.

In 1936 he appeared once again with a re-worked design, the 'Type 96'. This was an improved 'Taisho 11', doing away with the hopper and using a removable 30-round box magazine of conventional form. It was still chambered for the 6.5mm cartridge, since this was an infantry squad weapon and the 7.7mm rifle was still in the planning stage. The barrel could be rapidly changed to avoid overheating, a good feature, but still the cartridges had to be oiled. Indeed, the system used here was worse than the previous one; the oil pump in the gun was removed and replaced by an oil pump on the magazine loader, so that the cartridges were oiled as they went into the magazine. The result was, of course, that the machine gunner and his mate carried pouches full of oily cartridges all day in the dust of the China plains, virtually guaranteeing that the cartridges would be well-coated with grit before they ever got near the gun.

By the end of the 1930s there were a good number of sound designs of light machine guns around the world. As a result, the Japanese acquired some Czechoslovakian ZB26 guns, either by purchase or, more likely, by capturing some from the Chinese. This was one of the most outstanding machine gun designs ever put together – it was, for example, the father of the British Bren Gun – and the Japanese Army were quick to see its virtues. They set about copying it forthwith, to fire the 7.7mm rimless rifle cartridge, issuing it in 1939 as the 'Type 99'. By carefully observing the Czech tolerances and other design features, and adopting the new cartridge, they were able to do away with the need to oil the cartridges, and at last they had a reliable and powerful light machine gun. But by 1939 their industrial capacity was being stretched to its utmost and it was impossible to make the Type 99 in anything like the numbers needed. As a result it was rarely seen in action, the majority of Japanese service units retaining the older models all through the war.

1. Type 91 hand grenade, introduced in 1931. It could be used as an anti-personnel weapon or with a Type 89 grenade launcher. Below is the charge for launching the grenade.

2. Type 99 hand grenade was used also as a rifle grenade with a Type 100 grenade launcher fixed on the muzzle of a Type 99 short rifle.

3. Type 2 rifle grenade discharger was introduced in 1942. It was a copy of the German Gew. Pz. Gr., plans and prototype of which were presented to Japan by courtesy of Adolf Hitler.

4. Type 100 sub-machine gun modified. This 1944 example of the 1940 model was a simplified version of its predecessor, but was

introduced too late in the war to have much value. It had no bipod and a fixed sight. It shot 800 rounds per minute with a caliber of 8mm.

5. Four experimental Japanese automatic rifles. None were put into mass production, as they were too expensive to use as a standard weapon.

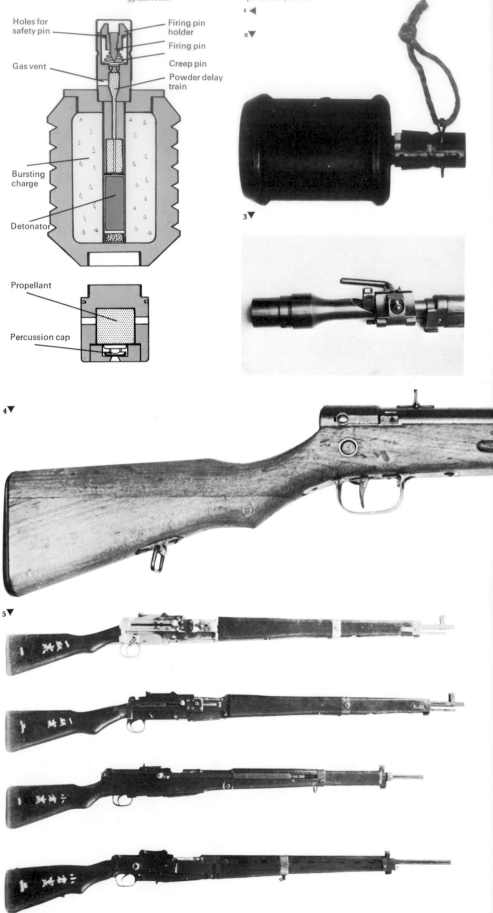

Holes for safety pin — Firing pin holder — Firing pin — Creep pin — Powder delay train — Gas vent — Bursting charge — Detonator — Propellant — Percussion cap

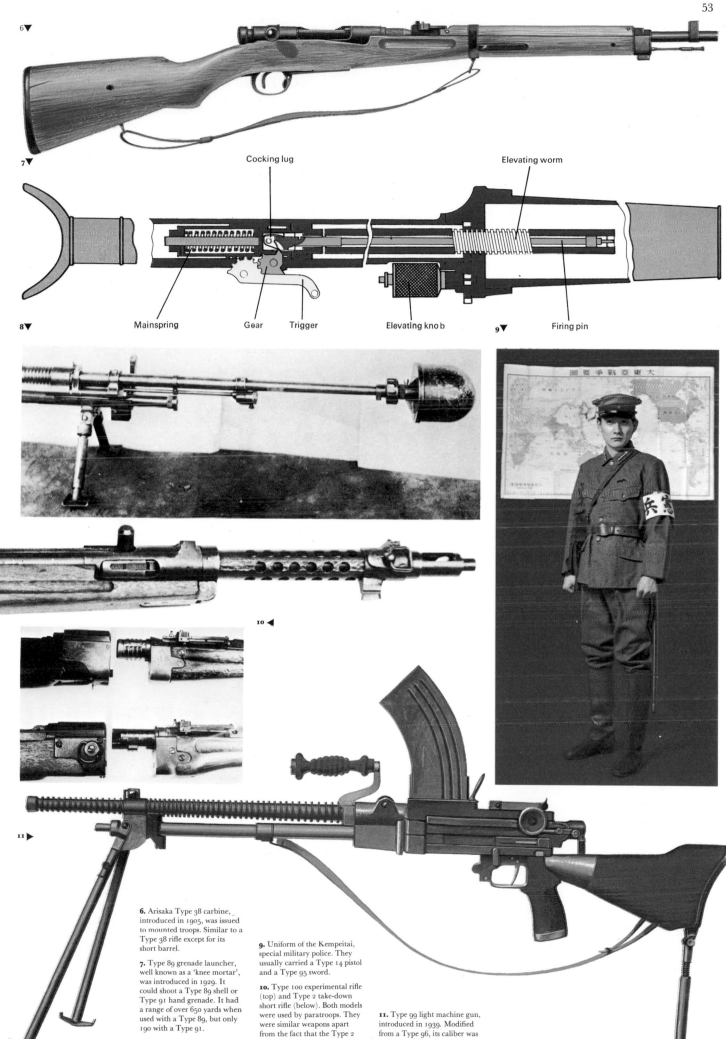

Cocking lug

Elevating worm

Mainspring    Gear    Trigger

Elevating knob    Firing pin

**6.** Arisaka Type 38 carbine, introduced in 1905, was issued to mounted troops. Similar to a Type 38 rifle except for its short barrel.

**7.** Type 89 grenade launcher, well known as a 'knee mortar', was introduced in 1929. It could shoot a Type 89 shell or Type 91 hand grenade. It had a range of over 650 yards when used with a Type 89, but only 190 with a Type 91.

**8.** Rifle grenade fixed on a Type 97 anti-tank rifle.

**9.** Uniform of the Kempeitai, special military police. They usually carried a Type 14 pistol and a Type 95 sword.

**10.** Type 100 experimental rifle (top) and Type 2 take-down short rifle (below). Both models were used by paratroops. They were similar weapons apart from the fact that the Type 2 could be taken apart more quickly.

**11.** Type 99 light machine gun, introduced in 1939. Modified from a Type 96, its caliber was enlarged from 6.5mm to 7.7mm.

FROM TOP TO BOTTOM: Type 100 sub-machine gun introduced as a paratroop weapon. This is an early version with an adjustable sight; Type 99 short rifle, widely used during the Pacific War. This early type had a monopod under the forearm; Type 2 paratrooper's takedown short rifle, which could be broken down into two parts so it could be carried in a small space; Type 38 carbine; Type 100 grenade launcher on a Type 99 short rifle; Type 44 carbine; Type 38 rifle; mechanism of a Type 96 light machine gun; Type 99 short rifle and rifle. Both were modified versions of the Type 38 and were widely used in the Pacific.

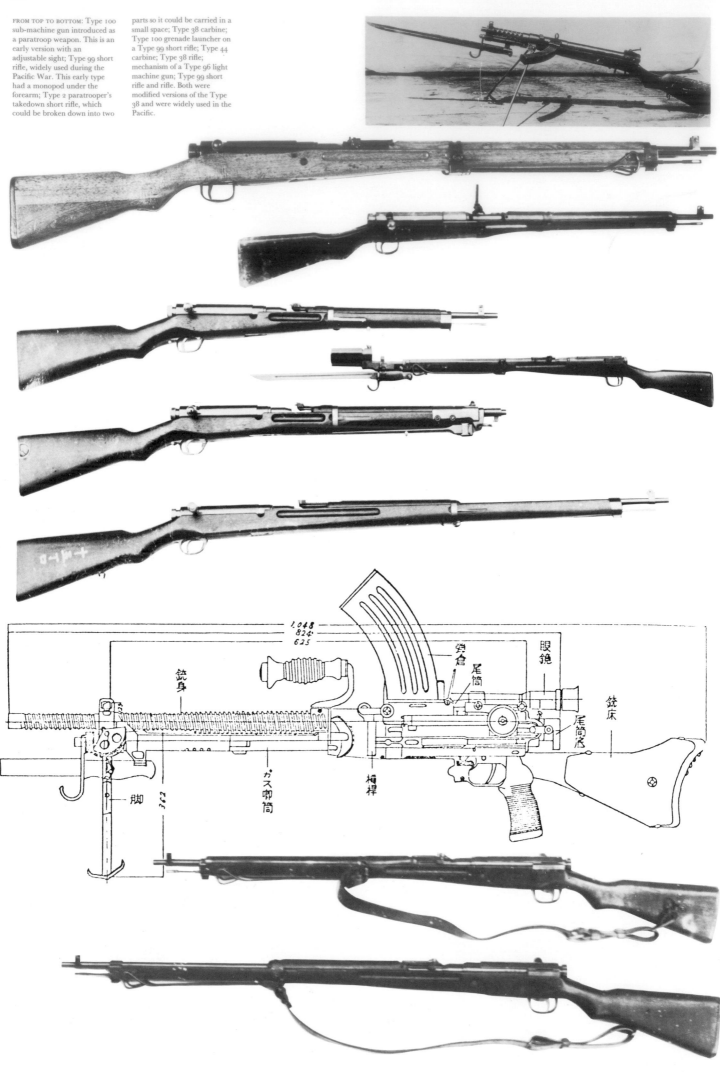

LEFT: Type 11 light machine gun, introduced in 1922. It had a complicated magazine and feed system; too sensitive for battle use, it was a notoriously bad weapon.

BELOW: Type 98 anti-aircraft heavy machine gun, introduced in 1938, was used extensively in the Manchurian campaign against the Soviet Union.

## Artillery

To Western eyes, Japanese artillery appeared anachronistic. In the first place most of its guns were, by Western standards at least, obsolescent. In the second place, although it was organized into regiments and batteries in the conventional manner, it rarely fought in such formations, and there seems to have been little attempt at fire control of grouped formations above the level of two or three adjacent batteries. The reasons for this lay not in any backwardness of Japanese artillery doctrines nor in any default in their artillery science. It was simply that they regarded artillery purely as a *direct* supporting arm of the infantry. All armies regard artillery as an infantry support, of course, but they implement this for the most part by massing their guns to blast away at long range and swamp the enemy by weight of shells, swinging their massed fire around as the situation demanded. Not the Japanese; if an infantry company were about to make an attack, they were given a battery of guns which was under the direct control of the infantry commander. If a major attack were being made, then two or three batteries might fire simultaneously in preparatory fires, after which they would follow the orders of their individual infantry commanders once more. This was largely due to lessons learned in the fighting in Manchuria and China; there the mere possession of a piece of artillery was enough to deter some Chinese warlords or even decide the course of an engagement without necessarily opening fire. Heavy pre-arranged fire was rarely needed, and the sprinkling of shells from four or six guns would suffice to give the necessary support to a limited attack. Such tactics remained valid in later years in the jungles of Burma and New Guinea, where the closeness of the country militated against bringing up or deploying large masses of artillery. Even the British Army, which

was probably the most expert manipulator of field artillery during the war, never pursued its policy of massed fires in Burma because the terrain was against it. The only time when Japanese forces in the field were able to employ large masses of artillery was in defensive battles in the Pacific islands where the guns were emplaced beforehand, the ground well surveyed, possible targets well located, ample ammunition available, and there was absolutely no chance of maneuvering.

As to the obsolescence of the equipment; it really stemmed from the employment. If artillery was to be used in such a manner there was really no need to worry about up-to-date pneumatized designs, super long-range guns or super-heavy howitzers. The tactics simply didn't call for them. And in spite of the apparent antiquity of the Japanese guns, there was always one outstanding feature about

their specification; their long range in relation to their light weight. By Western standards the factor of safety in Japanese guns was on the low side; the amount of metal in the weapon rarely appeared to be commensurate with the violence of the explosion which went on inside it to hurl the shell. As a result, Japanese guns and howitzers usually outranged their Western equivalents, even though the design of their shells was less scientific and less effective. This latter point, however, is a textbook one; the difference between a Japanese 105mm shell and an American 105mm shell landing ten feet away from one is, at best, academic. The effect on the unfortunate recipient is indistinguishable.

The most widely used field piece was the 'Meiji 38 Improved' gun, a 75mm weapon which had originated as a Krupp design in 1905. The improvements, designed during the First World War, in-

## Japanese Artillery
### Anti-tank, Mountain and Field

| Weapon | Model | Caliber | Length of bore (cals) | MV fs | Shell Type | Weight (lbs) | Range max (yds) | Elevation | Depression | Traverse | Weight in action (lbs) | Trail | Remarks |
|---|---|---|---|---|---|---|---|---|---|---|---|---|---|
| Anti-tank gun | "94"–1934 | 37mm (1.45") | 40 | 2300 | AP HE | 1.54 | ˉ500 | 27° | 10° | 60° | 815 | Split | |
| Anti-tank gun | "1"–1941 | 47mm (1.85") | 53.7 | 2700 | AP HE | 3.37 3.08 | 8400 | 19° | 11° | 60° | 1660 | Split | Pneumatic tyres. Adapted for towing by MT |
| Mountain gun | "94"–1934 mtn gun | 75mm (2.95") | 21 | 1265 | HE Shrapnel Chemical AP | 13.4 | 9080 | 45° | 10° | 45° | 1180 | Split | Also hollow charge amn. |
| Field gun | "38"–1905 | 75mm (2.95") | 30 | 1675 | HE AP Shrapnel Smoke | 14.3 | 9025 | 16° | 8° | 7° | 2083 | Box | Obsolescent in 1938 |
| Field gun | "38"–1905 improved | 75mm | 31 | 1978 | HE AP Shrapnel Smoke | 14.3 | 13,080 | 43° | 8° | 7° | 2497 | Open box | |
| Field gun | "90"–1930 | 75mm | 44 | 2296 | HE AP Shrapnel Smoke | 14.3 | 16,350 | 43° | 8° | 43° | 3300 | Split | Prominent muzzle collar. Very uncommon |
| Field gun | "95"–1935 | 75mm | 31 | 1640 | HE AP Shrapnel, Smoke Chemical | 14.3 | 12,000 | 43° | 8° | 50° | 2438 | Split | Derived from a French Schneider design of 1933. |
| Field Howitzer | "91"–1931 | 105mm (4.14") | 24 | 1790 | HE AP Shrapnel | 35 | 11,700 | 45° | | 50° | 3300 | Split | Also hollow charge amn. |

### Medium, Field Heavy and Siege

| Weapon | Model | Caliber | Length of bore (cals) | MV fs | Shell Type | Weight (lbs) | Range max (yds) | Elevation | Depression | Traverse | Weight in action (lbs) | Trail | Remarks |
|---|---|---|---|---|---|---|---|---|---|---|---|---|---|
| Medium Howitzer | Taisho 4 (1915) and later models | 150mm (5.90") | 22 | 1350 | HE AP CW Shrapnel Smoke | 68 | 10,460 | 65° | 5° | 6° | 6175 | Box | Travels in two loads |
| Medium Howitzer | "96" (1936) | 150mm (5.90") | 22 | 1780 | HE AP Shrapnel Smoke | 69 | 12,970 | 65° | −7° | 30° | 9108 | Split | |
| Medium gun | "14" (1925) | 105mm (4.14") | | 2040 | HE AP Shrapnel Chemical | 35 | 14,500 | 43° | −5° | 30° | 6850 | Split | Obsolescent in 1938 Tractor drawn. Very few were made |
| Medium gun | "92" (1932) | 105mm (4.14") | 45 | 2500 | AP HE Chemical Smoke | 35 (HE) | 20,100 | 48° | 10° | 36° | 6600 | Split | Tractor drawn |
| Gun | "89" (1929) | 150mm (5.90") | | | HE AP Shrapnel | 88 | 22,000 | 43° | 5° | 47° | 22,900 | Split | Tractor drawn |
| Howitzer | "45" (1912) | 240mm (9.44") | | 1200 | HE | | 400 | 11,000 | | | | | Transported in 10 vehicles |
| Rail gun | | 240mm (9.44") | | 3560 | HE | | 440 | 54,500 | | | | 35 tons | Several types reported |
| Howitzer | "7" Short (1918) | 30cm (11.8") | 16·4 | 1310 | HE | | 880 | 12,750 | 73° | 3° | 360° | 14.7 tons | |
| Howitzer | "7" Long (1918) | 30cm (11.8") | 23.7 | 1600 | HE | | 1100 | 16,700 | 73° | 3° | 360° | 19.7 tons | |
| Siege Howitzer | | 41cm (16") | 538" | 1760 | HE | | 2200 | 21,200 | 45° | | | 80 tons | Unconfirmed |

## Japanese Infantry Support Weapons

| Weapon | Model | Calibre | Length of bore (cals) | MV fs | Shell Type | Weight (lbs) | Range max (yds) | Elevation | Depression | Traverse | Weight in action (lbs) | Trail | Remarks |
|---|---|---|---|---|---|---|---|---|---|---|---|---|---|
| Anti-tank gun | "94"–1934 | 37mm (1.45") | 40 | 2300 | AP HE | 1.54 | 5500 | 27° | 10° | 60° | 815 | Split | |
| Anti-tank gun(1) | "1"–1941 | 47mm (1.85") | 53.7 | 2700 | AP HE | 3.37 3.08 | 8400 | 19° | 11° | 60° | 1660 | Split | |
| Battalion gun | "92" gun–1932 | 70mm (2.57") | 8.79 | 650 | HE Shrapnel Smoke | 8.36 | 3075 | 75° | 4° | 45° | 468 | Split | |
| Regimental gun | "Meiji 41"–1908 | 75mm (2.95") | 30 | 1672 | HE Shrapnel AP | 12.5 15 | 11,900 | 30° | 8° | 6° | 2158 | Single U | |
| Mountain gun | "94"–1934 mtn gun | 75mm (2.95") | 21 | 1265 | HE Shrapnel Chemical | 13.4 | 9080 | 45° | 10° | 45° | 1180 | Split | |
| Field gun | "90"–1930 | 75mm (2.95") | 44 | 2296 | HE AP Shrapnel Smoke | 14.3 | 16,350 | 43° | 8° | 43° | 3300 | Split | |
| Field Howitzer | "91"–1931 | 105mm (4.14") | 24 | 1790 | HE | 35 | 11,700 | 45° | 5° | 56° | 3300 | Split | |
| Medium Howitzer | Taisho 4 (1915) and later models | 150mm (5.90") | 22 | 1350 | HE AP CW Shrapnel Smoke | 68 | 10,460 | 65° | 5° | 6° | 6175 | Box | |
| Medium Howitzer | "96" (1936) | 150mm (5.90") | 22 | 1780 | HE AP Shrapnel Smoke | 69 | 12,970 | 65° | 7° | 30° | 9108 | Split | |

(1) The 47 mm (1.85") anti-tank gun was replaced by the 37 mm (1.45") towards the end of the war.

BOTTOM: Type 94 mountain gun, introduced in 1934, a modified version of the Type 41 mountain gun. Caliber: 75mm; Weight: 536kg; Muzzle velocity: 329m/sec.

volved changing the breech mechanism to a faster-acting type and altering the carriage to allow the gun to be elevated to 43°. This gave it a maximum range of 13,080 yards with a 14lb shell, for an all-up weight of 2500lb, a remarkably good combination; by comparison the famous French 75 fired a 16lb shell to 12,200 yards for a weight of 2600lb.

Infantry were provided with their own personal weapon in the shape of the 'Meiji 41 Mountain Gun' which, as the name suggests, started life in 1908 with the Mountain Artillery. This was another Krupp design, a 75mm firing the same 14lb shell as the '38 Improved' to a maximum range of 7700 yards for an all-up weight of an astonishing 1218lb in action. Moreover it could be rapidly stripped down into six pack loads, easily transportable by pairs of men with carrying poles, so that it could be taken anywhere that men could walk provided there was enough flat ground to emplace it. The infantry received this gun in 1934 when the mountain artillery were given a new design, the 'Type 94', which had a better maximum range of 9100 yards and a weight of 1160lb. This, too, could be stripped into six mule-pack loads or it could be further dismantled into 11 units, the heaviest of which was 210lb in weight, for man porterage.

The Infantry were also supplied with the tiny 'Type 92 Battalion Gun', a 70mm piece which weighed a mere 468lb. This fired an 8lb shell to just over 3000 yards, which may not sound much but was quite a useful performance from such a small weapon. In fact it was used more often as a form of mortar than as a gun, since it could elevate to 75° to drop shells into otherwise inaccessible places. It was also provided with a hollow-charge shell

RIGHT: Type 92 howitzer, introduced in 1932, was issued to the infantry and was one of the most commonly used howitzers in World War II. Caliber: 70mm; Weight: 204kg; Muzzle velocity: 197m/sec.

BELOW RIGHT: Some Japanese standards. First row, left to right: prince's standard, regent's standard, standard of the Empress, standard of the Emperor. Second row, left to right: cavalry regimental flag, infantry regimental flag, flag of the Crown Prince.

which gave it an anti-tank performance out of all proportion to its size, though there is little record of its use in that particular role. Some reports, notably those by Western intelligence agencies, spoke of it as being unreliable and disliked by its owners, but this strikes with the sound of whistling in a graveyard; there appear to be few records of complaints by the Japanese infantry who used it, and it could be found in the service of the Chinese Communist Army well into the middle 1950s.

Japanese field artillery prior to the First World War had all been built by Krupp, the Japanese having no facilities for producing this type of weapon at that time. But this defect was remedied during the war, as evidenced by the making of the 'Type 38 Improved'. In postwar years, doubtless due to the restrictions placed on Krupp by the Versailles Treaty, the Japanese switched to Schneider of France for their designs, and after purchasing some guns they proceeded to build the Schneider designs under license. The first of these to appear, part of the rearmament program which began in 1931, was the 75mm field gun 'Type 90'. This was quite a modern design, the carriage being of the split trail type and the gun being fitted with a muzzle brake. Two versions were made, one for horse-drawn batteries using the old-style wooden spoked wheels, and one for motorized batteries, using pneumatic tires. An interesting compromise was to issue horse-drawn guns to motorized batteries and transport them on a trailer having four pneumatic-tired wheels, allowing high-speed towing.

However, there is some question as to whether this gun was as good as it set out to be. Its performance was sound enough; 16,350 yards for an all-up weight of 3035

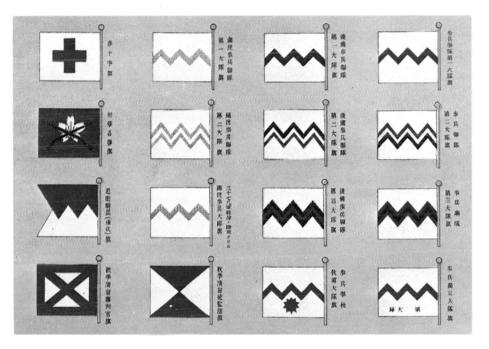

lb was very good. But few seem to have been built; they were rarely seen in the Burma or Pacific theaters, and it is reported that they were mostly issued to the Manchurian Army in 1936–37, later to be withdrawn and replaced by a 105mm howitzer. It is probable, though not confirmed, that the fault lay in the recoil system; Schneider designs used a hydropneumatic system of surpassing complexity, which required extremely precise manufacture to work well. When American companies of considerable technical ability attempted to build these mechanisms in 1917–18 they found themselves stretched to their utmost before they eventually succeeded, and it is likely that the fine tolerances and delicate workmanship were beyond the current state of the art in Japan. Moreover these systems

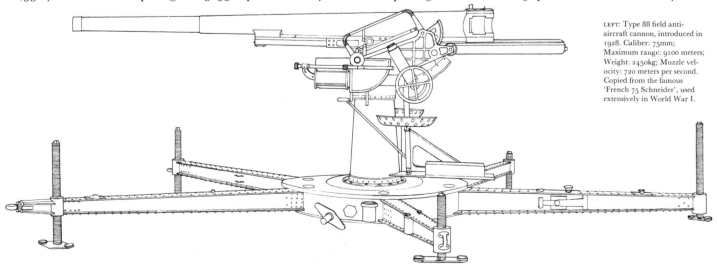

LEFT: Type 88 field anti-aircraft cannon, introduced in 1928. Caliber: 75mm; Maximum range: 9100 meters; Weight: 2450kg; Muzzle velocity: 720 meters per second. Copied from the famous 'French 75 Schneider', used extensively in World War I.

FAR LEFT: Type 94 anti-tank gun (1934), 37mm with metal wheels. Weight: 327kg; Muzzle velocity: 700 meters/sec; Maximum range: 6700 meters.

LEFT: Rear view of a Japanese 37mm Type 1 anti-tank gun on Guadalcanal. Maximum range: 6300 meters; Muzzle velocity: 780 m/sec.

BELOW: 150mm, 40 caliber naval gun, used for coastal defense on Kiska Island, which Japan seized when she invaded the Aleutians. It has a cruiser-type shield. Maximum range: 13,600 yards; Length of barrel: 21 feet.

BOTTOM: General Tojo visits the home of an officer killed in the war to offer his sympathy to his widow and son. A ceremonial cup of green tea is placed before the wartime Premier.

demand a highly sophisticated repair facility and extremely sympathetic battery mechanics to keep them working at their best, neither of which was likely to be apparent in Manchuria in 1937. It seems likely, therefore, that the Schneider design, good as it was, was a trifle too good for the Japanese at that time and it was replaced by weapons using the more primitive but more easily maintained system based on the older Krupp patterns.

The last field gun to appear was the 75mm 'Type 95'. This is said to have been derived from a Schneider design of 1933, but the connection seems tenuous. In reality it was little more than the Model 38 Improved mounted on a split-trail carriage derived from the Model 90. It had a maximum range of 12,000 yards and an all-up weight of 2450lb, and it

was intended to replace the Model 38 Improved, though production never achieved the volume necessary to achieve that aim.

The next step up was to the 105mm caliber, in which there was a gun and a howitzer. The gun was a long-barrelled model on a split trail, the 'Type 92', a cumbersome affair. The barrel was so long that it tended to whip in its bearings when being towed, and thus had to be disconnected and pulled some three feet back along the trail before being moved. This system has frequently been used on heavy guns, but it has no place in a weapon of this caliber. It fired a 35lb shell to 14,200 yards with its standard ammunition, and was provided with a special long-range shell and cartridge which could reach out to 20,000 yards

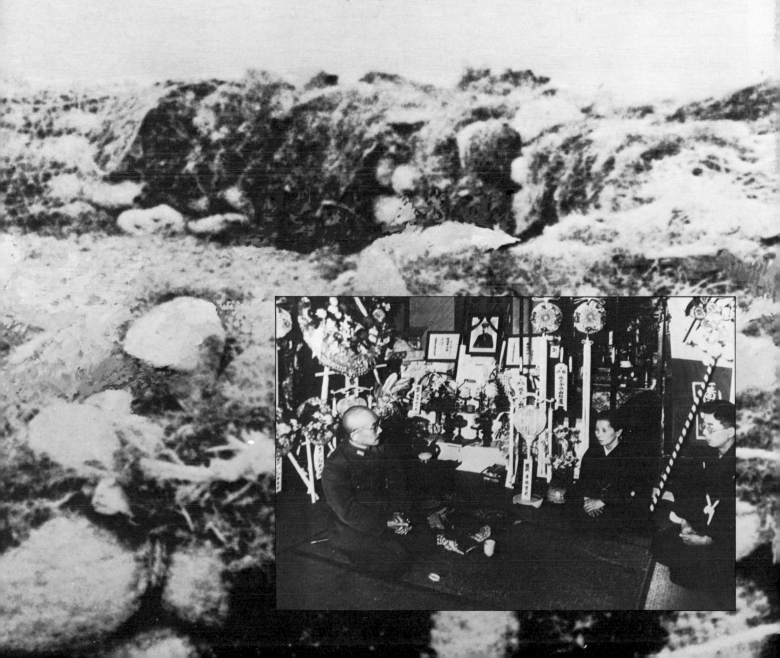

FAR LEFT: Type 3 tank developed for defense of the home islands. Introduced in 1943, only 61 of this type were built before the war ended and were never used in action. Equipped with a 75mm cannon, it carried a crew of five.

LEFT: 280mm coast defense howitzer, which had a range of about 8300 yards. There were normally four guns to a battery, and the overall length of the weapon was 17ft. 2 inches.

RIGHT: Twin Type 96 (1936) automatic anti-aircraft guns, which were usually laid in 2, 3 and 4-gun batteries.

BELOW: Type 96 (1936) dual purpose, 120mm, 45 caliber gun, used for anti-aircraft and coastal defense of Manila. An improved version of the Type 10 (1921) 120mm naval gun, it is mounted on a conical steel pedestal. It must be fixed in concrete. Maximum vertical range: 33,000 feet; Maximum horizontal range: 17,050 yards.

when needed. The 105mm howitzer 'Type 91' was more conventional, using a short barrel on a split trail carriage, and it fired a similar 35lb shell to the gun, giving it a maximum range of 11,750 yards.

The medium artillery used 15cm weapons; firstly the 15cm Gun 'Type 89', firing a 101lb shell to 22,000 yards, and, more frequently encountered, the 15cm howitzers 'Model 4' and 'Type 96'. The Model 4 dated from 1915 and appears to have been the first Japanese-designed and built artillery piece to see service. It was a peculiar weapon in one respect; the breech-block opened upwards, something never done on any other weapon until the OTO-Melara 105mm pack howitzer used by NATO in the 1950s. The opening of the block was helped by a spring while the closing was, of course, gravity-assisted. One is inclined to speculate on the number of recruit gunners who must have lost their fingers in this device over the years. Apart from this idiosyncracy, it had a generally odd look about it, the trail being extremely long in proportion to the rest of the weapon, but it threw a 68lb shell to 10,500 yards, which was quite reasonable for its day.

The 'Model 4' was augmented in 1936 by the 'Type 96', a more conventional design using a screw breech-block and firing the same shell to 13,000 yards. This model used a split-trail carriage with spring suspension, but although it was a much better design than the older Model 4 it never completely replaced it, due to the same old problem of production facilities being insufficient to allow the desired quantity to be made.

In contrast to the other belligerent nations, who commonly used artillery in the field of much greater calibers, Japan had no field army artillery bigger than the 15cm weapons. When one considers that they were the first people to put super-heavy artillery in the field, when they deployed 28cm howitzers against the defenses of Port Arthur in 1904, this seems surprising, but considering

the country in which they fought and their problems of communication and supply, there was good sense in letting well enough alone. For almost all their actions 15cm was sufficient, and the logistic problem of moving heavier ordnance over jungle trails was one they could have done well without.

In the anti-tank field the Japanese began, like almost everyone else, with a 37mm gun. This was the 'Type 97', which was known in the Japanese army as the 'RA 97', the 'RA' standing for 'Reinmetaru', the Japanese form of 'Rheinmettal'. For the gun was, in fact, the German 37mm Panzer Abwehr Kanone 37, made by Rheinmettal-Borsig and sold to Japan in 1937–39 in some numbers. In 1941 this was supplemented by a new design, the 47mm 'Type 1' which was, at first, assumed by Western observers to be little more than an enlargement of the RA 37. However closer examination leads to the belief that it was, more likely, based on the Soviet ZIK 45mm anti-tank gun. This, it is true, was little more than an enlarged copy of the Rheinmettal design, since these had also been bought by the Russians in 1936–37, and it seems probable that one or two of these may have been acquired by the Japanese in the Manchurian border clashes with Soviet troops in 1938–39. By copying the Soviet carriage design and adding the 47mm tank gun, which was then in production, the Japanese arrived at quite a good anti-tank gun. It fired a $3\frac{1}{2}$lb piercing shell at 2700 ft/sec to penetrate 70mm of plate at 500 yards range, and it remained the standard anti-tank gun for the remainder of the war, though it never completely replaced the 37mm model.

Bearing in mind the fact that almost every other major nation had, by 1939, a heavier anti-tank gun on the drawing-board, and had, by 1942, disposed of such calibers as 37mm and 45mm, it seems that the Japanese fell into a common error in designing their anti-tank guns; they took their own standard tanks as the norm to be beaten, built guns sufficiently good to

OPPOSITE LEFT: Searchlight, 150cm. with a mobile mount.

OPPOSITE RIGHT: Type 88, 75mm anti-aircraft gun, which was also used for coastal defense. The entrance to the right of the gun leads to underground barracks and a system of tunnels connecting all the guns in the battery of six. Weight: 2450kg; Maximum range: 9100 meters; Muzzle velocity: 720m/sec.

ABOVE LEFT: Type 92 (1932), 70mm howitzer, which was used in support of infantry. Maximum range: 3075 yards.

ABOVE RIGHT: Type 99 76.2mm anti-aircraft gun, also used for coastal defense. Weight: 6500kg; Maximum range: 10,000 meters; Muzzle velocity: 800m/sec.

BELOW: Type 94 (1934), 75mm mountain gun. It could be broken down into eleven units and transported on six pack horses. The elevating and transversing handwheels are on the left.

BELOW: Three greetings flags or banners. When Japanese soldiers arrived at a railway station, they were greeted by banners such as these. Admittedly this usually occurred when they returned home on leave.

do that, and then considered that good enough to beat anyone else's tanks. This sort of closed-loop technology appeared in other countries at various times, so it is not peculiar to Japan, but in this case it put the Japanese Army at a disadvantage when it met such machines as the British Matilda and the American Sherman, which were only vulnerable to an extremely lucky shot.

The same sort of limited-objective thinking appeared in Japanese anti-aircraft guns. Their performance was, by and large, up to par for the middle 1930s and it equated well with the performance of their own aircraft. But it was soon overtaken by developments in Allied aircraft, so that rates of fire, pointing speed and ceilings were insufficient to cope with the increased speeds and greater combat altitude of American airplanes. Moreover the development of Japanese radar was far behind that of the Allies. Their anti-aircraft fire relied on optical tracking and electro-mechanical computing to provide its fire control solutions, and by 1945 this simply was not good enough.

The standard Army AA gun was the 75mm 'Model 88' (1928), a terminology which led to some hilarious mis-assessments by Allied intelligence staffs in the early days of the war when, from study of captured documents, they heard of the 'AA Gun 88' and fearfully assumed the Japanese were using the dreaded German '88' anti-aircraft gun. In fact, later in the war a few of the improved German 88mm Flak 41 guns were sent to Japan,

which must have been a revelation to them, but although there was talk of putting a copy into production it never came off. The 'Model 88' was a good design for its day and appears to have been copied from a British Vickers model. It fired a 14lb shell to a maximum ceiling of some 29,000 feet; but its effective ceiling was generally quoted as being 21,000 feet. The difference between these terms is fundamental; *maximum* ceiling is the height to which the shell would go if the gun was to be pointed at 90° to the ground. The only things which come into this calculation are the muzzle velocity, the weight of the shell and the pull of gravity; in this case at 29,000 feet the pull of gravity overcame the momentum of the shell and it started back down again.

But this is a purely theoretical figure; in the first place the Model 88 could only elevate to 85°; in the second place the shell was fitted with a time fuse which ran out of time and detonated the shell before it could get to the theoretical maximum altitude. And in the third place, simple geometry shows that an anti-aircraft gun is only of any use when operating at less than its maximum ceiling, since it needs to be able to fire more than one shot at the enemy. The Japanese definition of the *effective* ceiling, as laid down by the Naval Gunnery School at Tateyama, was 'the maximum altitude at which a directly approaching aircraft flying at a ground speed of 300 mph can be engaged for 20 seconds, assuming the first round to be fired at 30 seconds time of flight and the

last at 70° elevation.' It was this sort of criterion which brought the effective ceiling down to 21,000 feet.

However, unlike the anti-tank guns, some effort went into trying to improve the state of affairs during the war and develop guns which would catch the American flyers. The 75mm model was improved into the 'Type 4' in 1944, the principal change being a longer barrel and more powerful cartridge to push the effective ceiling up to about 27,000 feet. There was also an '8cm Model 99' which, in spite of its confusing name, was still a 75mm gun and which had a performance slightly better than the 'Type 4', the difference being that the 'Model 99' was a naval service gun translated onto an army mounting as a sort of stop-gap measure. Another naval gun frequently used in shore installations and often found on Pacific islands was the 10cm 'Model 98', a really formidable weapon firing a 28 lb shell to a ceiling of 35,000 feet. Had this ever been adopted by the Army in place of their 75mm models, the Japanese air defenses would have been a very tough proposition. The Army did, in fact, have a 105mm gun, the 'Model 14' which dated from 1925 and was thus somewhat antiquated, having a performance no better than the 75mm 'Model 88'.

The Navy took AA gunnery very seriously indeed since they, as explained elsewhere, were under few illusions about just how effective aviation could be, and they produced guns of up to 15cm caliber. But instead of pursuing the obviously

BELOW: A series of armbands worn during World War II. Left column, from top to bottom: MP in the China campaign, MP in Singapore, MP armband in general use, naval shore patrol (SP) armband, Japanese Naval Press, Army hospital orderly, naval SP. Right column, from top to bottom: on leave (1943), on leave with car (1943), on leave with horse (1943), China campaign headquarters, Manchurian Storm Trooper, military press, Army propaganda trooper, military press (civilian).

wise course and adopting these weapons, the Army, doubtless due to the rivalry between the services, preferred to go its own way and began developing weapons of its own. Thus work began on a 120mm 'Type 3' to fire a 51lb shell to 35,000 feet and a 150mm, without title, which was to fire a 97lb shell to something in the order of 55,000 feet. There is a strong possibility that some of the inspiration for this latter gun came from Germany, where work on a 15cm gun with similar characteristics had gone on throughout most of the war without producing much success.

There is one field of Japanese artillery which is rarely mentioned, since it took no active part in the war, but which deserves study since it was technically far in advance of any other branch of Japanese artillery and equally far in advance of comparable artillery anywhere else in the world; the Japanese coast defenses.

Japan had always set great store by her coast defenses, an attitude which is understandable in an island nation surrounded by potential enemies. In the late 19th century extremely powerful batteries had been installed all round Japan's coastline at vulnerable points, great reliance being placed on heavy howitzers or mortars, concealed from the sea, which could drop piercing shells onto the thin decks of enemy warships. In fact it was some of these 28cm mortars which had been removed from their coast emplacements and turned into field army weapons to bombard Port Arthur in 1904 and usher in the age of super-heavy artillery.

After the First World War it was decided to bring the coast defenses up to date. At that time the guns emplaced were a heterogeneous collection dating from the 1880s, since it seems to have been the policy that once a gun was emplaced it was never scrapped until it wore out; as long as ammunition was available and it could still shoot, it stayed in place.

To bring the defenses into a more efficient state, designs of new guns were put in hand, but before these could be completed the Army had a windfall. As a result of the 1922 Washington Conference on Naval Limitation, the Japanese Navy found itself with a quantity of surplus battleship twin-gun turrets on hand. It offered these to the Army and they, realizing that their coast defense problem was thus practically solved, were very happy to accept them. The army then began drawing up plans for installing

these turrets in various important fortresses, and in 1928 the work began. Enormous pits were dug, into which were built labyrinthine complexes of magazines, crew quarters, engine rooms, fire control centers and air conditioning plants. When this installation was complete it was surmounted by a concrete shaft and the earth replaced. The turrets were then installed on the tops of the shafts and camouflaged. All that showed above ground was the turret, and this was concealed by a foot of earth on top, planted with weeds and bushes, while the guns lay in long pits in the ground, covered in netting.

The turrets comprised three mounting two 41cm guns, six mounting twin 30cm guns, and two each of 25cm and 20cm caliber. They were operated by the fire control system 'Type 88' which was a highly advanced electrical computing system which practically guaranteed a target shot with the first round at any range. With the exception of some German wartime installations, these Japanese turret systems of the early 1930s probably represent the most advanced coast artillery ever seen. But like so many coast artillery installations throughout the world, they were destined never to fire a shot in anger.

BELOW: Type 89 medium tanks were introduced in 1928 by the Army, but were also used by naval landing troops as in this photograph. They were equipped with a Type 90, 57mm cannon and had armor with a maximum thickness of 17mm.

BOTTOM: Experimental one-man panzer, used sporadically during the China campaign but too impractical ever to be put into wide-scale production.

## Armor

The last of the major military weapons which should be examined is the tank. Japanese involvement with armored vehicles began shortly after the First World War with the purchase of small numbers of British and French tanks for evaluation. After considering these vehicles and their possibilities, the first steps were taken in 1925 with the formation of two tank companies, one of which was purely an experimental unit for the study of tactics and technical trends. At the same time the Osaka Arsenal began designing their first tank, a 22-tonner armed with a

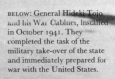

BELOW: General Hideki Tojo and his War Cabinet, installed in October 1941. They completed the task of the military take-over of the state and immediately prepared for war with the United States.

LEFT: Type 97 (1937) Chi-Ha medium tank, equipped with a Type 97, 57mm cannon, although later in the war a Type 1, 47mm was used. They carried 114 rounds of ammunition and were also equipped with a Type 97 heavy machine gun.

BELOW LEFT: Type 95 tanks in Malaya. Introduced in 1935, they were equipped with a

Type 94, 37mm cannon and a Type 97 heavy machine gun. Maximum armor was 12mm.

BELOW CENTER: Type 2, 10cm self-propelled gun. It was introduced too late in the war to be sent overseas, and was planned for defense of the home islands. It carried a crew of five, and was equipped with a V-12, 170hp engine which was air-cooled.

70mm gun in a central turret and with two smaller turrets at front and rear, each carrying a machine gun.

Between 1926 and 1932 more specimen tanks were purchased from abroad, including one Vickers 'Mark C' which had been designed to Japanese specifications. This was then used as a starting point for a fresh design, since the Osaka Arsenal model had run into difficulties, and in 1929 the 'Model 89A' the first Japanese design, entered service. This was an 11-tonner with a four-man crew, armed with a 57mm gun and two machine guns. Production began in 1931, when ten were built, and the first off the line were sent to Manchuria for service testing.

The Osaka design team had continued on their original 1925 design, re-working it to get things right, and in 1932 this appeared as the 'Heavy Tank Type 92', weighing 26 tons and armed with a 37mm gun. With a five-man crew this could manage 14 mph and had armor 15mm thick, which scarcely seems to add up to a 'heavy tank' image in anything except sheer weight. Its principal defect lay in its enormously complicated suspension, with no less than 34 bogie wheels.

What limited experience the Japanese had by now acquired in Manchuria tended to show that tanks were most useful as individual supporters of infantry units, and since the Chinese had little means of countering even the lightest type of tank, the Japanese army suddenly became enthusiastic about 'Tankettes', small but nimble vehicles armed with a heavy machine gun, capable of rapid movement about the battlefield to bring heavy support to bear when the infantry were pinned down; a sort of battlefield flying squad. This system was being promoted in the west too, but the Spanish Civil War was to reveal that against an enemy with any degree of anti-tank capability it was useless. But it suited the Japanese tactics and their current type of warfare, and after buying a number of Carden-Loyd tankettes from Britain the Osaka Arsenal made a few minor changes and produced

BOTTOM: Japanese infantry armor was introduced during the China campaign for the protection of grenadiers.

BELOW: Recruitment poster for the Army Tank Corps School. It urges volunteers to join up with inducements like free clothes, free food, and the handsome sum of four yen a month as well. In order to join one had to pass examinations in literature, mathematics and Japanese history.

the 'Type 92 Tankette', a three-man four-tonner which carried one machine gun in a small turret and another alongside the driver. This was built in small numbers and then rapidly succeeded by the 'Type 94 Tankette', a 2½-ton two-man model with a single machine gun. This could reach 25 mph and was powered by a cheap and simple four-cylinder petrol engine; the original British version had, in fact, been powered by the Ford Model T engine and gearbox. The cheapness and simplicity of the Tankette, plus its suitability to conditions in Manchuria, insured its success, and large numbers were made.

However, the Manchurian campaign was also bringing out some other lessons; the most important of these was the problem of operating motor vehicles in the extreme winter conditions of North Manchuria – which is, after all, practically part of Siberia. In seeking an answer to this the Japanese designers came up with an answer which put them ahead of any

## Japanese Tanks

| Type | Weight tons | Crew | Armor | Armament | Dimensions | Engine | Drive | Speed | Suspension |
|---|---|---|---|---|---|---|---|---|---|
| Tankette (Series M2592, 2594, etc.) | 3 | 2 | Turret 14mm (.55"). Hull front 14mm Hull sides 8mm (.31") | One MG in ball mounting in turret | Length 11' Width 5' 3" Height 5' 4" | Petrol 45-50 hp 4-Cylinder air-cooled | Front sprocket | 20-25 mph (max) | 4 bogie wheels each side, in pairs |
| Light Tank (Early Model, M2593) | 7 | 3 | Up to 22mm (.87") | One LMG in front turret. One LMG in front superstructure | Length 14' 8" Width 5' 10" Height 6' 0" | Petrol 85hp 6-cylinder air-cooled | Front sprocket | 28mph (max) | 6 small bogie wheels each side, in pairs |
| Light Tank (Series M2595, etc.) | Unladen 7, In action 8-9 | 4 | Turret 12mm (.47"). Hull front 12mm. Hull sides 10-12mm (.4-.47"). Hull rear 12mm. | One 37mm (1.45") gun in front turret. One MG right rear of turret. One MG in left front superstructure. | Length 14' 4" Width 6' 9" Height 7' 0" | Diesel 240hp at 2000 rpm air-cooled | Front sprocket | 28mph at 2000 rpm | 4 bogie wheels each side, in pairs. |
| Medium Tank (Early Model, M2594) | 14 | 4 | Front 17mm (.67"). Sides 11mm (.43") Turret 17mm | One 37mm (1.45") gun in front turret. One MG in rear of turret. One MG in front superstructure. | Length with tail 20' 10" Width 8' 4" Height 8' 6" | Petrol 160hp 6-cylinder air-cooled | Front sprocket | 28mph (max) | 9 small bogie wheels and protective skirting |
| Medium Tank (Series M2595, 2597, etc.) | Unladen 13½. In action 15 | 4 | Front 25mm (.98"). Sides 15mm (.59") Top 8mm (.31") | One 57mm (2.24") gun in front turret. One MG in turret rear. One MG in front superstructure | Length 18' 0" Width 7' 8" Height 7' 2½" | Diesel 12 cylinder air-cooled | Front sprocket | 25mph (max) | 6 medium sized bogie wheels each side |
| Heavy Tank (Early Model M2595) | 27 | 5 | Up to 35mm (1.38") | One 70mm (2.75") gun. One 37mm (1.45") gun and two MGs. | Length 21' 3" Width 8' 10" Height 9' 6" | 290hp | Front sprocket | 13½mph | 6 small bogie wheels each side in pairs |

BELOW LEFT: Japanese troops follow a tank on maneuvers in Manchuria.

RIGHT: Experimental anti-aircraft self-propelled gun for protection of troops from aerial attack. They never came into general production.

Western nation; they produced an air-cooled six-cylinder diesel engine for their next tank design, the light tank 'Type 95'. This new engine produced 114 hp and allied to the 6½-ton three-man tank produced a vehicle as fast and maneuverable as the Tankette but better armed, with a 37mm gun and two machine guns. This went into quantity production in 1936.

The 'Type 89A' medium tank was now fitted with the new diesel engine to become the Type 89B. By this time, 1936, Japanese tank production had reached 400 vehicles a year and in 1937, when the Sino-Japanese War broke out, the Army's tank strength was some 1050 tanks and tankettes organized into three tank regiments plus schools and reserves. Two of the regiments were in Japan while the third was with the Manchurian Army. With the start of the war with China the force was expanded, the Manchurian regiment becoming a tank brigade of three companies plus motorized infantry, artillery and engineer regiments attached.

Nevertheless, it was never destined to fight as a brigade, that is as an autonomous unit. Japanese doctrine still saw tanks simply as infantry support weapons. There was no thought of using tanks en masse as an armored force in order to achieve results by momentum and firepower as, for example, in the German panzer divisions. But this point of view was given a setback when Japanese commanders saw what the Soviets could do with properly organized armored forces in the border incidents at Nomonhan and Changkufeng. Further food for thought was provided by the activity of German armor in Poland and later in France. This, in 1940, led to the experimental formation of two armored divisions in Manchuria, though there is little or no evidence of their actual use in divisional strength.

Meanwhile, in 1937, the 'Type 97' medium tank had been introduced, probably the best Japanese design. This had better armor – 25mm – and a two-man turret mounting a 57mm gun. Driven by a 170hp air-cooled diesel it could reach 25 mph, weighed just over 15 tons, and had a four-man crew. Its worst defect lay in the gun, a low-velocity model which was well below contemporary thought on tank guns. The Japanese soon realized this and took steps to improve matters. The first move was to develop a high-velocity 47mm gun as a direct replacement; this was the same gun which later appeared as an anti-tank gun, and it was certainly better than the 57mm although of smaller caliber. In 1940 though the whole tank was completely re-designed to become the 'Type 1' or 'Chi-He' model; the armor was thicker and welded instead of riveted, and the engine was boosted to 240 hp. But the 47mm gun remained, since no replacement had yet appeared.

The invasion of Malaya was accompanied by about 300 tanks from the 3rd Tank Division, largely Tankettes and Type 95's, and numbers of these two types were also sent to the Philippines to assist in operations there. Some of the new 'Chi-He' models also appeared on the Bataan Peninsula in 1942. After the expansion of the tank forces, in 1942 they were re-organized once more, the two Manchurian divisions being formed into a 'Tank Army', but in fact the whole of this organization was a paper transaction. Many of the individual units were permanently detached for duty with other formations, and it is extremely doubtful if this so-called 'Tank Army' ever managed to assemble during the whole of its existence. One of the constituent divisions was used with some success in China in 1944, one of the few occasions when a major armored formation was used as an entity, but in the other theaters, Burma and the Pacific, tanks were thrown into action in ones and twos to support small infantry actions and, inevitably, were simply defeated in detail wherever they appeared.

During this period of the war the production of tanks in Japan almost came to a standstill. In 1942 1290 tanks had been built, the peak of production; in 1944 only 295 were built, since the Japanese economy had reached a point where it could no longer support the multifarious demands being made on it, and something had to suffer. Since by 1944 the priority was declared to be aircraft and anti-aircraft defenses, tank production had to take a low priority. This was doubly unfortunate since 1944 saw the last Japanese tank design appear, the 'Type 3 Medium' or 'Chi-Nu'. This was a 'Type 1' with some detail improvements, but with a major change in the adoption of a 75mm gun derived from the 'Type 90' field gun. This was a vast improvement, and is believed to have been suggested to the Japanese by their experiences with the US Sherman M4, also armed with a 75mm gun. But good as this new model was, by that time the production facilities were insufficient to make it in anything like the number needed; no more than 60 were ever built and few of them ever saw combat.

In general terms the Japanese tank forces were ineffective because of the peculiarly isolated position of Japan at the time their tactics and equipment were being worked out. In the eyes of postwar critics the principal faults were firstly the waste of effort on tankettes when such lightweights had been proved useless in the Spanish Civil War; and secondly the poor armament fitted in the tanks. Both these faults stemmed from the circumstances of fighting the Chinese in Manchuria, an enemy with little or no means of retaliation against even the worst tank and against whom virtually any sort of armored vehicle was certain of success. If it worked in Manchuria, the Army reasoned, it would work elsewhere. And this point of view seemed to be reinforced by experience in Malaya, where Japanese tanks found little opposition, largely because British experts had declared that tanks could not operate in such terrain and had thus neglected to provide either tanks or anti-tank capability for the British forces there. Early successes against the American Army also strengthened their opinions. They began to change their minds when better Allied tanks appeared against them. Their final disillusionment came in 1945 when the Soviet Army, with the formidable T34/85, destroyed the Manchurian Tank Army as if it were made of cardboard.

# THE IMPERIAL JAPANESE NAVY

BELOW LEFT: Admiral Isoroku Yamamoto, Japan's most brilliant naval leader, planned and executed the strategy which swept Allied navies from the Western Pacific in 1941–42. He warned the Imperial General Staff that war with the West would be fatal, but his advice was unheeded.

BOTTOM: The destroyers *Akebono* (right) and *Ushio* on maneuvers. The 20 units of the *Fubuki* Class, completed in 1928–29, set a new standard for all destroyers. For the first time they were armed with six 5-inch dual-purpose guns in gas-proof enclosed mounts. The provision of nine spare torpedoes doubled their fighting power in battle.

All navies are reflections of their parent countries' economic and political progress, but the Imperial Japanese Navy is the outstanding example. Like the Japanese Empire the Navy's meteoric rise and catastrophic fall happened in less than 80 years. The reasons for this rapid rise and fall are inextricably bound up with the history of Japan herself but as far as the Navy was concerned the turning point was the Battle of Tsushima. When Admiral Togo's fleet took the surrender of the battered Russian survivors Japan changed from an ambitious small nation to a front-rank naval power.

World War I stimulated the growth of the Navy even more. Japan's rulers astutely gave immediate backing to the British and French, despite attempts by the British to keep her neutral. The Anglo-Japanese Treaty carried no obligation upon Japan to intervene, and the British were afraid that Japanese ambitions against China would be hard to curb. The British were torn between the desire to restrain Japan's territorial ambitions and the need to use her large navy to help them protect their colonies and shipping in the Far East, and the Japanese government was quick to exploit the situation. The German colony of Tsingtao (Kiaochow Bay) in the Shantung Peninsula was quickly subdued, and Japanese warships joined in the hunt for Admiral Spee's squadron. But joining the war did much more for Japan's prosperity. Enormous demands from her Allies for munitions were followed by orders for ships. France ordered a dozen destroyers and Britain began negotiations for submarines. In 1916 Japan was asked to join in a giant merchant shipbuilding programme, part of a belated effort to replace U-Boat losses. No fewer than 236 ships were built for Britain and new shipyards had to be laid out. By the Armistice the Japanese mercantile marine comprised more then two million tons and there were 57 major shipyards.

Japan was able to finance the modernization of her heavy industries, build up her mercantile marine and displace European nations from their well-established markets in China, all out of her war profits. But this must not disguise the fact that the valor of her soldiers and sailors and the shrewdness of her rulers had played an equally important part. In 1854 Japan was a feudal nation apparently ripe for the same sort of brutal onslaught from Western trade and technology that dismembered China, yet by 1868, when the young Emperor Meiji accepted the resignation of the Tokugawa Shogun, Japan was still in charge of her own destiny. Within a year later the first students left for Europe to learn the secrets of Western civilization. The tiny navy placed orders for its first big ships in 1871 and a British technical mission arrived in Japan to train the fleet and set up a naval administration.

Although still small the Japanese Navy had no difficulty in destroying the Chinese fleet during the Sino-Japanese War in 1894, but the European nations forced Japan to return her territorial gains.

LEFT: The *Kagero* Class were the finest Japanese destroyers, with a large radius of action, high speed and heavy armament. The *Yukikaze* was the only survivor of a class of 18, armed with six 5-inch dual-purpose guns, eight 24-inch torpedo tubes, firing the dreaded long-lance torpedo, and had a top speed of 35 knots.

When these same gains were leased to Russia the Japanese knew that they had been tricked, and began to prepare for a new conflict. Although it seemed presumptuous for a small Oriental nation to take on one of the great European powers the Japanese had the technical backing of the British Royal Navy, whereas the Russian armed forces were in a chronic state of neglect and muddle. The impossible happened; David toppled Goliath and the Russians lost not only their new Manchurian possessions but their entire Baltic Fleet.

The collapse of Russia's fledgling Eastern Empire brought Japan tremendous prestige. Her Army had defeated the Russians in Manchuria and the siege of Port Arthur was hailed as a great feat of arms but Admiral Togo's victory over the Baltic Fleet was by far the most important element of Japan's triumph. In its annihilation of a large fleet by a smaller one the Battle of Tsushima ranked with Trafalgar as one of the greatest sea-fights of all time, and Togo was christened the 'Japanese Nelson'. With such praise in their ears the Japanese Navy could hardly be blamed for thinking themselves invincible, and even though they were denied the opportunity of major action in 1914–18 their self-confidence was unbounded. The news in 1921 that Britain was not anxious to renew the Anglo-Japanese Treaty, and that she and the US wanted Japan to cut back her Navy

ABOVE: The Battleship *Tosa*, cancelled to comply with the naval limitations imposed by the Washington Conference of 1921–22, was used as a target and sunk by the Japanese in 1925. Her sister *Kaga* was converted to an aircraft carrier.

was therefore all the more insulting.

At the Washington Naval Disarmament Conference in 1921–22 the Japanese delegation fought in vain for parity with the British and Americans, and finally accepted a 5:5:3 ratio with reluctance. Yet the Imperial Japanese Navy was now the third largest in the world. Her army was second only to that of France and, whereas the British and Americans were limited to their existing bases Japan now had control over a large number of ex-German islands in the Western Pacific. The British reserved the right to fortify Singapore and the Americans had Pearl Harbor, but it was clear that both navies would find it very difficult to wage an effective naval war against Japan.

74

Although there was great admiration for the Royal Navy the Japanese rightly suspected that the British refusal to renew the Anglo-Japanese Treaty was only to comply with American demands, and British prestige suffered as a result. Although the might of the United States was respected there was already a long history of friction. The annexation of Hawaii had been resented and the exclusion of Japanese subjects from California had caused great indignation. America in her turn opposed the annexation of Korea, and supported the 'open door' policy in China. When in 1915 Japan tried to coerce the new Republic of China with a series of truculent demands which would have reduced her to a vassal state the United States objected. The 'Twenty-One Demands' were withdrawn but the loss of face was not forgotten.

The Washington Naval Disarmament Treaty of 1922 did more than restrict national aspirations; it put a severe brake on the growing size of warships by im-

## Japanese Shipyard Production

**1937 3rd Replacement Program**
(excluding auxiliaries and minor warships)
2 battleships *(Yamato* and *Musashi)* completed 1941–42
2 fleet carriers *(Shokaku, Zuikaku)* completed 1941
1 seaplane carrier *(Nisshin)* completed 1942
15 destroyers *(Kagero* Class*)* completed 1939–41
14 submarines (4 types) completed 1940–42
4 escorts *(Shumushu* Class*)* completed 1940–41

**1938 Supplementary Estimates**
2 training cruisers *(Katori* Class*)* completed 1940–41

**1939 4th Replacement Program**
2 battleships *(Shinano, No. 111) Shinana* converted to carrier, *No. 111* cancelled Dec 1941
1 fleet carrier *(Taiho)* completed 1944
6 light cruisers *(Agano* and *Oyodo* Classes*)* 5 completed 1942–44, 1 not laid down
1 training cruiser *(Katori* Class*)* completed 1941
22 destroyers (5 types) completed 1941–43
25 submarines (3 types) completed 1942–43

74

FAR LEFT: Admiral Toyoda advocated the 'southern strategy' which led Japan into war with the U.S.

LEFT: The naval leaders of Imperial Japan. Front row, from left to right: Admirals Shimizu, Hosogaya, Takahashi, Kondo, Yamamoto, Takasu, Nagumo, Tsukahara and Inoue.

CENTER LEFT: The biggest battleship built by any navy in World War II, the 64,000 ton *Yamato*, on trials in 1941.

RIGHT: Vice-Admiral Kondo, C-in-C of the Second Scouting Fleet based on Hainan, at the time of Pearl Harbor.

BELOW: The coast defense ship *Idzumo*, a veteran of Tsushima, off the Shanghai Bund.

posing limits on tonnage and armament. In common with the other navies the Japanese set about planning a new generation of warships to comply with the limitations, but in their boundless self-confidence they tried to produce ships which were superior to all possible opponents. Unfortunately the Japanese Navy soon ran into trouble, and the new ships displayed a number of faults. To rectify them the ships were frequently altered after completion, and if the result was an increase in displacement tonnage this additional figure was not revealed. The result was that foreign observers marveled at a series of unorthodox warships which apparently incorporated speed and gun and torpedo-armaments superior to all other navies. The really astonishing point about this phenomenon is that it misled even trained observers. It is a recognized axiom of ship-design that two ships of similar tonnage and date will only be able to carry the same weight of weaponry and machinery. If there is a marked discrepancy it can be taken for granted that the figures quoted are not correct. This is not to say that the Japanese Navy began by cheating on the Treaty conditions; the tasks set by their constructors were too difficult to achieve, but the Navy was not prepared to accept any reduction of armament, and so the extra weight of improvements had to be concealed.

The advances in weapons were much more important, for in this field Japanese designers achieved much more. Their outstanding mechanical achievement was to design an oxygen-driven torpedo with greater speed and range than any contemporary. Known as the 'Long Lance', the project was started when news leaked out of British experiments, and while the British abandoned the idea the Japanese perservered until they had eliminated all the dangerous faults. Not

only did a 24-inch 'Long Lance' deliver a 500-kg warhead at 36 knots over a distance of 40,000 yards, but the oxygen bubbles dissolved and left no tell-tale wake. Knowledge of its potential remained a close secret, the existence of this rugged and reliable weapon conferred important tactical advantage in the Pacific in 1942–43. Another example of Japanese foresight in weapon development can be seen in the introduction of a dual-purpose (surface/anti-aircraft) gun-mounting for destroyers. Six years before the Americans introduced this feature Japanese destroyers could boast a gun-mounting that was not only capable of firing against aircraft but was also proof against gas attack. To exploit the advantages of the 'Long Lance' torpedo destroyers were equipped with reloading gear, another unique feature which enabled Japanese destroyers to spring several surprises in action.

But the Treaty limitations still irked the Japanese Navy, and by 1934 its constructors told the Staff that any further improvement in the quality of the Fleet's matériel could only be achieved by ignoring those limitations. Now it has been widely thought that the Imperial Japanese Navy at this period was more moderate, more pro-British and less rabidly anti-American than the Army. In modern jargon the Navy 'doves' were supposed to be a restraining influence on the Army 'hawks'. Certainly Navy officers were better educated and more broad-minded, and less infatuated by admiration for Prussian-style military efficiency. However, this cosy picture ignores the complex web of intrigues and factions which made the Japanese military and political hierachy.

At the time of the Meiji Restoration in 1868 the Emperor's powers were enshrined in a series of Imperial Precepts and Ordinances, and even when a constitution was granted in 1889 the new German-style Diet had no control over the Army and Navy. Thus there was nothing improper in the ceaseless lobbying which went on behind the scenes, based on philosophies, regional interests or even family connections. But even more important was a wholly Japanese phenomenon, the *chuken shoko*, the influence of 'middle rank' officers. In other words a good deal of the pressure for changes in policy came from majors, lieutenant-colonels and colonels in the case of the Army, or lieutenant-commanders, commanders and captains in the case of the Navy. This was an honored precedent dating back to 1867–68, when young samurai of middle rank engineered the downfall of the Shogunate and the restoration of the Emperor.

Such a combination of freedom from political control and an exaggerated deference to the opinions of relatively junior officers presented both the Japanese Government and the Emperor Hirohito with severe problems in framing policy. The Navy was better controlled than the Army and there was no equivalent of the 1936 mutiny of younger army officers, but throughout the 1930s the middle rank officers became more and more determined to force a showdown against the Americans, British and Dutch whose possessions seemed so inviting. Their ambitions were not purely for military glory. Japan's industrial growth demanded enormous imports of raw material, 20 per cent of its food, 24 per cent of its coal, 88 per cent of its iron ore, and over 90 per cent

---

## Strength of The Imperial Japanese Navy in Dec 1941

Figures in parenthesis indicate ships under construction.

**10 Battleships** (+3)[1]
4 *Kongo* Class completed 1913–15[2]
2 *Fuso* Class completed 1915–17
2 *Ise* Class completed 1917–18
2 *Nagato* Class completed 1920–21
[1]3 *Yamato* Class, of which a fourth had been cancelled in 1941.
[2]Ex-battlecruisers completely rebuilt as fast battleships 1934–40.

**8 Aircraft Carriers** (+8)[1]
1 *Hosho* completed 1922[2]
1 *Kaga* completed 1928[3]
2 *Hiryu* Class completed 1937–39
2 *Shokaku* Class completed 1941[5]
1 *Akagi* completed 1927[4]
1 *Ryujo* completed 1933
[1]*Shoho* and *Zuiho* converting from high speed oilers, and 6 liners and tenders about to begin conversion. [2]Brought back to front-line duties on outbreak of war but later relegated to training. [3]Ex-battleship. [4]Ex-battlecruiser. [5]Still working up.

**18 Heavy Cruisers** (+1)[1]
2 *Furutaka* Class completed 1926–27
2 *Aoba* Class completed 1926–27
4 *Myoko* Class completed 1928–29
4 *Takao* Class completed 1932
4 *Mogami* Class completed 1935–37[2]
2 *Tone* Class completed 1941[3]
[1]1 *Ibuki* Class, not yet laid down. [2]Completed as 6-inch gunned cruisers 1936 but rearmed with 8-inch guns. [3]Designed as light cruisers but altered during construction to heavy cruisers.

**20 Light Cruisers** (+9)[1]
2 *Tenryu* Class completed 1919
5 *Kuma* Class completed 1920–21
6 *Natori* Class completed 1922–25
1 *Yubari* completed 1923
3 *Jintsu* Class completed 1924–25
[1]3 *Katori* Class, of which 1 was cancelled, 4 *Agano* Class, 2 *Oyodo* Class.

**108 Destroyers** (+43)[1]
3 *Momi* Class completed 1920–22[2]
13 *Minekaze* Class completed 1920–22[3]
7 *Wakatake* Class completed 1922–23
4 *Kamikaze* Class completed 1922–24
12 *Mutsuki* Class completed 1925–27
20 *Fubuki* Class completed 1928–31
4 *Akatsuki* Class completed 1932–33
6 *Hatsuharu* Class completed 1933–35
10 *Shiratsuyu* Class completed 1936–37
10 *Asashio* Class completed 1937–39
18 *Kagero* Class completed 1939–41
1 *Yugumo* Class completed 1941
[1]27 *Yugumo* Class and 16 *Akitsuki* Class. [2]Most others of class converted to patrol vessels by 1940. [3]2 others converted to patrol vessels 1940.

BELOW: Insignia of the Imperial Japanese Navy. First column left, from top to bottom: Good conduct badges, fifth grade to first; second column, from top to bottom: first class sergeant; 2nd class sergeant; 3rd class sergeant; 1st class private; 2nd class private; 3rd class private. Third column: naval paymaster, rankings from top to bottom as in column two.

Fourth column: hospital orderly, same as above. Fifth column: naval air corps. Sixth column: naval mechanic. Seventh column: sailor. Eighth column, top four: lieutenant junior grade, lieutenant, cadet, cadet (dress), from top to bottom. Ninth column, top four, from top to bottom: Captain, Commander, Lieutenant Commander;

Lieutenant Senior Grade. Tenth column, top four, top to bottom: Admiral, Vice Admiral, Rear Admiral. Bottom six on the far right, left top to bottom: cap badge for commissioned officer, cap badge for NCO, cap band for seaman; right top to bottom: cap for commissioned officer, cap for NCO, cap for seaman.

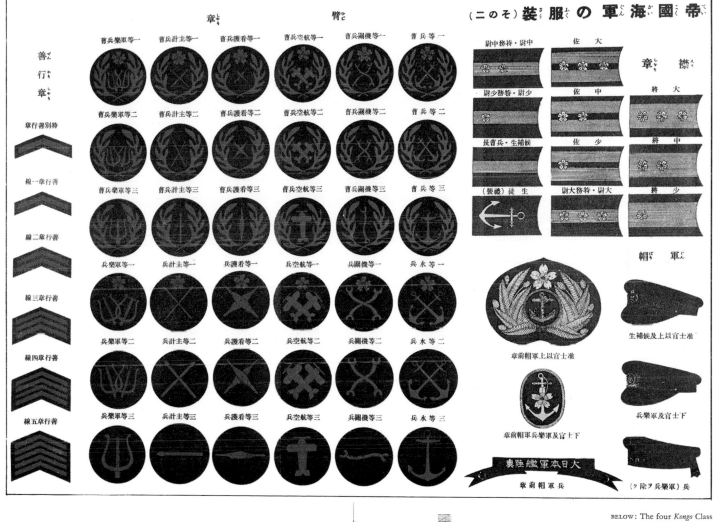

BELOW: The four *Kongo* Class battlecruisers underwent a series of modernizations between 1930 and 1940 to transform them into high speed battleships. Their speed was increased from 26 to 30 knots to make them suitable escorts for the carrier groups.

BELOW: The battleship *Yamato* was 863 feet long and had a beam of 127 feet. Her main armor belt was 16 inches thick, and the turrets for the nine 18-inch guns had armor of 20–25½ inches thickness. No other battleship ever built has matched *Yamato* for firepower, weight and armored protection.

78

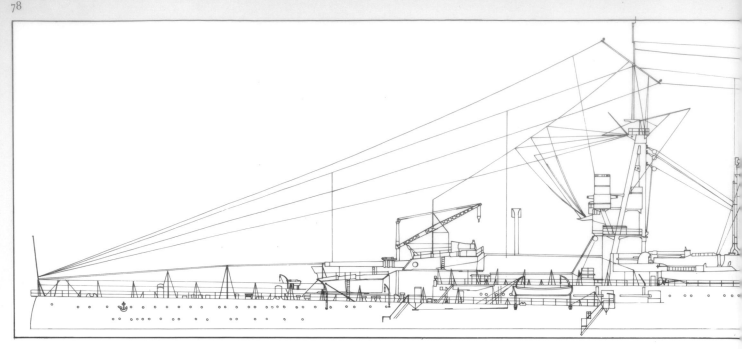

of its oil. Yet the Western Powers held the riches of Southeast Asia, the rubber and tin of Malaya and the oil of Sumatra and Jarva. It was clear to the Japanese that the colonial forces which had won such victories over Oriental armies with ridiculously small forces were now but a shadow of their former might. The British and Dutch colonial empires were ramshackle in the extreme, a bitter truth which only became evident to their inhabitants and rulers with the fall of Singapore and the conquest of the East Indies.

## Battleships

The first fruits of this internal dissent and pressure flowered in 1934, when Japan announced that she was giving the required two years' notice of her withdrawal from the Washington Treaty. Immediately work began on a design for battleships which would be more powerful than any possessed by the USA or Great Britain. The other powers had concluded further treaties in a desperate attempt to stave off a naval arms race, and they were bound by tonnage and numerical limitations until 1940. Thus the Japanese Navy reasoned that if it could somehow complete a class of giant battleships in secret by 1940 it would be able to defeat the American battle fleet or even overawe the United States' government to the point where the Americans would negotiate rather than risk defeat. To avoid the risk of the Americans building

their own super-battleships there was a further twist to the Japanese reasoning. Their battleships would be built to such a size that any possible opponent would be too big to pass through the Panama Canal, thus robbing the Americans of their great advantage of being able to transfer ships from the Atlantic to the Pacific rapidly.

The battleships were part of what might be called the traditional strategic plan, one based broadly on Admiral Togo's masterful campaign against the Russians. The American Fleet would be lured across the Pacific, exposing itself to attrition through destroyers and submarine attacks, hence a strong emphasis on torpedo- and submarine-warfare. When the numerical superiority of the US Fleet was whittled down to something approaching parity the main Battle Fleet would be thrown in to accomplish its destruction. Another factor, however, was promoting the development of a potent new force of aircraft carriers. This faction, a very influential one, wanted to whittle down or even annihilate American strength by means of swift, far-ranging air strikes from carrier task forces. The Army, in complete contrast, hankered after operations on the mainland of China as a counter to Russian land forces in Mongolia.

The new battleships were to be called the *Yamato* class, and the first plans were drawn up in 1935. Finally in 1937, when the order was about to be placed, the

designers discovered that the novel high-speed diesel engines were not reliable. In frantic haste the ships were altered and given four-shaft steam turbines, a change which resulted in lower endurance than originally planned. Only two of the seven projected were completed, but they were the most powerful battleships ever built. With an overall length of 863 feet, a beam of nearly 128 feet and a draught of 34 feet, the displacement totalled 64,000 tons. The thickest armor carried was $25\frac{1}{2}$ inches thick and the deck armor alone was 9 inches in places. The effort required to build these two, the *Yamato* and *Musashi* and a third which became an aircraft carrier, put a tremendous strain on the Japanese shipbuilding and steel industries, and it is arguable that the money could have been better spent on four smaller ships or even on aircraft carriers, because the Japanese needed numbers above all else.

In addition to these new monsters there were ten older ships. The oldest were the four *Kongo* class, completed early in World War I to a British design. Between 1934 and 1940 they were rebuilt as fast battleships, with a great increase of speed to allow them to act as escorts for the aircraft carriers. Two of them, *Hiei* and *Kirishima*, were sunk in night action off Guadalcanal in November 1942, but the other two survived to fight at Leyte Gulf in 1944. The *Kongo* was torpedoed off Formosa, and the *Huruna* succumbed to the final overwhelming air attacks against

LEFT: The *Mutsu*, as well as her

Japanese battleships to survive
the axe of the Washington
Conference. Both ships were
rebuilt in 1934–36 with new
machinery and protection. The
*Mutsu* had eight 16-inch guns
and steamed at 25 knots.

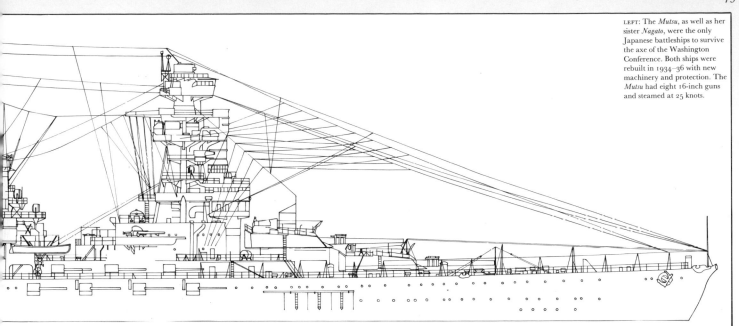

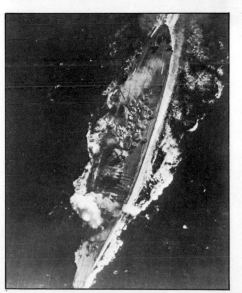

ABOVE LEFT: The *Yamato* nears
completion at Kure in
September 1941.

ABOVE RIGHT: Vice Admiral
Takeo Kurita played an
important role in the decisive
Battle of Leyte Gulf in 1944.

RIGHT: *Yamato* under attack at
Leyte Gulf with a US aircraft
bomb exploding on the
forecastle.

BELOW: The *Yamato* running
her trials off Sata Point in
October 1941

RIGHT: The *I.58* was a fleet submarine of the B3 Type, equipped with a seaplane in a hangar foreward of the conning tower and a catapult.

RIGHT: The Type C midget submarine was 80 feet long and was armed with two 18-inch torpedoes.

FAR RIGHT: The *I.400* Class were the world's largest submarines, when they were completed in 1945. Their three floatplane bombers were intended to attack the Panama Canal, but vessels like the *I.402* seen here were completed too late to accomplish much.

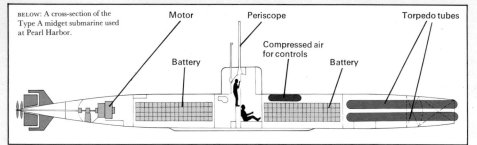

BELOW: A cross-section of the Type A midget submarine used at Pearl Harbor.

Motor

Periscope

Torpedo tubes

Battery

Compressed air for controls

Battery

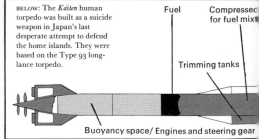

BELOW: The *Kaiten* human torpedo was built as a suicide weapon in Japan's last desperate attempt to defend the home islands. They were based on the Type 93 long-lance torpedo.

Fuel

Compressed for fuel mixt

Trimming tanks

Buoyancy space / Engines and steering gear

BELOW: The *I.176* Class fleet submarines were completed in 1941–42. They were armed with six 21-inch torpedo tubes and had a surface speed of 23 knots. All ten units were lost.

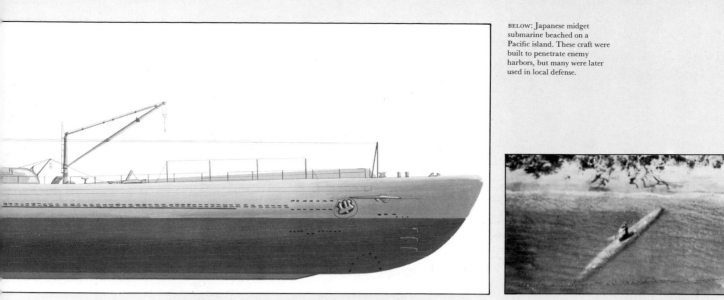

BELOW: Japanese midget submarine beached on a Pacific island. These craft were built to penetrate enemy harbors, but many were later used in local defense.

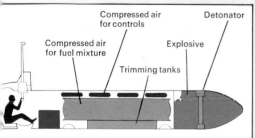

Compressed air for fuel mixture

Compressed air for controls

Detonator

Explosive

Trimming tanks

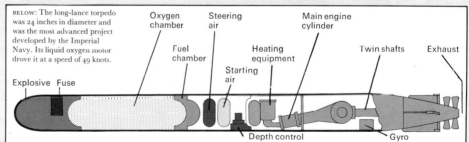

BELOW: The long-lance torpedo was 24 inches in diameter and was the most advanced project developed by the Imperial Navy. Its liquid oxygen motor drove it at a speed of 49 knots.

Explosive    Fuse

Oxygen chamber

Steering air

Fuel chamber

Heating equipment

Main engine cylinder

Starting air

Twin shafts

Exhaust

Depth control

Gyro

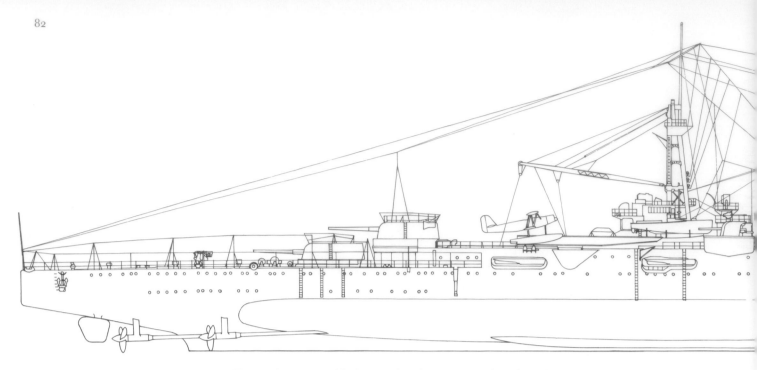

Japanese homeland bases in 1945. The *Fuso* and *Ise* classes were four elderly units of World War I vintage, but like the *Kongo* class they were completely reconstructed to bring them up to modern standards. The two most modern units were the *Nagato* and *Mutsu*, which were the first battleships in the world armed with 16-inch guns. They were relatively fast and well-protected, but even they underwent a massive reconstruction as part of the program to provide maximum fighting power within each class.

The reconstructions were ingenious but one can doubt if they all justified themselves. For all their alterations the *Hiei* of the *Kongo* class was sunk by American cruisers, since the original thin side armor had been retained. Similarly there was little room for really effective re-armoring in the *Fuso* and *Ise* group; as built they had 50 per cent more armament than the *Kongo* class on only 2000 tons more displacement tonnage.

### Aircraft Carriers
The Japanese laid down their first aircraft carrier in 1919, the 7400-ton *Hosho*. Although too small for work with the fleet

she was still in service in 1941 and survived the war. The first effective fleet carriers were the *Akagi* and *Kaga*, both ex-capital ships salvaged from the wreckage of the Washington Treaty. Originally the Treaty had allowed the Japanese to convert the hulls of the 40,000-ton battlecruisers *Akagi* and *Amagi* to carriers, but after the *Amagi* was damaged during the 1923 earthquake the slightly smaller battleship *Kaga*'s hull was substituted. As completed they both displaced 29,600 tons in standard condition (announced as 28,100 tons) and carried 60 aircraft. Like the American *Saratoga* and *Lexington* they took maximum advantage of the clause in the Treaty about armament, and had 8-inch guns, a dubious asset to any aircraft carrier. As built *Kaga* had immense horizontal funnels running below the flight deck port and starboard, to discharge smoke aft, whereas *Akagi* had two on the starboard side, one curving downwards and the other upwards. Neither ship was an unqualified success, apart from having good aircraft capacity, and in 1934–38 both ships were taken in hand for reconstruction. This altered them completely, and increased their aircraft capacity to 90

aircraft. The loss of both ships at Midway with their crack air groups was a disaster from which the naval air arm never recovered.

In April 1941 the Foreign Minister Yosuke Matsuoka signed a non-aggression pact with Russia to remove worries about Japan's northern frontiers. Although it had the desired effect Japan was put in an embarrassing position when her Axis partner Germany launched the invasion of Russia only two months later. With all the other factors apparently favorable the Japanese hoped to be able to reach a settlement with the Americans, but the economic embargo imposed by President Roosevelt in July, the freezing of Japanese assets, was the last straw. The Navy's plans had to be accepted, and the greatest naval war in history was virtually inevitable.

As the Washington Treaty limited Japan to having 80,000 tons of aircraft carriers but did not restrict carriers of under 10,000 tons, the designers were told to design an 8000-ton type (announced as 7100 tons). This was the *Ryujo*, which emerged with a displacement of 10,600 tons but continued to be listed under her

RIGHT: *Akitsuki* was the first of a new class of high speed, anti-aircraft escorts designed to screen carriers. She was armed with eight 100mm dual purpose guns and four 24-inch torpedo tubes.

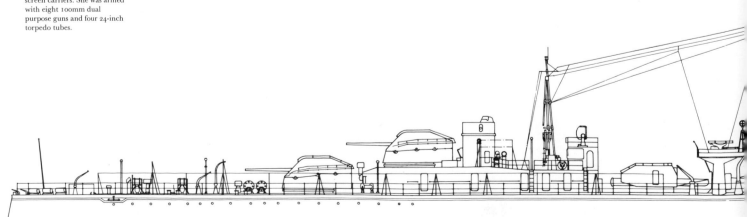

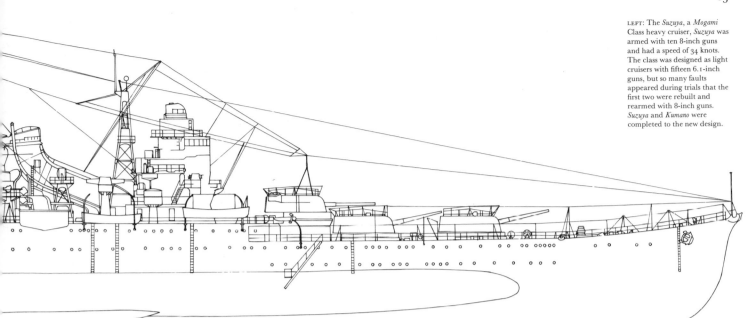

LEFT: The *Suzuya*, a *Mogami* Class heavy cruiser, *Suzuya* was armed with ten 8-inch guns and had a speed of 34 knots. The class was designed as light cruisers with fifteen 6.1-inch guns, but so many faults appeared during trials that the first two were rebuilt and rearmed with 8-inch guns. *Suzuya* and *Kumano* were completed to the new design.

ABOVE: The *Akagi* was converted from the hull of a battlecruiser cancelled by the Washington Treaty. She was the flagship of the Carrier Fleet under Admiral Nagumo and was sunk at Midway.

ABOVE CENTER: The *Shokaku*, and her sister *Zuikaku*, were the most successful Japanese aircraft carriers in World War II. *Shokaku* took part in most of the major battles in the Pacific except Midway and was launched in 1939. She carried 84 planes and steamed at 34 knots.

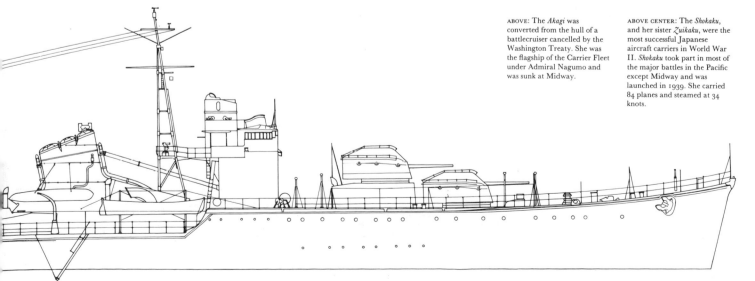

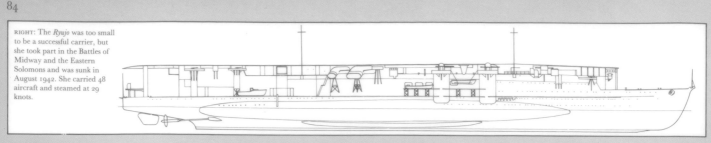

RIGHT: The *Ryujo* was too small to be a successful carrier, but she took part in the Battles of Midway and the Eastern Solomons and was sunk in August 1942. She carried 48 aircraft and steamed at 29 knots.

misleading displacement. But this time the designers over-reached themselves, and in 1934 the ship was taken in hand for drastic modifications to improve stability. Two years later she was in dock again to have her forecastle built up to improve seaworthiness, and all the while *Jane's Fighting Ships* listed her displacement as 7100 tons. The mistakes were rectified in the *Soryu*, ordered in 1934, but again the tonnage was understated at 10,050 tons when she was actually 15,900 tons. Her sister *Hiryu* had a slightly broader hull and displaced 17,300 tons, as the Treaty restrictions had been abandoned by the time she was ordered. Like *Akagi* the *Hiryu* adopted an island on the port side, despite having her funnels on the starboard side. The theory was that two sister ships could land aircraft using approach circuits well clear of one another, but as the funnels were on the starboard side in both ships the unfortunate pilots had to contend with two areas of turbulence. Normally Japanese carrier designers paid little attention to such details but the *Hiryu*'s scheme proved so dangerous that the idea was never repeated.

After the abrogation of the international treaties Japanese constructors were free to build the carriers that they wanted, and the result was the 25,000-ton *Shokaku* and *Zuikaku* ordered in 1937–38 and completed three months before the outbreak of war. In these ships the Japanese achieved a good balance of aircraft capacity (84), high speed and heavy defensive armament, and they were probably the best all-round warship design produced by the Japanese Navy in the inter-war years. An even larger type, the 29,000-ton *Taiho* was ordered in mid-1941. The most important difference was the inclusion of an armored flight deck, similar to that planned for the contemporary British *Illustrious* class. Like the British carriers she had to sacrifice a deck to save topweight, and she carried the resemblance further by having an enclosed or 'hurricane' bow for better airflow over the flight deck. Unfortunately the fuel handling arrangements in Japanese carriers were not all that they should be, and in 1944 the *Taiho* demonstrated this tragically by blowing up with the loss of nearly 1700 men.

Despite all this expansion the number of carriers remained too low for comfort. While the London Naval Treaty was still in force the Japanese made provision for future needs by designing fleet support vessels such as submarine tenders which could be rapidly converted to carriers. In this way the high speed oilers *Tsurigizaki* and *Takasaki* became the carriers *Shoho* and *Zuiho* between January 1940 and January 1942. Similarly the liners *Idzumo Maru* and *Kashiwara Maru* became the *Hiyo* and *Junyo* and the submarine tender *Taigei* became the *Ryuho*.

**Cruisers**

In 1922 Vice-Admiral Hiraga, the Chief Designer, produced a design for a revolutionary small cruiser capable of firing as many guns on the broadside as existing ships of twice her displacement. When she appeared in 1923 the new ship, called *Yubari*, marked a new departure in cruiser-design; on a nominal displacement of only 2,890 tons she carried six 5.5-inch guns and steamed at $35\frac{1}{2}$ knots. Although she was a remarkable combination of speed and gunpower on a

ABOVE: The *Kaga* was similar to the *Akagi* and in 1924–28 had been converted from the hull of a battleship. This carrier operated 90 aircraft and was armed with ten 8-inch guns.

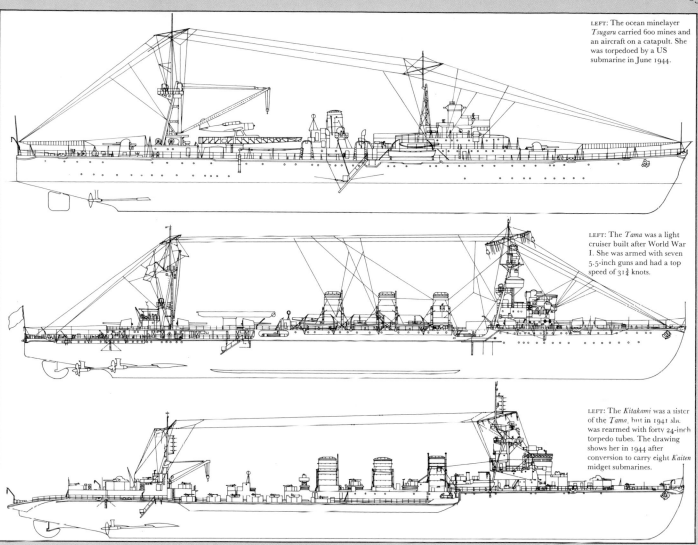

LEFT: The ocean minelayer *Tsugaru* carried 600 mines and an aircraft on a catapult. She was torpedoed by a US submarine in June 1944.

LEFT: The *Tama* was a light cruiser built after World War I. She was armed with seven 5.5-inch guns and had a top speed of $31\frac{3}{4}$ knots.

LEFT: The *Kitakami* was a sister of the *Tama*, but in 1941 she was rearmed with forty 24-inch torpedo tubes. The drawing shows her in 1944 after conversion to carry eight *Kaiten* midget submarines.

ABOVE LEFT: The *Kaiyo* was converted to an escort carrier in 1942–43 from the hull of a luxury liner. She is seen here heavily damaged by aerial attack in 1945.

ABOVE: The heavy cruiser *Haguro* was armed with ten 8-inch guns and steamed at $33\frac{3}{4}$ knots. She was sunk by British destroyers in the East Indies in May 1945.

LEFT: The *Akagi* as she appeared on completion in 1928.

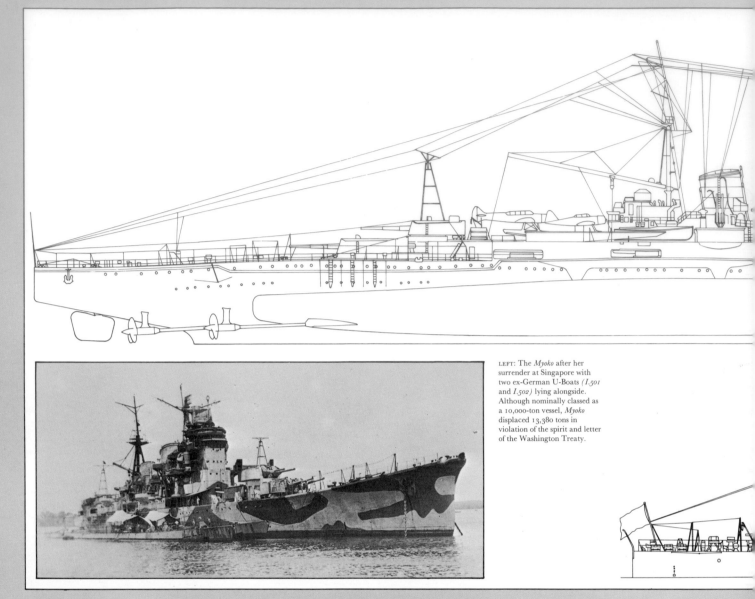

LEFT: The *Myoko* after her surrender at Singapore with two ex-German U-Boats (*I.501* and *I.502*) lying alongside. Although nominally classed as a 10,000-ton vessel, *Myoko* displaced 13,380 tons in violation of the spirit and letter of the Washington Treaty.

small hull her actual displacement was nearer 3,500 tons and her speed in service did not exceed 32 knots. Nevertheless she inspired a series of much bigger heavy (8-inch gunned) cruisers which soon hypnotized the world. The first of these were the *Furutaka* and *Kako*, which were credited with having six 8-inch guns on no more than 7,100 tons. The British Director of Naval Construction, for example, was criticized for failing to match such expertise in the British cruiser *Exeter*, and it would have helped his case if it had been known that the actual displacement on completion was 8100 tons. Nor did reconstruction improve matters; displacement rose to 9150 tons and speed fell from a nominal $34\frac{1}{2}$ to 33 knots.

Undeterred the Japanese built more heavy cruisers, culminating in the *Chokai* class of 1927–32, which were credited with ten 8-inch guns on a displacement of only 9850 tons, whereas the original displacement of 11,350 tons soon rose to 13,400 tons, even after the hull had been fitted with 'bulges'. By Western standards the disposition of gun armament was idiosyncratic to say the least, with No. 3 8-inch gun turret sited forward of the

superstructure where it had only limited arcs of fire. Like the battleships the cruisers carried a big outfit of floatplanes for reconnaissance when detached from the main fleet.

As they had with the carriers the Japanese tried to increase their numbers of heavy cruisers by conversion at a later date. This led to the fiasco of the *Mogami* class, laid down in 1931–34 as light cruisers but rearmed with 8-inch guns

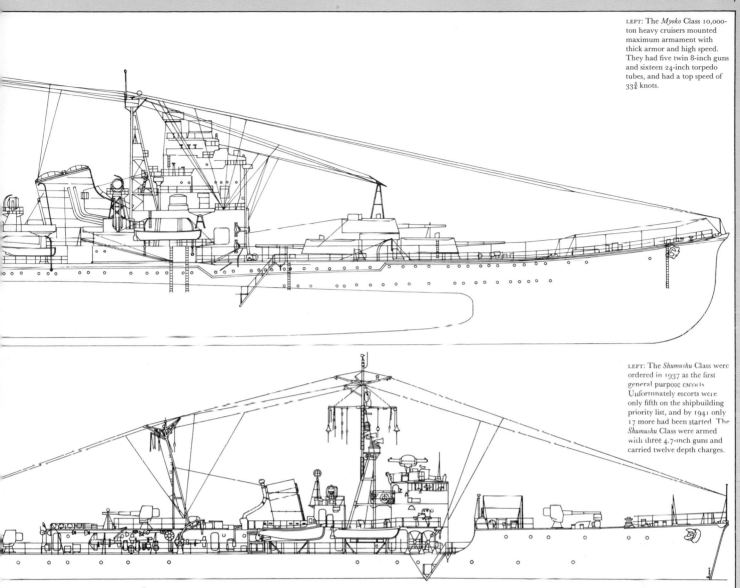

LEFT: The *Myoko* Class 10,000-ton heavy cruisers mounted maximum armament with thick armor and high speed. They had five twin 8-inch guns and sixteen 24-inch torpedo tubes, and had a top speed of 33¾ knots.

LEFT: The *Shumushu* Class were ordered in 1937 as the first general purpose escorts. Unfortunately escorts were only fifth on the shipbuilding priority list, and by 1941 only 17 more had been started. The *Shumushu* Class were armed with three 4.7-inch guns and carried twelve depth charges.

in 1939. When the *Mogami* appeared in 1935 she was hailed as the wonder ship of the decade, with fifteen 6.1-inch guns on only 8500 tons, and yet carrying heavy armor and capable of steaming at 37 knots. Yet the gunnery trials of the *Mikuma* and *Mogami* showed that poor-quality welding had resulted in deformation of the hull, and the welded seams had split. To cure the faults riveting had to be applied over the welds and external 'bulges' had to be added, increasing displacement to 11,200 tons and reducing speed. In 1939 a further reconstruction was necessary to increase the bulge, and this time displacement rose to 12,400 tons and speed dropped even further. Two near sisters, *Chikuma* and *Tone* were com-pleted with 8-inch guns from the outset and displaced 11,215 tons. As the British D.N.C. had always maintained, it was *not* possible to build a balanced heavy cruiser design on 8500 tons.

## Destroyers

To provide effective strength in surface torpedo-attack a series of big destroyers was started under the 1923 Program. Known as the *Fubuki* class or the 'Special Type', the first vessels displaced 1750 tons and were armed with six 5-inch guns and nine 24-inch torpedo-tubes. It was this class which first used the oxygen-driven 'Long Lance' torpedo, which replaced their compressed air-driven Type 90 weapons in 1933. As with the cruisers they

BELOW: The *Chokai* firing her 8-inch guns during a practice shoot in 1933. This heavy cruiser served from 1941–44 with the Combined Fleet, often as a flagship.

LEFT: About 84 *Koryu* midget subs at a drydock in Kure in 1945. Some 500 of this type were planned for local defense, but only 115 units had been completed by the time of Japan's surrender in August 1945.

BOTTOM LEFT: The *L.68* Class fleet submarines were started in 1931. In 1942 the survivors were converted to transports to supply the isolated garrisons in the Solomons. Later renumbered *I.168* this boat sank the USS *Yorktown* in the Battle of Midway.

BOTTOM RIGHT: *I.55* was typical of the large fleet submarines built after 1920. By the summer of 1942 the boats of this class were renumbered, *I.55* becoming *I.155* and relegated to training. Their size and slow diving made them easy targets for Allied escorts.

failed to justify the optimism of their designers in service. In 1935 the Fourth Fleet was overwhelmed by a typhoon, during which the *Hatsuyki* lost her bow, and other vessels of the class reported that they were in danger of capsizing. During 1935–37 the hulls had to be strengthened, extra ballast was added, and the reload torpedoes were reduced from nine to six. Tonnage rose to 2090 tons and speed fell to 34 knots.

A series of developments followed, from the *Akatsuki* class to the *Yugumo* class ordered under the 1939 Program, but all were basically similar. The first radical change came in 1939, when the first of the *Akitsuki* class ultra-large destroyers was ordered. Known as the 'Type B', they were designed primarily as anti-aircraft fleet escorts. Displacing 2700 tons they were armed with a new type of high-angle 100-mm gun, and had separate fire control positions forward and aft, a luxury which their great size permitted. Having all three funnel uptakes trunked into one large funnel made them look remarkably like the small cruiser *Yubari* already mentioned, and when they first appeared in mid-1942 American intelligence reports contained numerous sightings of the *Yubari*.

## Submarines

Japanese submarine design was strongly influenced by the German cruiser-submarines of World War I, despite the lack of success of that type in actual combat. Year after year the yards turned out massive submarines, some equipped with floatplanes and catapults to provide long-range reconnaissance. As in other categories their potential was greatly exaggerated. To cite one example, the *I.1* was supposed to have an endurance of 25,000 miles on the surface, but only had 17,000 miles' range in practice. But the worst failure was in tactics and employment. Training was devoted to attacks on warships, not merchant ships, and wartime experience showed that American anti-submarine escorts had little trouble in mastering Japanese submarines; the brand-new American destroyer escort *England* sank six submarines in twelve days. The answer of the Naval Command was to throw submarines in against heavily defended targets such as amphibious landing forces, and later to fritter them away in carrying supplies to isolated garrisons. High hopes were entertained for midget submarines, and the first were built in 1934. Their main use was to be the penetration of enemy harbors, but their first operation against Pearl Harbor was a failure.

Despite the apparent strength of the Japanese economy it was not strong enough to support three widely divergent and expensive military efforts. The extreme militarism fostered in the civilian population made it acquiescent in the matters of taxation and living standards, but as other dictatorial governments found, a high level of apparent peacetime efficiency could not easily be raised any further in wartime. Despite a massive infusion of capital in 1917–18 the shipyards had ignored ideas of mass-production of ships, and even welding was inhibited by a lack of suitable welding rods. Japanese warship design had fostered ingenuity at the expense of simplicity, and little could be done to speed up construction. The Japanese economy might have been able

## Japanese Shipyard Production

**1940 Estimates and 1940 Urgent War Program**
2 training cruisers (*Katori* Class) Cancelled 1941, another not laid down
18 submarines (2 types) Completed 1942–44
2 aircraft carriers (*Junyo* Class) Conversion from liners completed 1942

**1941 Emergency Program**
1 aircraft carrier (*Unryu* Class) Completed 1944

1 heavy cruiser (*Ibuki* Class) Conversion to carrier begun 1943, not completed
14 destroyers (2 types) Completed 1942–44
33 submarines (4 types) 26 completed 1943–44, 7 cancelled

**1941 Additional Program**
31 submarines (6 types) 10 completed 1944, 1 not completed and 20 not begun

to sustain a large Army and a tactical Air Force, or a big conventional fleet or yet again a Navy of aircraft carriers and light strike forces, but it could never do justice to all three. Yet this is what was attempted, and the subsequent performance of the Imperial Japanese Navy must be judged against this fundamental problem.

The tables shown give some idea of how far Japanese shipyard production lagged behind requirements. Although wartime showed up the full deficiencies it is clear that even the peacetime targets could not be met.

### Naval actions before 1941

Although the Army hankered after operations on the mainland of China it was the Navy which first seized the opportunity to act. In the summer of 1931 Chinese indignation over the Mukden Incident led to a boycott of Japanese imports. Shanghai was the center of the agitation, which reached such a pitch in January 1932 that the Municipal Council of the international settlement proclaimed a state of emergency. But the local Japanese commander, Admiral Shiozawa, went further and issued an ultimatum to the mayor of Shanghai to the effect that the local societies organizing the boycott had to close by January 29. At the last moment the mayor, General Wu Teh-chen, agreed to carry out the demands,

but before it could be done the ultimatum expired and Japanese Marines occupied the Chapei district which adjoined the Japanese settlement. In the process they exchanged shots with Chinese soldiers, but no serious injuries resulted.

To Shiozawa this mattered little, and he reacted to the 'insult' by ordering the aircraft carrier *Hosho* to launch a strike against the troops in Chapei. The Japanese described the action as 'drastic measures in a possible minimum degree' but public opinion in Great Britain and the United States regarded it as an indiscriminate attack on a densely populated civilian area. The Chinese resisted fiercely, and after weeks of fighting the Japanese had to withdraw, but the incident had wider repercussions. The Japanese Navy had flexed its muscles, and the United States had protested strongly, although Britain had refused to support her stand. To the Japanese Navy it was proof that the international treaties were no guarantee of Japan's naval security, while the British attitude showed that the Western powers would not make a concerted stand. In the purely naval sense the successful use of the *Hosho*'s aircraft strengthened the influence of the carrier lobby, for the strike had been devastating, economical and speedy.

In July 1937 the Army got its chance when the so-called 'China Incident' provided an excuse for intervention. Within

two months 150,000 troops were deployed in a massive drive down the coast of China, and by the very nature of the campaign the Navy became fully involved in these operations. Although there were no heroic battles to be won against the tiny Chinese Navy, the Japanese gained invaluable experience in actual warfare. The importance of this experience must not be underestimated, for it helps to explain the confidence and skill with which Japanese forces overran the East Indies and Philippines in 1942. But equally important was the experience gained in amphibious warfare. In 1934 the Navy completed the *Shinshu Maru*, the world's first ship designed as an amphibious transport. This remarkable vessel was based on a whaling factory ship, and like the Anglo-American Land-

**1942 5th Replacement Program (Cancelled after Midway)**
3 battleships (*Yamato* Class)
2 battlecruisers (Type 'A')
3 carriers         32 destroyers
2 cruisers        46 submarines

**1942 Modified 5th War Replacement Program**
20 aircraft carriers (15 *Ikoma* Class,
5 *Taiho* Class) 2 completed 1944, 3 launched 1944, 15 not laid down
2 heavy cruisers (Type 'B') Not laid down
31 destroyers (2 types) Not laid down
130 submarines (5 types) 4 completed 1944–45 rest not completed or cancelled
12 escorts (*Yaku* Class) None completed

**1942 Additional Program**
42 escort destroyers (*Matsu* Class) 31 completed, 11 not laid down
11 cargo submarines (*I.361* Class) Completed 1944

**1943–44 War Program**
10 escort destroyers (*Matsu* Class) 1 completed 1945, rest cancelled
121 submarines (4 types) 25 completed 1944–45
294 escorts (3 types) 122 completed 1944–45

**1944–45 War Program**
Over 800 escorts and submarines were projected but none ordered.

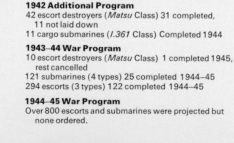

FAR LEFT: Rear Admiral Osami Nagano, Chief of the Japanese Naval Staff during the Second World War.

LEFT: A Japanese naval officer aboard the old coast defense ship *Idzumo* scans Chinese positions during the sweep down the China coast in 1937. Note the twin 25mm anti-aircraft gun in the background.

BOTTOM: Some of the latest Japanese submarines lying at Kure in October 1945. On the left are *HA.203* and *HA.204*, small high-speed submarines similar to the advanced Type 21 German U-Boats. In the center is *I.203*, a larger type with high underwater speed, and on the right is the *HA.106*, one of a class of subs designed purely as transports for Army garrisons.

BELOW: Admiral Mineichi Koga, C-in-C of the Combined Fleet 1943–44.

ing Ships Dock (LSD) could put her own landing craft afloat through a stern well. Apart from the US Marine Corps no other navy in the world was so adept in the techniques of transporting soldiers and landing them at random on an enemy coastline.

The Navy also gained in influence by helping the Army. At the time of the Anti-Comintern Pact there had been wild talk in Army circles of occupying the Navy Ministry to force the Navy to 'reconsider' its opposition to the pact. But its role as handmaiden to the Army in 1937–38 checkmated Army demands for a cut in the naval budget. Although the Army did not relinquish its dreams of conquering China it learned that it could do far more in conjunction with the Navy than without it. When in 1939 it became clear that

the Army had become bogged down in what was virtually an unwinnable colonial war, the Navy's ideas for more ambitious operations elsewhere looked inviting. The Navy had no wish for a war against either Great Britain or the United States, but both these powers controlled the natural resources, particularly oil, which were needed for survival. The outbreak of war in Europe made a reduction of British strength in the Far East inevitable, and the swift German successes in France in May and June 1940 helped to convince Japan that Germany would be able to keep the British fully occupied.

In August 1940 the Operations Section of the Naval General Staff drafted a plan for an advance into Indo-China; its purpose was to secure raw materials and strategic vantage points to give some chance in a war against the United States. It was recognized that America's first weapon against Japan would be a total trade embargo on Japanese manufactures, and this would compel Japan to seize the oilfields in the Dutch East Indies. Yet, and this would horrify any Western naval officer or politician, such a drastic plan was not presented to any highly placed officials in the Japanese Government – it was purely the product of 'restless' middle-rank officers. By April 1941 it was felt within the Navy that this unrest would only be quelled if an attack was launched against Malaya and the

East Indies. The departmental chiefs in Tokyo concurred, and the Emperor gave his approval. The Pearl Harbor attack was now inevitable, and although the Government searched in a haphazard way for a means of achieving peace its efforts could hardly be called coherent. Japanese foreign policy had been thrown out of gear by the cynical Molotov-Ribbentrop Pact in 1939. Here was her anti-Comintern ally signing a pact with the arch-foe, without prior warning. In the words of the Prime Minister, Baron Hiranuma, he was resigning because the world situation had become 'too complicated to be understood'. If the motives and intentions of a fellow-Axis partner could not be accurately judged it is hardly surprising that Japanese diplomats misjudged the climate of opinion in the United States. Right up to the moment of Pearl Harbor it was believed that American isolationism and President Roosevelt's interest in the fate of Great Britain would force the US Government to negotiate. Only when it was too late did the Japanese realize that there would be no deal in the Far East.

# THE ROAD TO PEARL HARBOR

On the night of 18 September 1931, a Japanese patrol engaged a small Chinese force in a firefight near Mukden following the investigation of explosions in the area which had slightly damaged a railway line leading into the city. The next morning, units of Japan's Kwantung Army occupied Mukden, Changchun, and laid siege to the city of Kirin which fell two days later. The Manchurian Incident had begun.

In retrospect, it is clear that the minor clash which occurred between Japanese and Chinese forces on the night of 18 September was a rather flimsy pretext for what quickly developed to become a full-scale invasion of Manchuria. Under normal circumstances, such a fracas would probably never have been reported. However, normal circumstances did not prevail at the time. Commanders of the Kwantung Army, Japan's crack force in

Manchuria, had long hoped for the opportunity to engage Chinese forces in the area and their army had been placed on alert at least three days prior to the incident of the 18th, suggesting that what occurred in Manchuria after September 1931 was hardly a spontaneous response to a local crisis. On the contrary, it was a cold and calculated gesture, taken without prior notification and/or approval from the government in Tokyo.

By the time that the news of the situation in Manchuria reached Tokyo, reinforcements had been sent to Manchuria from Korea and the Cabinet was faced with a *fait accompli*. Try as they might, government leaders found themselves powerless to halt the advance of Japanese forces in Manchuria since field commanders simply ignored their orders, arguing that local conditions produced operational necessities which required

93

BELOW: Chinese civilians flee to the International Settlement to avoid Japanese aerial attack on Shanghai in 1932. The Chinese quarter was subject to bombardment, while the largely European section of the city which was not subject to the laws of China escaped. Western tourists went up to the roofs of their hotels to watch the action.

BELOW: Prince Konoye, who was unable to stop the lurch toward general war when he served as Premier of Japan in 1940–41.

BOTTOM: Banzai, banzai was the Japanese cry of victory as they seized another enemy position in their advance through China.

BELOW: Japanese AA gunners
search for Chinese aircraft in
the early stages of the China
campaign.

RIGHT: Aerial bombardment
of a bridge near Canton,
4 November 1937. The bridge
formed an important railway
link between Canton and
Wuchang, the industrial center
of China Proper.

BELOW: Victorious Japanese
cry 'banzai' as they move into
northern China in the summer
of 1937.

BELOW: The Marco Polo
Bridge between Manchuria
and China that the Japanese
surged across on the morning
of 7 July 1937, opening the
China Incident which lasted
for eight years. The invasion of
China bogged Japan down in an
unwinnable war which forced
her to expand elsewhere to obtain
the raw materials necessary
to fight the war in China.

action contrary to orders from Tokyo. Furthermore, field commanders in Manchuria were supported by the General Staff and the War Ministry.

The invasion of Manchuria was a bad omen of things to come. Japanese forces successfully completed their occupation of the area by the end of the year in spite of decisions made in Tokyo. Put in other words, the Manchurian Incident inaugurated a series of episodes in which decisions which vitally affected the course of Japanese history and diplomacy were made by army officers in the field while the government in Tokyo stood by powerless to act except in response to *faits accomplis*.

By January 1932 hostilities in Manchuria were concluded but the *de facto* war between the Chinese and Japanese continued, spilling over into China proper where rival forces clashed in Shanghai and Nanking. Powerless to protect their interests by force, the Chinese appealed to the League of Nations, hoping for some kind of action to stop Japan's advance and return Manchuria to Chinese control. Responding to this appeal, the League appointed an investigatory committee headed by Lord Lytton of Great Britain. This investigation was initially approved by the Japanese government which publicly denied China's charges of aggression but privately hoped that the force of world opinion might have a restraining influence on ambitious officers in the Imperial Army.

If some political leaders in the Diet

hoped that League of Nations' intervention would put a damper on further incursions of the Imperial Army into the realm of foreign policy, they were mistaken. In March 1932, even as the Lytton Commission was conducting its investigation, Pu Yi, the last Emperor of the Ch'ing (Manchu) dynasty, was resurrected and placed on the throne of a new state, Manchukuo, created by military fiat. Needless to say, this event aborted the possibility that the Lytton Commission might succeed and ultimately resulted in the first major crisis faced by the League of Nations.

As might have been expected, the report of the Lytton Commission was highly critical of Japanese activities in Manchuria. The report, which was submitted to the League in September 1932, condemned Japan and called for a voluntary Japanese withdrawal from all areas occupied by force in Manchuria. Since such a suggestion was totally unacceptable to the Imperial Army and the general public, the Japanese government had little choice but to denounce the Lytton Report and withdrew from the League of Nations in February 1933. Whatever reservations members of the Cabinet and Diet may have had about the whole affair, they dared not criticize the military for fear of their lives as well as their careers.

Although the international ramifications of the Manchurian Incident were serious, domestic political repercussions were even more critical. The

Wakatsukii government was forced to resign in December 1931, following which a series of successors grappled with the constitutional crisis posed by military activities in Manchuria. Making matters even more ominous for Japan's civilian political leaders was the rash of violence and assassination plots launched by political radicals following the Manchurian Incident. Between February and May 1932 at least three major political figures were assassinated, including Prime Minister Inukai who was shot in his official residence. These terror tactics did not succeed in laying the ground work for an immediate military *coup d'état* as their perpetrators may have wished but they bode ill for the continuation of a viable parliamentary system in Japan.

The assassins of Prime Minister Inukai were brought to trial in the summer of 1933, but rather than being condemned by the public and the court, they were lauded as patriots. Their trial became a focus for expounding patriotic doctrines in defense of Japanese expansion on the continent. To foreign observers, it appeared as if it was the government and not the assassins who were on trial and the sentences handed down by the court seemed to confirm this view. Of the men involved in Inukai's murder and other assassination attempts, only one received a long jail sentence. The others received little more than token sentences or verbal reprimands. Such leniency by the courts could hardly have encouraged party

BELOW: Japanese Marine landing troops carefully progress down a street in Shanghai, which they seized early in the China war.

leaders in the Diet and those who opposed the trend of events. Members of patriotic societies, on the other hand, were buoyed up by the court's decision and continued their brazen attacks on the political system.

One immediate result of the Manchurian Incident and subsequent domestic violence was the end of effective party government. Discouraged and frightened by what was happening, leaders of the major political parties feared to take strong stands in opposition to the military. Furthermore, they found it impossible to form viable governments given the unwillingness of the Army and Navy to participate in the Cabinet by releasing men from active service to serve as Ministers of the Army and Navy. As a result, it was necessary to resort to the device of coalition Cabinets headed by non-party men acceptable to extremists in the military. Indeed, the two men who followed Inukai as prime ministers were both admirals, their choice based upon the assumption of the party men that they would be easier to control than more radical types in the Imperial Army. Unfortunately, the party men were naïve in their assumption that such a compromise would buy time to restore civilian control of the government.

Japanese expansion on the mainland continued in 1933. Undaunted by the League of Nations censure, the worsening of Japanese-American relations, and the continuation of political agitation at home, the Kwantung Army added the province of Jehol to the Kingdom of Manchukuo at the beginning of the year. In May a demilitarized buffer zone south of Manchuria was created as a result of the Tangku Truce with China, a pact negotiated by military men and not the Foreign Ministry. Compared to the dramatic territorial gains of 1931 and 1932, these advances were on a small scale but still represented a continued usurpation of power by the military. Such a situation continued to prevail in the years that followed when the provinces of Hopei and Chahar in China fell victim to Japanese control. As 1936 dawned, the Imperial Army was well on its way to making China a Japanese protectorate.

By the beginning of 1936 the question of who controlled the Japanese government, the party men or the military, had been resolved in favor of the military. Another question, however, remained to be answered. That was which faction controlled the military, particularly the

Imperial Army. Just as the Diet was divided into two major parties plus various factional groups, so too was the Army divided. One group, the Imperial Way faction or Kodo, called for continued expansion in Manchuria and a more aggressive stance vis-à-vis the Diet. Another group, the Control or Tosei faction, was more concerned with the situation in China and seemingly preferred to work within the existing political system to effect change. Members of these factions also differed with regard to the definition of Japan's enemies, the Kodo faction seeing the Soviet Union as Japan's primary adversary while the Tosei clique viewed China as Japan's principal enemy, at least for the moment. Both groups, however, shared the view that the Japanese government should pursue a positive foreign policy which called for continued expansion of Japanese interests on the continent.

During 1935 and 1936 the Kodo and Tosei factions waged an internal war for control of the Imperial Army. At the time, the Kodo faction enjoyed a more favorable position, its leaders Generals Araki and Mazaki serving as Minister of War and Director-General of Military Education respectively. In 1935, however, Tosei advocates were seriously threatening Kodo dominance. When General Nagata, leader of the Tosei clique, secured the dismissal of General Mazaki in July 1935, the quiet political battle for control of the Imperial Army became violent.

On 12 August 1935 General Nagata was assassinated by a young officer of the Kodo faction. When the assassin was court-martialed and tried for murder, Kodo adherents once again resorted to force. On the morning of 26 February 1936, approximately one thousand troops of the First Division which guarded Tokyo and was commanded by Kodo supporters attempted to take over the city, attacking the residences of the Prime Minister and other government officials. Although the Prime Minister was not killed this time, many others were, including the Finance Minister, the Lord Privy Seal, and the new Director-General of Military Education.

The attempted coup d'état was aborted on 29 February when the Imperial Guards and selected units of the Imperial Navy were called to Tokyo. Taking unusually prompt and decisive action, government leaders arrested and tried the leaders of the ill-fated rebellion, thirteen of whom were executed. Unlike the show trials of 1932, the defendants were not permitted to use the courtroom as a soapbox for the propagation of ultranationalism. Furthermore, even those leaders of the Kodo faction not directly involved in the affair of 26 February were punished, Generals Araki and Mazaki being retired from active service and placed on reserve. Other officers remained on active service but were transferred to 'safe' posts.

Although discipline was returned to the Imperial Army, a dear price was paid

FAR LEFT: Foreign Minister
Matsuoka addresses the
meeting of the members of the
Anti-Comintern Pact.
The Rome-Berlin-Tokyo Axis
had been created.

LEFT: Japanese prostitutes
attract curiosity from Chinese
civilians in Tientsin in 1938.
The Japanese made it a matter
of policy to bring prostitutes
with them to keep their troops

happy, whether on the
battlefield or, as in this case, in
occupation of a foreign city.
There was a superabundance
of professionals in that line of
work in Tientsin even before
the Japanese invasion.

BELOW: Japanese round up
Chinese citizens suspected of
espionage for the Kuomintang
(Chinese Nationalists) in a
village in South China in 1938.

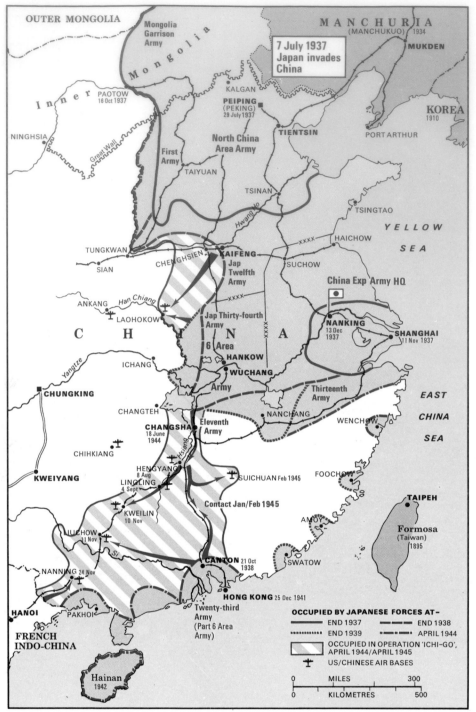

RIGHT: Japanese camp followers wade across a river during the advance into Shansi province in 1939.

FAR RIGHT: Troops roll up the Chinese defenders of Shansi as well as their trousers as they wade across the Fen River in August 1939.

BELOW RIGHT: Chinese Nationalist troops display some trophies of war from the Japanese they have slain. The Chinese fought back hard when they chose to fight.

BOTTOM RIGHT: Japanese infantry are strafed with machine gun fire as they proceed along a riverbank in Shansi in February 1939.

Nanking were hard-fought contests with Chinese forces putting up fierce resistance to Japanese troops for the first time in modern history. Eventually, such resistance failed, Shanghai and Nanking falling to the Japanese by the year's end.

Unaccustomed to resistance from Chinese armies, the Japanese sustained very heavy casualties in their quest for Shanghai and Nanking and retaliated by going on a rampage of death, destruction, pillage, and rape after taking these cities, particularly Nanking. Such behavior was widely criticized in the West. More important, it seemed to fortify Chiang K'ai-shek's will to resist. Thus, Japanese efforts to negotiate a settlement with the Chinese fell on deaf ears in 1937 and 1938. This fact pleased some Japanese commanders who grew less interested in a negotiated settlement of the China Incident as Japanese victories continued. They demanded nothing less than the total capitulation of the Chinese including the resignation of Chiang K'ai-shek as preconditions for ending hostilities in China. Needless to say, given this set of preconditions, serious negotiations were impossible.

In 1938 Japanese forces continued their advance in China, forcing the Chinese to evacuate the major urban centers along the Yangtze River as well as all coastal ports from Shanghai south to Canton. With the exception of the provinces of Szechwan and Yunnan, most of China proper was in Japanese hands. Despite this fact, Chiang K'ai-shek's government refused to capitulate to the Japanese, thus posing economic and political problems for the Imperial Army. Although the China Incident had dragged on longer than had originally been anticipated, the full resources of the Japanese had not been marshalled to secure a military victory. As one observer pointed out at the time, the war in China was more nearly akin to a colonial war of attrition than to a total war. Nevertheless, the longer the China Incident dragged on without result, the more war weary the Japanese became. Furthermore, if the military effort was to be continued, the domestic economy would be subject to increased strain. Whether the Japanese people would accept such a situation without protest remained questionable.

Fearing that further extension of the conflict in China would have adverse effects at home, Japanese leaders re-evaluated the situation in China in 1939,

for the restoration of order. The new leaders of the Army, almost all members of the Tosei faction, demanded a free hand in matters relating to China as a reward to their suppression of the Kodo revolt and forced the government to accede to their demands by refusing to participate in the Cabinet unless given *carte blanche* in questions relating to national security. Since no Cabinet could function without a Minister of War, military leaders were able to exercise a *de facto* veto over government decisions to an extent hitherto unknown.

With the Tosei faction safely ensconced in the War Ministry, it was only a matter of time before renewed Sino–Japanese hostilities became a reality. The wait was short. In July 1937 a clash between Chinese and Japanese troops near Peking provided the rationale for yet another expansion of Japanese interests in China.

The Marco Polo Bridge Incident was a relatively minor one, but Japanese commanders did not need much of an excuse to renew hostilities with the Chinese. Once again, despite the reluctance of the government to use the Marco Polo Bridge Incident as a pretext for a full-scale confrontation with Chiang K'ai-shek, local commanders dictated what action was to be taken, plunging Japan into a long and costly struggle in China.

Within a month after the initial encounter between Chinese and Japanese forces at the Marco Polo Bridge on 7 July 1937, Japanese troops had successfully occupied Peking and Tientsin. By the beginning of September over 150,000 Japanese troops were stationed in China. What is more important, they were being moved south to confront Chinese Nationalist armies defending Shanghai and Nanking. The battles for Shanghai and

ultimately deciding to abandon further military offensives in favor of a policy of consolidation and cooperation with various puppet regimes in occupied China. At the same time, the Japanese launched a diplomatic effort to isolate the regime of Chiang K'ai-shek by closing supply routes into Free China from Burma and Indochina, thereby making it impossible for the Chinese Nationalists to continue their resistance.

After 1938 there were only two routes over which supplies could be carried into Free China. The first was through the port of Haiphong and over the Haiphong–Hanoi–Yunnan railway line. The second was through the port of Rangoon and over the Burma Road, an even more circuitous and difficult route. If the Japanese could persuade the British and French to close these access routes, China would surely capitulate.

BELOW: Japanese troops wind their way through Western China. The mountainous terrain prevented an easy Japanese victory far more than the army of the Kuomintang.

LEFT: Japanese troops guard defenses outside Shanghai after they seized China's principal port in 1937.

BELOW: A 'Kate' torpedo plane takes off from one of the Japanese carriers for its mission to Pearl Harbor as the crew cheers them on with cries of 'banzai' at dawn, 7 December 1941.

Japanese diplomats pressed their case with the British and French in 1939 and 1940. At the same time, less subtle pressures were exerted. In February 1939 Japanese forces occupied Hainan Island, a French interest, off the China coast. Three months later, Japanese forces briefly blockaded the British and French concessions in Tientsin. If these acts were not sufficient to persuade the European powers to accede to Japan's demands, the outbreak of war in Europe in September provided a more compelling reason to do so. By the end of 1940 both the British and Vichy French governments had agreed to close the ports of Rangoon and Haiphong to goods bound for Free China. At year's end, it looked as if victory was in sight.

With the prospect of continued Chinese resistance hopefully eliminated as a result of Japan's arrangement with the British and the French, the Japanese government and military were seemingly free to turn their attention to the Soviet threat in the north. Clashes between Japanese and Russian forces along their long common border north of Manchuria had occurred with increased frequency in 1938 and 1939, causing great concern in Tokyo. Since these incidents were not minor skirmishes but involved relatively large numbers of men and mechanized units on both sides and the Japanese had not fared well in these engagements, they were quite fearful of another Russo–Japanese war.

Fear of the Soviets led the Japanese to reconsider their relationship with Hitler and the German government. The Anti-Comintern Pact which the Japanese had signed with Germany in November 1936 provided a defensive alliance against Russia under certain limited circumstances plus a rather meaningless pledge against the spread of Communism. Since neither of these provisions provided much assurance of German intervention in the event of a war between Japan and the Soviet Union, many officers in the Imperial Army urged the negotiation of a bilateral defense pact which would provide insurance against a Russian attack. Accordingly, the Japanese Ambassador in Berlin, General Oshima Hiroshi, was instructed to initiate discussions with the German government in June 1938.

Preliminary Japanese–German talks

got nowhere. The Germans showed little interest in the idea of a bilateral agreement, preferring a broader accord involving others, particularly the Italians. The Japanese government balked at this, but talks were continued. However, with the announcement of the Nazi–Soviet Pact in August 1939, talks were quickly broken off not to be resumed until after the outbreak of war in Europe.

Although disappointed by the failure of the initial Japanese–German negotiations, Japanese leaders continued to lean toward a German alliance. Germany's early victories over Poland, Belgium, the Netherlands, and France only served to strengthen this view. Furthermore, the need for some kind of agreement with Hitler seemed even more pressing, considering the opportunity for expansion into the Southeast Asian colonies of France and Holland which had been so recently defeated by the Germans. The Japanese were very much interested in the mineral resources of the area but before they made any move, they had to know the intention of the Reich *vis-à-vis* these colonies. Thus, in July 1940, the Japanese government reopened discussions with the Germans.

Under the watchful eye of Japan's new Foreign Minister, Yosuke Matsuoka, Japanese–German negotiations proceeded rapidly, culminating in the signing of the Tripartite Pact with Germany and Italy on 27 September 1940. With

the signing of this agreement, the Japanese turned their attention to the Soviet problem. Convinced that a war with the Russians would be a disaster, the Foreign Ministry initiated discussions with the Soviets which led to the conclusion of a Russo–Japanese Neutrality Agreement in April 1941. The signing of this agreement with the Soviets ended the immediate prospect of a war in Manchuria and permitted the government to take advantage of the power vacuum in Southeast Asia created by the preoccupation of the powers with the European war.

The idea of Japanese military expansion into Southeast Asia was not a new one. It had been discussed by military leaders throughout the 1930's. The rich reserves of oil, tin, rubber, bauxite, and rice known to exist in the region made it increasingly attractive to military men who were only too keenly aware of Japan's dependency on imports of such items from the United States and other sources. As long as Japan remained dependent upon such imports in large quantities, she would be vulnerable to blackmail by those who controlled the supply of such vital prerequisites for modern industry. Although this fact did not seem to bother Japanese business leaders, many senior officers were obsessed by the matter. Thus, when war broke out in Europe, considerable pressure was put on the government to take advantage

of the situation to acquire more direct access to vital resources by seizing the colonies of the European powers.

On 27 July 1940 the question of expansion of Japan's interests in Southeast Asia was raised at an Imperial Liaison Conference. It was decided at that time to take advantage of the preoccupation of the powers with the war by initiating discussions with these powers and their colonial government with an eye toward increasing the quotas of vital raw materials shipped to Japan from these colonies. Although the conference did not approve military preparations for a move south, it was clear that if diplomatic efforts failed, force would follow.

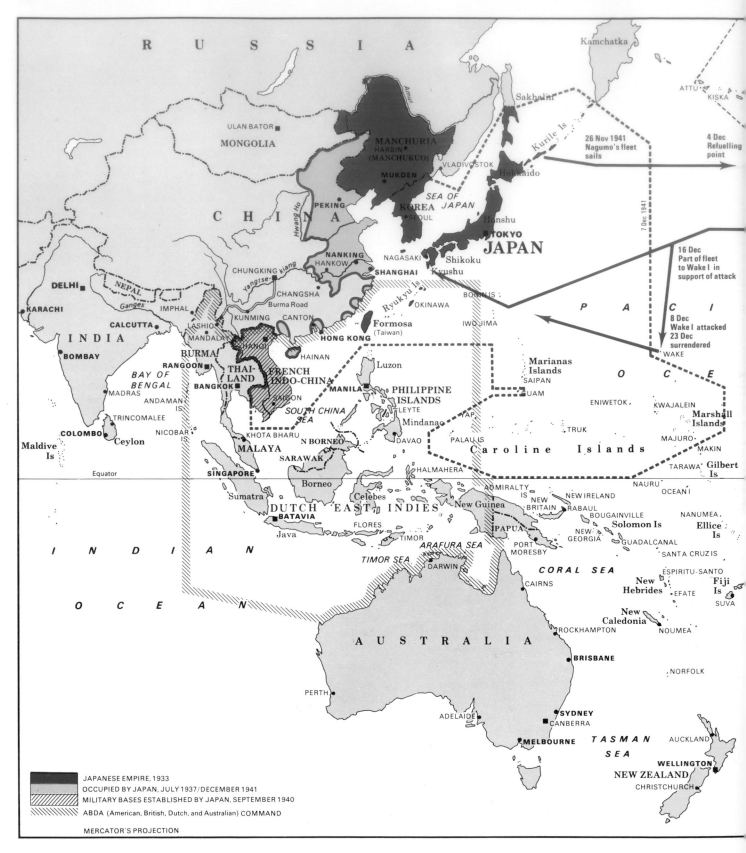

The Foreign Ministry lost no time in implementing the decision of the Liaison Conference. In August 1940 Japanese and French diplomats began talks which resulted in an agreement in September permitting the Japanese to establish military and naval installations in Tonkin and to move troops through Indochina in the event of war with another power. In return for these concessions, the Japanese promised to continue to recognize French sovereignty in Indochina. Negotiations with Dutch colonial officials in the Indies proved less fruitful. Despite their even more precarious position than the French, Dutch officials in Batavia refused to accept Japan's demand for special economic and political privileges in the Islands, leaving the impression in Tokyo that only the use of force would provide Japan with all of the petroleum products she needed from the Dutch.

Discussion of Japanese expansion into Southeast Asia was based upon pragmatic considerations but also fit neatly into the ideological rationalizations for such expansion on the continent, e.g. the concept of a New Order in East Asia. As originally envisaged by Prime Minister Konoye in 1938, this New Order would link Japan, Korea, China and Manchuria in an economic and political commonwealth dominated by Japan. Such a pan-Asian ideal could easily be expanded to include the colonies and states of Southeast Asia and this was what was suggested by Japanese propagandists in 1940 when they called for the creation of a Greater East Asia Co-Prosperity Sphere

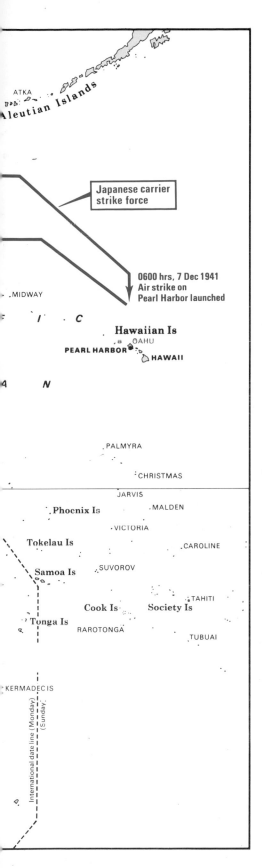

RIGHT: Joseph Stalin and Foreign Minister Matsuoka after they signed the Soviet-Japanese Neutrality Pact in Moscow, 13 April 1941. In his visit to Berlin Matsuoka was told nothing of Germany's plans to invade Russia in June, so he decided to close one flank in preparation for action on the 'southern strategy' to attack Western holdings in the Pacific.

**Japanese carrier strike force**

0600 hrs, 7 Dec 1941
Air strike on
Pearl Harbor launched

support among the military, in the government, and among the general population. The most ardent proponents of the Co-Prosperity Sphere called for immediate and vigorous action to realize their dream, pointing out that the British, Dutch, and French were in no position to halt Japan's advance. Had it not been for the fact that the United States remained aloof from the war and in a position to oppose further Japanese expansion, the Japanese expansionists might have had their way in 1940. Such, however, was not to be the case.

As of 1940, Japanese leaders were unwilling to risk a war with the United States as the price for southward expansion, at least not until the position of the American government relative to Japan's new role in Asia was clarified. Although it was no secret that the Americans opposed Japan's occupation of China after 1937 in a manner consistent with their earlier response to the Manchurian Incident, the United States had taken no action to break off diplomatic relations with Japan nor to impose economic sanctions of an effective nature. On the other hand, the Japanese could not assume that this would continue to be the case in the future. Indeed, there were tell-tale signs that such action might be taken in the event of a Japanese occupation of the Southeast Asian colonies of the European powers. In 1939, for example, the United States refused to discuss renewal of the Japanese–American Treaty of Commerce which was due to expire in 1940. Furthermore, in the face of mounting opposition to Japanese expansion, the Roosevelt administration inaugurated a licensing system for exports of vital materials to Japan in 1940. Although Roosevelt did not immediately choose to embargo exports to Japan, he was eventually forced to do so, placing a ban on the export of all scrap metals in September and adding iron and steel exports to the embargo list after the election of November 1940 in the United States.

Given the fact that American firms supplied Japan with at least 65% of her petroleum imports, which as of January 1941 were not placed on the embargo list, Japanese leaders sought to obtain a diplomatic agreement relative to their New Order before resorting to force. Their occupation of southern Indochina later that year led President Roosevelt to freeze all Japanese assets in the United States, bringing trade between Japan and the United States much to the horror of

many Japanese. This action, more than any other, convinced Japanese leaders of the resolve of the American government and the need to make one last effort at a negotiated settlement with the United States. Accordingly, Japan's new Ambassador to the United States, Admiral Kichisaburo Nomura, was instructed to open up a dialogue with Secretary of State Cordell Hull.

Ambassador Nomura was a well-known proponent of Japanese–American rapprochement. His appointment was designed to reassure the United States of Japan's desire for peaceful solutions in Asia and to provide a climate in which meaningful negotiations might take place. Before leaving Tokyo, Nomura had been instructed to inform Hull and Roosevelt that Japan was ready to renounce further use of force in Asia if the United States moved to restore normal economic relations with Japan and served as an intermediary in arranging peace talks with the Chinese Nationalists. This message was conveyed in the first round of Secretary of State conversations between Nomura and Hull.

American response to Nomura's message was cool, Secretary of State Hull suggesting that before progress could be made in resolving Japanese–American differences, the Japanese would have to recognize four basic principles, these being: 1) respect for the territorial integrity and sovereignty of all states in Asia; 2) a promise not to interfere in the internal affairs of any Asian state; 3) acceptance of the Open Door principle; 4) renunciation of the use of force to achieve economic and/or political ends.

Hull's response to Nomura's initiative was unacceptable to the Japanese. If accepted, Hull's preconditions would have meant a renunciation of all Japanese activities since 1931 and a withdrawal of Japanese forces from Manchuria, China

in place of the New Order. If anything, the idea of the Co-Prosperity Sphere was even more attractive than the earlier call for the creation of a New Order in East Asia because of the economic potential of this larger unit. Furthermore, it would be relatively easy to add the Southeast Asian colonies to Japan's orbit, given the preoccupation of the powers with the European war and the anti-colonial prejudices of the people of the region.

The concept of the Greater East Asia Co-Prosperity Sphere found considerable

BELOW: The destroyer *Shaw* blows up as fires reach her forward magazine during the Pearl Harbor attack.

BOTTOM: The battleship *Pennsylvania* (background) and the destroyers *Cassin* and *Downes* lie damaged in dock after the Pearl Harbor raid.

and Indochina. No government could long survive in Tokyo if it accepted such terms. On the other hand, the Japanese were not ready to give up the idea of a diplomatic settlement with the United States. Thus, Japanese–American talks continued throughout the spring and early summer of 1941. In the meanwhile, plans for war was prepared and discussed. When President Roosevelt refused Prime Minister Konoye's call for a conference in August 1941, the die was cast.

In preparing for war with the United States, two considerations were primary, weather conditions and Japan's stockpile of vital commodities. Given the limitation of resources at their disposal, the Japanese could not endure a prolonged war nor could they expect a total victory over the

BELOW: Salvage work begins at Pearl Harbor. Many of the damaged ships were returned to service including six of the eight battleships.

BOTTOM: Wrecked aircraft lie strewn all over Hickam Field after the Japanese strike. Most of the American aircraft were caught parked in unprotected positions and easily destroyed.

RIGHT: A view from a Japanese
plane of Battleship Row on
Pearl Harbor Day.

BOTTOM: The remains of a B-17
after it was destroyed on the
ground at Hickam Field.

combined might of the United States, the
United Kingdom, and the Netherlands.
What was called for was a limited pre-
emptive strike designed to neutralize the
Pacific Fleet of the United States at Pearl
Harbor while Japanese forces simul-
taneously invaded Burma, the Dutch
East Indies, Malaya, and the Philippines.
Once this was achieved, it was assumed
that a permanent diplomatic settlement
with the United States and the other
powers would follow.

If economic realities dictated a limited
war to neutralize American forces in the
Pacific, weather conditions necessitated
that action be taken no later than the
beginning of December 1941. This was
reported to the Supreme War Council in
Tokyo on 6 September 1941, at which
time preliminary plans for the simul-
taneous attacks on Pearl Harbor and
Southeast Asia were presented and discussed. These plans were accepted at that
time, and war games off the Japanese
coast commenced later that month.

As preparations for war continued,
Prime Minister Konoye was forced to
resign, being replaced by General Hideki
Tojo on 18 October 1941. Tojo's rise to
power eliminated what little influence
party men exercised within the govern-

## III

US AIRFIELDS

MILES 0 — 8
KILOMETRES 0 — 12

First Wave (Fuchida)
Second Wave (Shimazaki)

0740 hrs 7 Dec 1941
0850 hrs

0945 hrs Japanese attacks end

OAHU

HALEIWA
43 Fighters
35 Fighters
7 Dive-bombers
54 High-level bombers

40 Torpedo-bombers
51 Dive-bombers

WHEELER FIELD
KANEOHE

PEARL HARBOR
Navy Yard
BELLOWS FIELD

49 High-level bombers
EWA
HICKAM FIELD
HONOLULU

PACIFIC OCEAN

PEARL CITY

Destroyers
Destroyers and tender
Blue

Destroyers and tender
Phoenix

Solace

Destroyers
Medusa
Detroit
Raleigh
Utah
Tangier
Curtiss

Allen, Chew

Novada

Ford Island
Arizona
Tennessee
Vestal
Maryland
W Virginia
Oklahoma
California
Neosho

Avocet
Sacramento
Ramapo
Argonne
New Orleans
Helena
San Francisco
Pelias
Oglala
Honolulu
Submarines
Shaw
Cachalot
Bagley
Sumner
Signal tower
St Louis
Castor
Pennsylvania
Cassin,
Downes
US naval station
Dry docks
Oil storage tanks

Minesweepers

HQ CINCPAC

**Pearl Harbor**

BELOW: Rescue work gets under way as the battleship *California* begins to sink at her moorings.

BOTTOM: The battleship *Arizona* capsizes after taking many hits. Despite the damage to the Pacific Fleet's battleships the carriers were away and escaped unscathed.

RIGHT: Rescue team rushes to the burning USS *West Virginia* after it was hammered by Japanese bombs and torpedoes at Pearl Harbor.

BOTTOM: A Type A Japanese midget sub beached on the island of Oahu after the Pearl Harbor attack.

OVERLEAF: Seamen on the capsized *Oklahoma* are rescued.

ment and facilitated the effort to mobilize the country for war with the United States. While such mobilization went on, however, one last effort at diplomacy was tried with the dispatch of the Kurusu Mission to the United States.

The Kurusu Mission had little chance of success since the Tojo government was unwilling to make any concessions beyond those originally offered by Ambassador Nomura several months before. As might have been expected, Secretary of State Hull rejected Kurusu's program but not before several weeks had elapsed during which both sides completed last minute preparations for war. Five days after Hull formally rejected Kurusu's last offer on 26 November 1941, the Imperial War Council in Tokyo ordered plans for the attack on Pearl Harbor to proceed. The point of no return had been reached.

In fact, the Japanese armada which attacked Pearl Harbor had put out to sea even before Hull's response to the Japanese on 26 November. Consisting of six carriers, two battleships, three cruisers, and dozens of smaller vessels and support ships, the Pearl Harbor attack force pursued a circuitous course toward the Hawaiian Islands unnoticed by the Americans despite the fact that American intelligence reports indicated the imminence of some form of attack. Although it is true that the time and place of such an attack were uncertain, American authorities in Hawaii had done little to prepare for a Japanese attack.

If the Americans were unprepared for a surprise attack, the Japanese task force steamed toward Pearl Harbor without leaving any clues behind as to their destination. In planning what route was to be taken to the Hawaiian Islands, the Imperial Navy had taken great pains to avoid sea lanes normally traversed by merchant shipping. Likewise, they avoided having the fleet pass near any American naval air installations from which spotter planes might safely operate. Although such considerations called for the passage of the Japanese task force through heavy seas and foul weather, the Japanese fleet moved toward its target without being detected, arriving off the coast of Oahu on the evening of 6 December 1941.

The Japanese fleet reached its attack position some 275 miles north of Pearl Harbor the next morning, 7 December, at 0600. An hour later, the first wave of attack planes were sent aloft and on their way to Pearl Harbor. Except for the absence of the four carriers of the fleet, the entire Pacific Fleet was present at Pearl Harbor when the first wave of Japanese planes passed over shortly before 0800. Thanks to local intelligence operatives in Hawaii, the Japanese knew the precise position of their victims and had to waste little time completing their mission. Within less than two hours, Japanese pilots had completed their mission successfully, sinking two battleships, the *Arizona* and the *Oklahoma*, and badly damaging the other six battleships in port, the *California*, *Maryland*, *Pennsylvania*, *Tennessee*, *West Virginia* and the *Nevada*, which had managed to get underway before being hit.

By mid-day, the Japanese task force retreated, leaving American officials to tally the destruction wrought by their surprise attack. The toll was grotesquely impressive. In less than 120 minutes, the Pacific Fleet of the United States had been neutralized. The Japanese attack was a tactical success. War was not merely a possibility, it was now a fact.

# JAPANESE AIR POWER

The yellowing pages of scores of prewar English-language publications bear witness to America's folly. The 1941 editions of *Jane's All The World's Aircraft, Aerosphere*, or official armed forces aircraft recognition manuals, all show an incredible, almost willful Anglo-American ignorance of the menace of Japanese airpower right up to the moment of the Pearl Harbor attack.

Not that they were unwarned. Their intelligence sources, such as they were, had tried to sound numerous alarms. In early 1941, General Claire Chennault, American air advisor to Chiang Kai-shek, tried vainly to interest Washington information about a fearsome new fighter plane that had recently appeared in the skies over China – the Zero. Equally disturbing reports from British military observers in Japan were routinely ignored

in London and Singapore. The official Western view remained that Japanese warplanes were, though perhaps fairly numerous, mostly derivative and emphatically second rate. Of the truth – that the Japanese airforces were among the most formidable on earth – there was not the slightest recognition. Certainly the US was guilty of complacency; probably of chauvinism; possibly, even of an unconscious racial arrogance. For this the price to her in treasure, blood and humiliation would be nearly unbearable.

To be sure, the Japanese assisted Western ignorance in every possible way. Japanese military security was excellent; among the world's great air powers only the Russians were equally unforthcoming with published information or, for that matter, were as intentionally deceptive. Even the Japanese method of designating

military aircraft types was obfuscatory (though this was not entirely deliberate) – so much so that to this day a certain confusion persists.

There was and is no avoiding the problem. The first condition of any meaningful discussion of Japanese military aviation in World War II is still that we understand something of the nomenclature involved.

## Japanese aircraft designations

When the war began the Japanese were using three distinct systems for designating military aircraft: an 'interservice' code system, an Army code system and a Navy code system. Later on, they began naming their planes as well. The Allies found this so confusing that they assigned English Christian names to all Japanese aircraft, thereby creating still another

system. Thus a Japanese World War II military aircraft may be properly designated by its 'interservice' code name, its service code name, its Allied code name, its Japanese name, or even its unofficial Japanese nickname. The accompanying chart attempts to show how all this worked in practice, but a few summary explanations might help to make things clearer.

What we have called the Japanese 'interservice' system of designation – it is usually called the Type Number system – was in fact meant to be used in all public or official references to military aircraft made outside the services themselves. Used since the late 1920s, it was a relatively straightforward affair, whereby a plane might, for example, be called simply 'The Type 97 Army heavy bomber'. The number refers to the last two

digits of the Japanese calendar year – in this case the year 2597 – in which the plane was accepted into service. 2597 on the Japanese calendar is 1937 on the western calendar. Thus 'Type 97' would be a plane of 1937; 'Type 98', of 1938; and so on. After 1940, only one digit was used, e.g. 'Type 2' for 1942. Progressive modifications were indicated by the addition of an Arabic numeral and/or the successive Kanji symbols *Ko*, *Otsu* or *Hei* (e.g. Type 2 Army fighter Mod. 2 *Otsu*).

This slightly clumsy system worked well enough before the war, but after hostilities commenced the increasing tempo of production threatened to create situations in which one service might accept, in a given year, two or more types with the same basic function – e.g. two aircraft that might properly be described as, say, 'Type 3 Navy carrier fighter'. A way

TOP LEFT AND CENTER: A series of posters urging young Japanese to join the Navy and/or the naval air force.

TOP RIGHT: Young Japanese pilot wears his ceremonial sword into battle. This photograph came from the cover of a fortnightly magazine published in Japan describing the course of the war, initially stressing Japanese conquests, and subsequently boosting morale by stressing the courage of Japanese arms against superior forces.

LEFT: A Zero A6M3. It had 20mm cannon on each wing and a 7.7mm machine gun on the port side near the engine cowling.

OVERLEAF: Type 4 fighters on the production line, one of the newest built by the Army. This was one of the first photographs printed for public consumption of this Nakajima Ki-84 *Hayate* (nicknamed Frank). She had a top speed of 388mph and excellent maneuverability.

might have been found around this hypothetical difficulty, but neither of the services had ever much liked the Type Number system anyway, and after mid-war it fell increasingly into desuetude, the Navy abandoning it completely after 1942.

The designation code used by the Japanese Army Air Force (JAAF) was simplicity itself. From 1933 on, each proposed new Army aircraft was allotted in sequence a *Kitai* (airframe or, simply, design) number. Abbreviated to *Ki*, it would appear as Ki-21, Ki-45 or whatever. Major modifications were indicated by the addition of a Roman numeral or the word *Kai*; minor modifications by the

successive Kanji characters *Ko*, *Otsu*, and *Hei* (*e.g.* Ki-44-II-*Ko*). Of course, unless an outsider knew what plane was being referred to in the first place, none of this elaboration was very helpful, for there was no inherent indication of mission, manufacturer, date of acceptance or much else.

The Japanese Navy Air Force (JNAF) aircraft designations, by contrast, were fully informative. Following the code used by the US Navy, the Japanese gave their naval aircraft designations consisting of alternating letters and numbers. The first letter stood for the plane's purpose – A = carrier fighter; B = carrier attack plane; D = carrier dive bomber;

G = land-based bomber; J = land-based fighter; N = floatplane fighter; and so on. The second letter stood for the manufacturer: M = Mitsubishi; N = Nakajima; K = Kawanishi; A = Aichi; Y = Yokosuka. The number in between, like an adjective modifying two nouns, indicated the series number of the aircraft designed for the mission in question. Thus in the basic three-unit code group A6M – the JNAF name for the redoubtable Zero fighter – one could read 'the sixth carrier fighter to be accepted by the Japanese Navy Air Force, designed by Mitsubishi'.

The numbers and letters following the initial three-unit group referred to various modifications. The second *number* re-

FAR LEFT: Aichi D3A (Type 99) Val carrier dive bomber, similar in many ways to the German Ju-87 Stuka.

CENTER LEFT: Mitsubishi A6M5 Zero, perhaps the most famous Japanese fighter in World War II. This final version had a top speed of 351 mph and was surpassed by Allied aircraft by the time it appeared in 1944, but its predecessors were as good or better than anything the Allies had in 1940–42.

LEFT: Mitsubishi G4M2 medium bomber developed teething troubles that were never fully resolved, making it as dangerous for Japanese pilots as for their targets.

LEFT: An unusual photograph of a Zero. The pilot is wearing a white *hachimaki* around his helmet, indicating that he is a *kamikaze* suicide pilot, but the fuselage carries a US emblem, while the wings carry the Japanese Rising Sun.

FAR LEFT: Japanese airmen in their round of daily exercises.

BOTTOM: Japanese pilots salute the colors before a mission.

ん い 報に 忌君クレ一

ABOVE: The Mitsubishi G4M
bomber, nicknamed Betty by
the US Air Force. Both the top
and underside views are shown.

BELOW: Work continues on the
fuselage of a Japanese bomber.

RIGHT: Japanese women
worked in their millions in
aircraft factories and in other
industries as Japanese
manpower was stretched to its
limits later in the war.

BOTTOM: Side view of a Betty.

ferred to progressive developments of the basic design: an A6M3 would therefore be a more advanced version of the Zero design than an A6M2. If the third *letter* were upper case, it would indicate a conversion that modified the aircraft's mission itself: thus the A6M2-N was a conversion of the basic Zero into a floatplane ('N'). If the third *letter* were lower case, it would refer to a minor variation: thus the A6M5c differed from other A6M5's only in its armament. A variation of intermediate importance might be given a special modification number (*e.g.* the A6M2 mod. 32 had clipped wing-tips; the A6M2 mod. 22 had rounded wing-tips).

In addition to the three original designation systems used by the Japanese, a fourth system came into being after the Pacific war began. The widespread use of nicknames started with the A6M Type 0 Navy carrier fighter. The Japanese press soon began to call this most famous of Japanese warplanes the *Reisen* (Zero fighter), and later, borrowing a word from Japan's enemies, the *Zero-sen*. Now that the floodgates had been opened, virtually every Japanese warplane subsequently produced received a sobriquet, each more poetic than the last. The Ki-43 Type 1 Army fighter became also the *Hayabusa* (Peregrine Falcon); the B6N Type 2 Navy attack bomber became also the *Tenzan* (Heavenly Mountain); and so it went. From 1942 on, the Navy, at least, recognized these names officially.

Given this profusion of Japanese nomenclature, it is probably no wonder that the bewildered Allies, who had only an imperfect grasp of *any* of the Japanese systems, should opt to devise a new system of their own. In 1942 the American Technical Air Intelligence Unit; headed by Col. Frank MacCoy, decreed that all Japanese military aircraft should thenceforward be referred to by an assigned Christian name. Thus the Ki-43 Type 1 Army Fighter *Hayabusa* now also became 'Oscar'; the B6N Type 2 Navy attack bomber *Tenzan*, 'Jill'; and so on. Variants were characterized by Arabic mod. numbers. Inevitably, some errors crept into

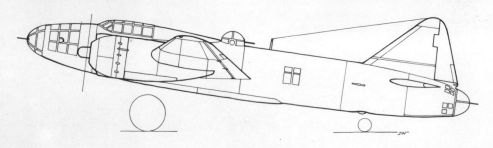

LEFT: A Zero A6M3 in flight. These planes were nicknamed Zekes by the Americans, but were generally called Zeros by all nations, even eventually the Japanese who nicknamed them Zero-sen.

BELOW LEFT: Heavy bomber factory operated by the Mitsubishi *zaibatsu*, one of the multi-faceted conglomerates of Japanese industry which dominated the economy of Japan.

BELOW RIGHT: Another Mitsubishi plant in which the engines and their casings were built.

BOTTOM: Final assembly of the aircraft.

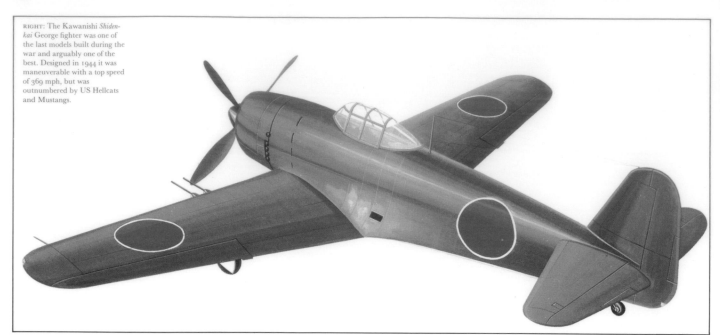

RIGHT: The Kawanishi *Shiden-kai* George fighter was one of the last models built during the war and arguably one of the best. Designed in 1944 it was maneuverable with a top speed of 369 mph, but was outnumbered by US Hellcats and Mustangs.

the system. For example, the *Zero-sen* was christened 'Zeke', but when the clipped-wing version of the *Zero-sen* appeared, the Allies mis-identified it as a new type and called it 'Hap'. Then, when USAAF General 'Hap' Arnold objected to this use of his own nickname, the plane was re-christened 'Hamp'. Finally, when it was discovered that 'Hamp' was really 'Zeke', the plane had to be re-named again, ending the war as 'Zeke 32'.

For the reader bemused by the complexities of all these competing designation systems, we can only suggest again that the accompanying chart may prove helpful.

## Growth of Japanese air power

During the period 1940–45 the Japanese produced so many new types of military aircraft (well over 100) that Allied code-namers were hard put to keep up with them. An industrial establishment capable of such creativity was clearly neither a Johnny-come-lately to the aviation business nor in any sense second rate. Indeed, however dim prewar Western perceptions of the fact may have been, the Japanese aviation industry had been developing apace with its Western counterparts for nearly two decades.

The Japanese Army bought its first airplane (a French Farman) in 1910,

but serious Japanese interest in military aviation dates from the 1914–18 war. The Japanese followed the fulminating growth of airpower during World War I with avid interest and, as it turned out, admirable insight. Immediately the war was over the Japanese began buying up surplus examples of Allied warplanes – Sopwith 1½ Strutters, Nieuport Bébés, and especially Spads. In a remarkably short time they put these imports into service, so rapidly, in fact, that they were able to use them operationally in the so-called Vladivostok Incident of 1920.

But the Japanese had no intention of permitting themselves to become dependent on foreign manufacture. The Nakajima Company soon negotiated licenses to produce both the French Nieuport 24 and the 29C.1, as well as the Hispano-Suiza in-line engine. And soon thereafter Nakajima acquired other licenses to build the British Gloster Gambet and its Bristol Jupiter radial engine.

While similarly manufacturing license types, Mitsubishi embarked on a somewhat more adventurous course, inviting Herbert Smith of the British Sopwith Company to confect an original design to meet a 1921 Japanese Navy requirement. It is worth noting that this requirement was for a *carrier-based* fighter – this

at a time when carrier aviation was everywhere in its feeblest infancy. Smith obligingly delivered a trim little biplane fighter, somewhat reminiscent of Britain's wartime SE.5, and, subsequently, original designs for a reconnaissance plane and a torpedo bomber.

A third company, Kawasaki, used both approaches. Kawasaki began by manufacturing French Salmson bombers under license and then, in 1923, installed as its Chief Designer Dr Richard Vogt, a German engineer, to produce original designs. Vogt's first effort, a Type 88 (*i.e.* 1928) Army bomber powered by a license-built BMW engine was easily up to prevailing Western standards.

The final short step to technological self-sufficiency was accomplished before the end of the decade of the 20s. The aircraft usually cited as the first all-Japanese warplane was a small Nakajima parasol fighter built to meet a 1927 Army specification. Entering service at the Type 91 Army fighter, both the plane and its engine were entirely designed and produced by Japanese technicians.

In addition to Mitsubishi, Nakajima and Kawasaki, new firms were constantly popping up – Tachikawa, specialist in trainers and light planes; Aichi, producer of seaplanes and Japan's first dive bomber; Kawanishi, founder of a distinguished line of seaplanes and flying boats; and several more. Meantime, the armed services themselves had begun to develop their own design facilities, such as the naval arsenals at Hiro and Yokosuka and the Army Rikugun design center at Tachikawa. By 1935 the inventory of combat aircraft available to the Japanese airforces was both relatively large and sophisticated.

As with the machines, so with the men. In both the Army and Navy air forces training and ground support were well developed, and in one important respect – experience – Japanese aircrews led the

RIGHT: The Mitsubishi A5M4 Claude carrier fighter was an early design with an open cockpit, which was subsequently replaced by more sophisticated models once the war began.

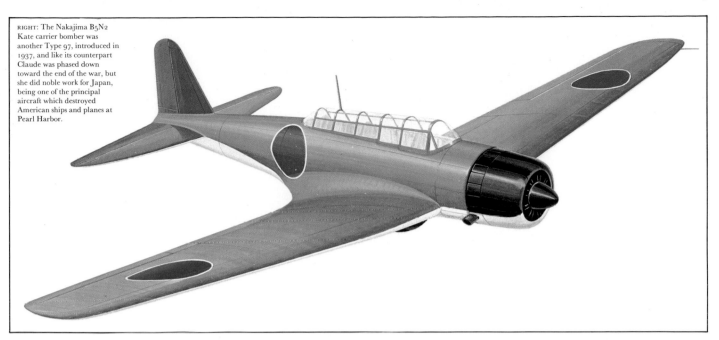

RIGHT: The Nakajima B5N2 Kate carrier bomber was another Type 97, introduced in 1937, and like its counterpart Claude was phased down toward the end of the war, but she did noble work for Japan, being one of the principal aircraft which destroyed American ships and planes at Pearl Harbor.

world. Since the end of World War I Japan's bellicose foreign policy had provoked a stream of international 'incidents' – at Vladivostok in 1920, at Tsinan in 1928, in Manchuria in 1931, at Shanghai in 1932 (Japan's first experience in air-to-air combat), in Jehol Province in 1933; and the biggest 'incident' of all, the invasion of China in 1937. These provided a nearly continuous series of opportunities to test men and equipment under full operational operations. Even before the beginning of the Sino-Japanese War, the Japanese air forces were staffed with combat veterans.

They were also very efficiently organized. Accumulating operational experience had prompted the Japanese to make progressive refinements of their command structures throughout the decade of the 1930s, and by 1940 they had established the basic structures they would use throughout the Pacific War. The Army Air Force heirarchy of command descended through Armies, Divisions and Brigades to Air Regiments – called *Sentais* – the basic tactical units, roughly comparable to British or American Groups. Fighter *Sentais* consisted of 45–48 planes; bomber and reconnaissance *Sentais*, anywhere from 27–36. Individual *Sentais* were usually made up of three Air Companies (*Chutais*), the equivalent of squadrons. The colorful tail markings of wartime Army planes almost always referred to the *Sentai* to which they belonged, often taking the form of a kind of elegant visual pun on the *Sentai*'s numerical designation (*eg.* the 5th *Sentai* used a tail design based on a highly stylized Roman V). The color in which the *Sentai* tail design was rendered differentiated the *Chutai*.

The organization of the Japanese Navy Air Force was somewhat more complex, since the command heirarchy branched into two parallel lines, depending on whether the establishment ultimately re-

## Japanese AA Weapons
### (including Dual Purpose and Naval)

| Model | Caliber | Range, max (a) Vertical (ft) (b) Horizontal (yds) | Rate of fire practical | Weight in action | MV fps | Ammunition | Weight of projectile | Remarks |
|---|---|---|---|---|---|---|---|---|
| "92" (1932) | 7.7mm (.303") | (a) 4000 (est) (b) 4600 | 300–350 | 122 lb | 2400 | Ball, AP, Incendiary Tracer | .47 oz | The infantry MG fitted with AA adaptor, Hotchkiss type (1), and special AA sights. |
| "93" (1933) | 13.2mm (.52") | (a) 13,000 (b) 7000 (Ground sight to 3,600 meters) | 250–300 | 7½ cwt (double) Gun alone 87 lb | 2250 | Ball, AP, Tracer | .114 lb | Single (pedestal) mount. Double (tripod) mount. 30-rd magazine. |
| "98" (1938) | 20mm (.79") | (a) 12,000 (b) 5450 | 120–150 | 836 lb without wheels | 2720 | HE, AP, Tracer, HE tracer (SD) | .55 lb | Dual purpose AA/Atk weapon, carried by machine cannon units (2) |
| "96" (1936) | 25mm (.98") | (a) 14,000 (b) 5700 | 175–200 | 5330 lbs (triple mount) Single gun only 246 lb | 2978 | HE, AP, HE tracer (SD), HE white phosphorous | .55 lb | Single mount. Twin (pedestal mount). 15-rd magazine. |
| "91" (1931) | 40mm (1.57") | (a) 13,000 (b) 5000 | 60–100 per barrel | 1960 lb single 3130 lb twin | 2000 | Tracer, AP, HE. HE with time fuse | 1.52 lb | Vickers type, single and double (pedestal) mounts. |
| "11" (1922)) 35 cals | 75mm (2.95") | (a) 19,600 (b) 11,000 | 10–12 | 4800 lb | 1800 | HE | 14.5 lb | Obsolescent |
| "88" (1928) 40 cals | 75mm (2.95") | (a) 30,000 (b) 15,000 | 20 | 5390 lb | 2360 | HE Incendiary HE Shrapnel | 14.6 lb | Principal Army AA gun. |
| "10" (1921) 40 cals | 76.2mm (3") | (a) 25,000 (b) 12,000 | 15 | | 2220 | HE Incendiary HE Shrapnel | 12.7 lb | Pedestal mount, Navy AA gun. |
| "14" (1925) | 105mm (4.14") | (a) 36,000 (b) 20,000 | 8 | 7 tons | 2300 | HE | 35 lb | |
| "89" (1929) | 127mm (5") | (a) 35,000 (b) 15,000 | 8–10 | | 2370 | HE, AP, fixed and semi-fixed | 50 lb | Single (pedestal) and double mount. |

(1) The Japanese also used a Model "92" (1932) 7.7 mm (.303") MG almost identical with the LEWIS, which fired British .303", Mk VII ammunition.   (2) The Japanese also used a 20 mm (.79") AA MG, OERLIKON Model.

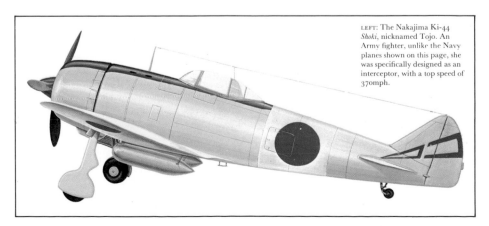

LEFT: The Nakajima Ki-44 *Shoki*, nicknamed Tojo. An Army fighter, unlike the Navy planes shown on this page, she was specifically designed as an interceptor, with a top speed of 370mph.

FAR LEFT AND LEFT: Work on aircraft frames and propellers later in the war. Women were utilized extensively, from the design stage to and including the assembling of parts and the shipment of the goods from the factories.

FAR LEFT: The shipping room of a spare parts factory for aircraft.

LEFT: Japanese workers assemble components at high speed. Masks were worn for protection against fumes.

BELOW LEFT: Workers sign in at the factory and proceed to the assembly line (near left).

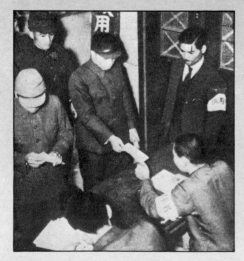

LEFT: A Zeke carrier based Navy fighter, which had the best maneuverability of any fighter in the world.

RIGHT: An Aichi D3A2 Val carrier dive bomber. This type, which became increasingly obsolete as the war progressed, was used in the last year of the war for *kamikaze* missions.

ferred to was land-based or carrier-based. The essential land-based tactical unit was the Air Corps (at first called *Kokutai* and later, *Koku Sentai*), an assemblage of aircraft usually (but not always) of the same type and mission, that could range in size anywhere from a handful of planes up to 70 or 80. The seagoing counterpart of the Air Corps was the Carrier Air Group (*Koku Sentai*). In 1941 the Air Groups embarked aboard the six big fleet carriers were made up of a mixture of fighters, dive bombers and level bomber/torpedo planes. For example, *Akagi*, flagship of the fleet carriers, embarked 18 'Zero' fighters, 18 'Val' dive bombers and 27 'Kate' bomber/torpedo planes. The three smaller carriers generally carried only two types of aircraft, fighters and bomber/torpedo.

It is easier to talk about the structure of the Japanese air forces than about their size. With respect to aircraft available, total figures tend not to be very meaningful, since they make no distinction between first- and second-line types and do not take into account whether a plane is significantly 'in position'. On the eve of World War II the Japanese Army Air Force was composed of about 50 *Sentais* and a scattering of independent *Chutais* – on paper a force of 1600 aircraft. A more realistic figure, composed of first-line aircraft in position, might be about 1375. Similarly, the Navy figures for December

1941 indicate a total of 3029 aircraft in hand, of which only about 1380 were first line and in position. This means that in first-line aircraft alone, Japan began the war with a quantitative advantage of better than 2:1 over the in-position aircraft of all her adversaries combined. Her qualitative advantage was, of course, much higher still.

## Japan's air forces in World War II

The story of how, in the final years of the 1930s, the Japanese moved from a position of dubious air parity to one of decisive superiority, and then, in the 40s, slid into defeat and ruin, forms one of the more arresting sub-plots of the vast, sinister drama of World War II. It is a story whose threads begin in the early 1930s.

The three years between 1933 and 1936 were a kind of watershed in the history of military aviation: the gestation period of all the air forces of the Second World War. It was a time when the doctrines of World War I experience fought their final battle with the logic of technology and lost. The lessons of 1914–18 were the dogma of senior air staffs everywhere – that fighter planes should, above all else, be maneuverable, that bombers should operate primarily in support of ground troops, and so on. But the internal dynamic of aviation progress took no account of these pieties. The insistent thrust in airplane design was for

BELOW: Air arm trainees sport
their dexterity and physical
prowess before their peers.

BELOW CENTER: Pilot trainees
were whirled around in these
contraptions to give them
greater balance in order to
inure them to the twists and
turns they would experience in
the air.

more power, greater speed, larger size, longer range. Finally, the contradictions could no longer be resolved. For example, the most maneuverable kinds of fighters were biplanes and triplanes, but these were inherently low-speed designs, and if they could not catch the fast, powerful new bombers that were beginning to be produced, what good were they? Only by holding back the clock of progress everywhere could the old doctrines be maintained.

So the old doctrines gave way, and the world's airpowers embarked on a belated orgy of 'modernization'. How successfully each was able to respond to the new technical challenges would have much to do with its subsequent fortunes in World War II.

Initially the Japanese response was cautious, misleading some Western observers into concluding that it was also ineffective. The first new-style Japanese warplanes, the result of decisions made two years earlier, began to enter service in 1936. Of these, the one destined to become most famous was the Mitsubishi G3M Type 96 Navy medium bomber, known later to the Allies as 'Nell'. Lean of fuselage, twin-engined and twin-tailed, sporting curious tortoise-back bulges at the dorsal and waist gun positions, the G3M could carry up to 1765lb of bombs or an externally mounted torpedo. Its Mitsubishi Kinsei engines delivered 840 hp, and a maximum speed of 234 mph (later upgraded to 1000 hp and 258 mph).

Why Western observers should have ignored what little they knew about the G3M is inexplicable. The plane was at least up to the standards of, say, the well-publicized contemporary British Bristol Blenheim or the Russian SB–2 that won fame in the Spanish Civil War. And in the Sino-Japanese War the G3M soon established records by conducting trans-oceanic raids in Hankow and Nanking from bases in Japan and Formosa. Certainly, after Pearl Harbor, the 'Nell' became very well-known indeed: within hours it was plastering American bases in the Philippines and within days, helping to annihilate the British Far Eastern fleet with the sinking of *Prince of Wales* and *Repulse*. In fact, G3Ms continued to serve, albeit with diminishing effectiveness, right through to the end of the war.

The other major Type 96 airplane, the Navy's Mitsubishi A5M carrier fighter, and its 1937 Army counterpart, the Nakajima Ki-27 Type 97 Army Fighter, were both superficially less impressive than the G3M. Western standards now dictated that modern fighters should be fast and sleek – low-wing monoplanes with enclosed cockpits and retractable landing gear and, if possible, in-line engines (which permitted streamlined 'pointed-nosed' designs.)

The A5M and the Ki-27 failed these criteria on several counts. Both were, to be sure, low-wing monoplanes, but they had blunt radial-engined noses and fixed, spatted landing gear; and the A5M even had an open cockpit. In addition, both had relatively low top speeds – well under 300 mph – and light armament – two rifle-caliber machine guns. Yet despite their conservative designs, both planes were highly sophisticated pieces of engineering and were spectacularly successful in pre-World War II combat. From the day in December 1937, when A5Ms shot down ten Russian-built 1–16 Chinese fighters in a matter of minutes, until the outbreak of the Pacific war, the little Mitsubishi fighter dominated the skies over China. Even more impressive was the performance of the Ki-27s in the so-called Nomonhan Incident in the summer of 1939. This marvelously stupid dispute between Russia and Japanese forces in Manchuria over a desolate part of the Mongolian border lasted for 120 days and involved both major ground fighting and the largest air battles seen since 1914–18. In the end, the Japanese claimed the destruction of 1260 Russian aircraft for the loss of 168 of their own. These claims are almost certainly lies (they were hotly disputed by the equally mendacious Russians), but they suggest both the scale of the fighting and the extraordinary success of the Ki-27.

Both the A5M (later codenamed 'Claude') and the Ki-27 ('Nate') soldiered on into the early months of World War II, until they were replaced by more advanced types. Indeed, that had prob-

BELOW: First stages of
parachute training; learning
how to land.

BELOW CENTER: The first
practice drop. . . .

BOTTOM: . . . and the landing.

BELOW LEFT: Parachute
trainees practice landings from
a greater height indoors before
attempting the real thing from
an aircraft.

BELOW RIGHT: The anxious
moment before the jump.

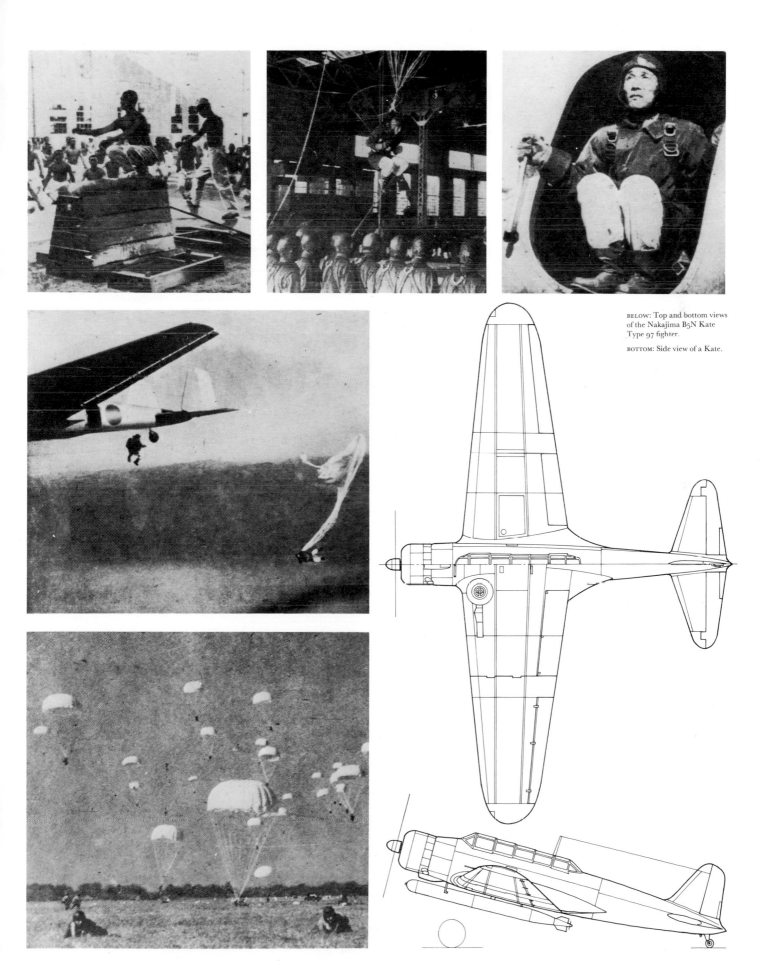

BELOW: Top and bottom views
of the Nakajima B5N Kate
Type 97 fighter.

BOTTOM: Side view of a Kate.

ably been their most significant function – to serve as test-beds for the truly extraordinary fighter designs that followed.

The Ki-27 was by no means the only important Type 97 airplane; indeed, 1937 was in some ways a banner year in Japanese military aviation. It also saw the introduction of the Army's counterpart to the G3M, a large twin-engined bomber known as the Ki-21, later to be christened 'Sally' by the Allies. Like the G3M, the Ki-21 was used extensively in the Sino-Japanese War, as well as in the Nomonhan fighting. Ultimately powered by 1490-hp radials (up from the original 850 hp) and capable of carrying 2205lb of bombs a distance of 1700 miles, 'Sally' was neither more nor less advanced than most of its Western contemporaries, but because the Japanese Army failed to develop a significantly better heavy bomber until late in World War II, the Ki-21 fought through to VJ-Day.

Other Type 97s that were to play important roles in World War II included a large reconnaissance flying boat, the Kawanishi H6K and a Mitsubishi single-engined light bomber, the Ki-30. But perhaps the most memorable of all the Type 97s was Nakajima's B5N Navy carrier bomber ('Kate'). This extraordinary machine was destined to be the first of the formidable trio of aircraft that would compose Japan's Carrier Air Groups at the beginning of World War II. At the time of its introduction into service it was unquestionably the most advanced plane of its type in the world. 'Kate' was a single-engined, two- or three-place monoplane that could carry either one 1764lb torpedo or three 550lb bombs.

During its long service career, it was powered by progressively more powerful radials ranging from 770 hp to 1115 hp, and its original design boasted many advanced engineering features, such as Fowler-type flaps, mechanically folding wings, retractable landing gear, variable pitch propellers and integral fuel tanks. Its impact on the course of history was considerable. 'Kates' were responsible for most of the damage done at Pearl Harbor, as well as for the subsequent near destruction of the US carrier force in the Pacific, since, by the end of 1942, B5Ns had been wholly or partially responsible for the sinking of *Yorktown*, *Lexington*, *Wasp* and *Hornet*. The B5N continued in first-line service into 1944 and they served in second-line service until the end of the war.

In contrast to 1937, the two following years added only a few new types of aircraft to the Japanese inventory, and of these, only two were particularly noteworthy. One was a Type 99 light-medium Army bomber, the Kawasaki Ki-48 ('Lily'), an undistinguished twin-engined design that nevertheless saw long service in the war and was produced in nearly 2000 examples. The other was much more important. The Aichi D3A Type 99 Navy carrier dive bomber ('Val') was to join the B5N ('Kate') as the second of the three types that would form the Navy's *Koku Sentais* at the outbreak of the war. Comparable in most technical respects to Germany's famous Stuka, the D3A gained world recognition for its part in the Pearl Harbor attack and in the battles of Midway, Santa Cruz, the Solomon Islands and many other actions. It

was specifically credited with the sinking of the British aircraft carrier *Hermes* and the cruisers *Cornwall* and *Dorsetshire* (the same *Dorsetshire* that had delivered the coup de grace to *Bismarck*). Like many other Japanese aircraft that drifted into obsolescence as the war progressed, the D3A ended its combat career in the lurid role of a *Kamikaze* suicide plane.

The third member of Japan's Carrier Air Group trio joined the Navy in 1940. Whatever the qualities of the other two, they paled by comparison. The Mitsubishi A6M Type O Navy carrier fighter, christened 'Zeke' by the Allied code namers but known everywhere as the 'Zero', was one of the greatest warplanes in the history of military aviation. Dr Jiro Horikoshi, Mitsubishi's head designer, was the man responsible for making the incredible leap from the stolid little A5M of 1936 to the dazzling Zero of 1940. It was a leap that entailed creating a fighter that was not only as good or better than the world's best, but designing it for carrier operations into the bargain – a combination most Westerners then considered a contradiction in terms. Indeed, the Zero made remarkably few concessions to the compromises that usually have to be made in warplane design – between speed vs. maneuverability, small size vs. long range, low weight vs. high power, and so on. The version of the Zero used at Pearl Harbor and during the early months of the war (the A6M2 mod. 21) was powered by a 925 hp Nakajima Sakai radial, had a top speed of 336 mph. and a (for a time) powerful armament of 2 rifle-caliber machine guns and two 20 mm cannon. Its maneuverability was

FAR LEFT: Chalking up victories.

CENTER LEFT: Nakajima B6N Type 2 Jill carrier bomber in flames after attacking the USS *Yorktown* Mark II in the Carolines, 29 April 1944.

BELOW LEFT: Reconnaissance biplane returns to its carrier.

BELOW: An aircraft engine factory. Instructor points out the intricacies of the engine to recruits.

BOTTOM: Japanese machine gunner spots an Allied bomber as his plane hovers above in preparation for the attack.

phenomenal – easily the best of any major fighter in the world – and its range was equally astonishing. When on the first day of the Pacific war Zeros appeared over the Philippines, the Americans could not believe that the planes had not been launched from carriers; in fact they belonged to the Tainan and 3rd *Kokutais*, making the round trip from their bases in Formosa 550 nautical miles away.

Yet the Zero design did, inevitably, include some compromises. For example, a superb climber, it was an indifferent diver; and a certain lightness of construction made it unable to sustain enemy gunfire for prolonged periods. But its greatest weakness was something more subtle, not readily apparent to anyone in 1941. It was one of those designs that for some reason did not lend itself easily to progressive improvement. Adored by its pilots and revered by the Japanese populace, the Zero was to be, in a sense, a victim of its early successes, kept in production long after it had exhausted its potential. The final major version of the Zero, the A6M5, had a top speed of 351 mph and an armament of 3 machine guns and two cannon, an insufficient advance over the specifications of the A6M2. By the time the A6M5 went into production (Spring 1944), it had been decisively surpassed by newer Allied fighters. But in the early days – at least up to the end of 1942 – the Zero ruled supreme in the Western Pacific.

Several other warplanes joined the Japanese airforces in 1940. The Mitsubishi Ki-46 ('Dinah') was a rather sauve twin-engined Army reconnaissance plane; the Nakajima Ki-49 *Donryu*

('Helen') was a not-very-successful attempt to improve on the old Ki-21 Army heavy bomber; the Aichu E13A ('Jake') and the F1M ('Pete') were single-engined seaplanes; but none of these other Type Os had a fraction of the importance of *the* Zero.

It was not until 1941 that the Army's counterpart to the Navy Zero fighter made its appearance. But for the Zero, the Nakajima Ki-43 Type 1 Army fighter *Hayabusa* ('Oscar'), might have been world famous. It was, by the standards of the time, an excellent plane, as maneuverable as the Zero and more effective than most of its early-war adversaries, but it lacked both the Zero's tech-

nical brilliance and its fierce exposure to history. The principal *Hayabusa* variant, the Ki-43-II-*Otsu* had only a fair turn of speed (320 mph) and inadequate armament (2 light machine guns), but all *Hayabusas* had superb handling characteristics and are affectionately remembered by their former pilots. More *Hayabusas* were produced than any other wartime JAAF fighter, and they served to the end of the war in every theatre where the Army fought.

The other major Type 1 aircraft was the Mitsubishi G4M (Betty), intended as a replacement for the Navy's G3M medium bomber of 1936. As befitted a replacement, the G4M was bigger, faster

and better armed than its predecessor, and could carry a heavier bomb load a longer distance. But it had one unpleasant weakness. In the interest of improved range, airframe construction had been made as light as possible and armor protection for the crew and gas tanks had been eliminated. Thus, for all its excellent qualities, the G4M soon acquired a reputation for being a 'flamer', and losses to allied gunfire were, in fact, high. 'Bettys' were nevertheless produced in large quantities and served throughout the Pacific until 1945.

Despite the Navy's sentimental unwillingness to replace the Zero, it moved swiftly enough to replace the other two

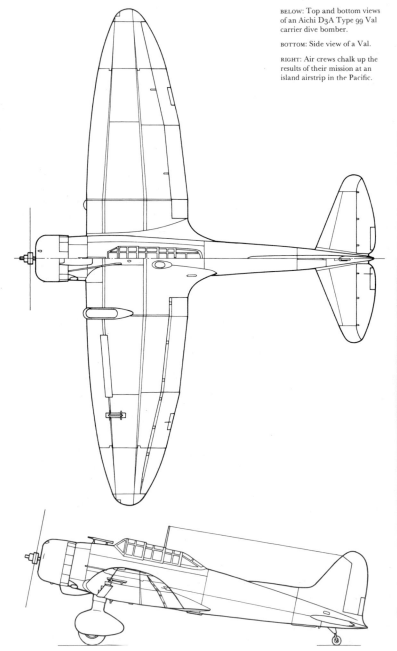

BELOW: Top and bottom views of an Aichi D3A Type 99 Val carrier dive bomber.

BOTTOM: Side view of a Val.

RIGHT: Air crews chalk up the results of their mission at an island airstrip in the Pacific.

## Famous Air Units

Apart from the *Koku Sentais* embarked aboard the big fleet carriers, the most famous Japanese naval air unit in the early part of the war was the Tainan *Kokutai*, its fame resting primarily on the exploits of its fighter component, which included an astonishing number of pilots who were to become great aces: Nishizawa, Sakai, Ohta, Sasai, Tanaka and several more. The Zeros of the Tainan *Kokutai* played an important part in the Philippine, East Indies and Guadalcanal campaigns, but their role in the Lae airwing on New Guinea, excitingly recounted by Saburo Sakai in his book *Samurai,* was perhaps the high point of their history.

Some other well-known Navy units were the Genzan, Mihoro and Kanoya *Kokutais,* whose bomber components sank HMS *Prince of Wales* and *Renown,* and the elite late-war 343rd *Kokutai* ('Genda's Circus'), a large air defense fighter unit commanded by Commander Minoru Genda, one of the chief planners of the Pearl Harbor raid.

Among the Army's more famous fighter units were the 64th *Sentai,* commanded by the national hero Lieutenant Colonel Tateo Kato, and the 50th *Sentai,* which included the Army's two top aces of the Pacific War: Anabuki and Sasaki. Both groups operated in Burma throughout most of the war. Belonging to the most famous of the Army's late-war air defense units were the colorfully painted 'Tojos' of Major Naboru Ikuda's 47th *Sentai* and the even more flamboyant 'Tonys' of Major Teruhiko Kobayashi's 244th *Sentai.* Kobayashi was, incidentally, one of the few Japanese pilots to win the rare Bukosho award for gallantry.

## The Leading Japanese Aces

| Name/Rank/Service | Confirmed Victories |
|---|---|
| Hiroyoshi Nishizawa, Warrant Officer, JNAF | 87 |
| Tetsuzo Iwamoto, Lt. (jg), JNAF | 80 (14 in China) |
| Shoichi Sugita, Petty Officer 1st, JNAF | 70 (approx.) |
| Saburo Sakai, Lt. (jg), JNAF | 64 (2 in China) |
| Hiromichi Shinohara, Warrant Officer, JAAF | 58 (all in Manchuria) |
| Takeo Okumura, Petty Officer 1st, JNAF | 54 (4 in China) |
| Satoshi Anabuki, Master Sgt., JAAF | 51 |
| Isamu Sasaki, Warrant Officer, JAAF | 38 |
| Mitsuyoshi Tarui, Lt., JAAF | 38 (28 in Manchuria) |
| Toshio Ohta, Petty Officer 1st, JNAF | 34 |
| Kazu Sugino, Warrant Officer, JNAF | 32 |
| Yasuhiko Kuroe, Major, JAAF | 30 (2 in Manchuria) |

## Nishizawa

Tall, pale and gaunt, Naval Warrant Officer Hiroyoshi Nishizawa was one of those odd characters whose like one finds surprisingly often near the top of aces' lists the world over. This greatest of Japanese fighter pilots was, on the ground, so habitually moody and withdrawn that his less complicated colleagues were sometimes hard put not to take offense. Once airborne, Nishizawa seemed to undergo a kind of demonic change of personality. According to his famous squadron mate, Saburo Sakai, "his reserve, his silence, his spurning of associates vanished... he became the Devil... a genius, a poet... Never have I seen a man with a fighter plane do what Nishizawa would do with his Zero." From Lae, through Rabaul and the Guadalcanal campaign, and on to the Philippines, Nishizawa blazed a brilliant, bloody trail that culminated in 87 official victories, with perhaps as many as 15 more unofficial kills. On 25 October, 1944, he died, a passenger aboard an unarmed transport shot down by enemy fighters.

carrier-based types. The successor to 'Kate' was the Nakajima B6N Type 2 carrier bomber *Tenzan* ('Jill'). Not unlike 'Kate' in general appearance, the *Tenzan* was a much superior plane, faster and with a 50 per cent greater range. Once again, it bid fair to be the best plane of its kind in the world. Similarly, the Yokosuka D4Y Type 2 carrier dive bomber *Suisei* ('Judy') was a considerable improvement over the Type 99 'Val', being, among other things, more than 100 mph. faster. Interestingly, the early versions of the *Suisei* were powered by in-line engines, the first time the Navy had broken faith with radials since 1932. Apparently the Navy's suspicions were confirmed, for the later versions of the *Suisei* were powered by the dependable Mitsubishi *Kinsei* radials.

Both the *Tenzan* and the *Suisei* demonstrated the ability of Japanese designers to keep pace with world standards, but the combat history of the two planes demonstrated something far less cheering for the Japanese. At the war's outset, one of the many conditions of Japan's frail hope for victory had been the destruction of the American aircraft carriers early in the war, while the Japanese carrier fleet remained largely intact. But by the end of 1942, the carrier fleets of both nations were a shambles. From that point

forward it was a race to see who could build the most carriers first – precisely the kind of production duel the Japanese were bound to lose.

The disastrous confirmation of this inevitable failure coincided, ironically, with the introduction of both the *Tenzan* and *Suisei* into major combat. On 19–20 June 1944, off the Marianas, history's greatest carrier battle was overwhelmingly won by the Americans. The Japanese lost 346 aircraft and two carriers against an American loss of just 30 planes. Perhaps if the Japanese Navy could have defended itself with a fighter more advanced than the Zero it might have made a better showing, but probably nothing could have saved it. In any case, from that point on the history of the Japanese carrier air arm was one of accelerating collapse. It now made little difference what the technical qualities of new Japanese carrier planes such as the *Tenzan* and *Suisei* might be. For Japan, only land-based aircraft could henceforth play significant roles.

As far as land-based Type 2 aircraft were concerned, two new Army planes were destined to play important parts in the closing stages of the war. One, the Nakajima Ki-44 Type 2 Army fighter *Shoki* ('Tojo'), was designed specifically as an interceptor – a tacit acknowledge-

ment, perhaps, that dark days might lie ahead. A conventional single-engined monoplane design, the *Shoki* conceded such traditional Japanese aerial virtues as maneuverability and range to high speed, heavy armament and rapid rate-of-climb. It was heavy and difficult to fly, but it had, in its most advanced version, a top speed of 370 mph and an armament of two heavy machine guns and two 40mm cannon. The *Shoki* was occasionally used in various theatres during 1942–44, with modest results, but it found its true vocation in 1945 as a bomber-killer, operating with such crack air defense units as the 47th *Sentai* and exacting a bloody price from the American Superfortresses and Liberators that were relentlessly beating Japan to its knees.

The other important Type 2 Army airplane was the two-place twin-engined Kawasaki Ki-45 *Toryu* ('Nick'), originally intended as a long-range escort fighter. It served with distinction in many areas, performing many unforeseen roles, but like the *Shoki* it is best remembered as an end-of-the-war interceptor operating in defense of the Japanese home islands.

The Navy's non-carrier Type 2 aircraft were a mixed bag. The least successful was originally intended to be an equivalent of the Army's *Toryu, i.e.* a twin-engined land-based escort fighter. But the

Nakajima J1N Type 2 Navy fighter proved ineffective in its originally-intended role and only marginally useful as a reconnaissance plane. It ended its career as a so-so night-fighter interceptor – the J1N1-S *Gekko* ('Irving').

Kawanishi's elegant H8K Type 2 flying boat ('Emily') was, from a design point of view, a very different story. An enormous four-engined bomber/reconnaissance plane with an impressive 4474 mile range, the 'Emily' was almost certainly the most sophisticated flying boat to see service anywhere in World War II. Over 160 models of all versions were built, being used throughout the Western Pacific until the end of the war.

The final Type 2 Navy plane was something of an oddity, but, as it turned out, an important one. Before the war the Navy planners had been convinced that floatplane fighters could one day play an important role in defending Japan's far-flung island empire. Accordingly, in 1940, the Navy commissioned Kawanishi to design a super floatplane fighter whose level of performance would approach that of its land- and carrier-based counterparts. While waiting for this design to

BELOW LEFT: Zeros await the signal to remove wheel chocks for the take-off on the air strike against Pearl Harbor.

BELOW: Zeros ready for take-off to attack Pearl Harbor.

BOTTOM: Captured Hamp, another nickname for the Zero, is flown alongside a US P-38 Lightning to compare its flying speed.

# Japanese Aircraft

Mavis 11

Emily 12

Tess 11

Nell 22

Sally 3

Irving 11

Kate 12

Nick 1

Dinah 3

Val 22

Tony 1

Rufe 11

Zeke 21

Judy 11

Zeke 52

Pete 11

Liz 11

Tabby 22

Betty 22

Topsy 1

Helen 2

Frances 11

Jake 11

Paul 11

Oscar 2

Jack 11

Tojo 2

## The Names of Japanese Warplanes

| Designer | Type Number | Designation | JNA Code | JAAF Code | Japanese Name (or nickname) | Allied Code Name |
|---|---|---|---|---|---|---|
| Mitsubishi | Type 96 | Carrier fighter | A5M | | | Claude |
| Mitsubishi | Type 96 | Heavy bomber | G3M | | ("Chukoh") | Nell |
| Mitsubishi | Type 97 | Heavy bomber | | Ki-21 | | Sally |
| Nakajima | Type 97 | Fighter | | Ki-27 | | Nate |
| Nakajima | Type 97 | Carrier bomber | B5N | | | Kate |
| Kawanishi | Type 97 | Flying boat | H6K | | | Mavis |
| Kawasaki | Type 98 | Light bomber | | Ki-32 | | Mary |
| Kawasaki | Type 99 | Light bomber | | Ki-48 | | Lily |
| Mitsubishi | Type 99 | Recco a/c | | Ki-51 | | Sonia |
| Aichi | Type 99 | Carrier dive bomber | D3A | | | Val |
| Mitsubishi | Type 0 | Carrier fighter | A6M | | Reisen; Zero-sen | Zeke; Hamp |
| Mitsubishi | Type 0 | Seaplane fighter | A6M2-N | | Suisen | Rufe |
| Aichi | Type 0 | Seaplane recco | E13A | | | Jake |
| Mitsubishi | Type 0 | Seaplane spotter | F1M | | | Pete |
| Nakajima | Type 0 | Recco a/c | | Ki-46 | | Dinah |
| Nakajima | Type 0 | Heavy bomber | | Ki-49 | Donryu | Helen |
| Nakajima | Type 1 | Fighter | | Ki-43 | Hayabusa | Oscar |
| Mitsubishi | Type 1 | Heavy bomber | G4M | | ("Hamaki") | Betty |
| Nakajima | Type 2 | Fighter | | Ki-44 | Shoki | Tojo |
| Kawasaki | Type 2 | Heavy fighter | | Ki-45 | Toryu | Nick |
| Nakajima | Type 2 | Carrier bomber | B6N | | Tenzan | Jill |
| Yokosuka | Type 2 | Carrier dive bomber | D4Y | | Suisei | Judy |
| Nakajima | Type 2 | Heavy fighter | J1N | | Gekko | Irving |
| Kawanishi | Type 2 | Flying boat | H8K | | | Emily |
| Kawanishi | Type 2 | Seaplane fighter | N1K | | Kyofu | Rex |
| Kawanishi | (1944) | Fighter | N1K2-J | | Shiden-kai | George |
| Kawasaki | Type 3 | Fighter | | Ki-61 | Hien | Tony |
| Mitsubishi | (1943) | Fighter | J2M | | Raiden | Jack |
| Yokosuka | (1943) | Light bomber | P1Y | | Ginga | Frances |
| Yokosuka | (1943) | Night fighter | P1Y1-S | | Kyokko | Frances |
| Mitsubishi | Type 4 | Heavy bomber | | Ki-67 | Hiryu | Peggy |
| Nakajima | Type 4 | Fighter | | Ki-84 | Hayate | Frank |
| Nakajima | (1943) | Carrier recco | C6N | | Saiun | Myrt |
| Aichi | (1943) | Carrier bomber | B7A | | Ryusei | Grace |
| Kawasaki | Type 5 | Fighter | | Ki-100 | | |

The chart above lists the most prominent Japanese warplanes. A given plane could be called by several different names: its Type Number designations, its Navy or Army code designation, its Japanese name (or unofficial nickname – shown in brackets and quotes) or its Allied code name. The Japanese Army used Type Number designations throughout the war; the Navy discontinued them after 1942.

LEFT: Japanese refuel a bomber in preparation for another mission.

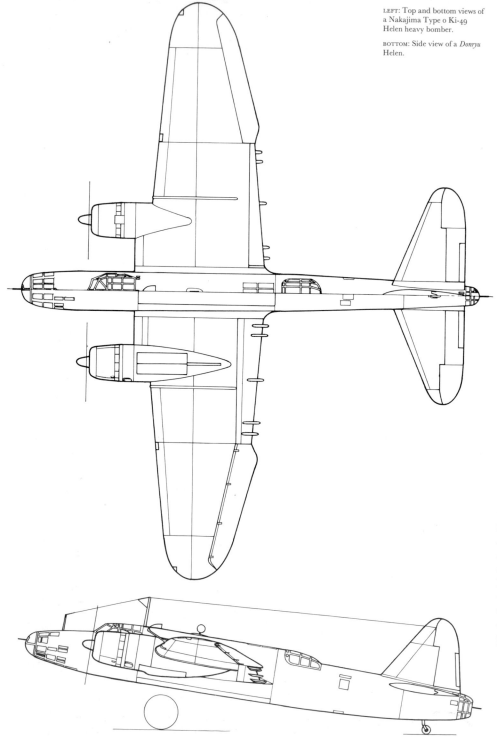

LEFT: Top and bottom views of a Nakajima Type 0 Ki-49 Helen heavy bomber.

BOTTOM: Side view of a *Donryu* Helen.

come to fruition, the Navy planned to use an interim expedient, a float-plane conversion of the Zero (the A6M2-N ['Rufe']).

But by 1942, when the Kawanishi N1K ('Rex') design was ready, the Navy had changed its mind. The experience with the 'Rufes' had been generally disastrous, the course of the war prompted a growing suspicion that there might not be all that many islands to defend after all, and the inherent impossibility of ever bringing a floatplane up to the performance standards of other fighters was at last being acknowledged. The orders for the Kawanishi floatplane were terminated after only 97 had been produced.

Dismayed but undeterred, Kawanishi set about the unpromising task of converting their floatplane into a land-based fighter. Against all odds, they succeeded brilliantly. The ultimate version of the Kawanishi design, the N1K2-J *Shiden-kai* ('George 21') of 1944, was to prove the best all-round Navy fighter of the war, giving a good account of itself over the Philippines, Formosa, Okinawa and the home islands, where it served with the large 343rd air defense *Koku Sentai*. Maneuverable, with a top speed of 369 mph and armed with four 20mm cannon, it was technically as formidable as the American Mustangs and Hellcats. In combat, however, it was always outnumbered and often poorly flown, the cadres of experienced Navy aircrews having by this time been murderously thinned.

When the *Shiden-kai* finally took to the air the Navy had already produced a second single-engined land-based fighter. This was the ponderous Mitsubishi J2M *Raiden* ('Jack'), which entered service in 1943. From the outset the *Raiden*, like the Army's Ki-44 *Shoki*, had been intended as an interceptor. Once again, range and maneuverability were sacrificed for speed, fire-power and rate-of-climb. The *Raiden* first entered combat in the Marianas in September, 1944, but it did not excel in the fighter vs. fighter role. Again, like the *Shoki*, it was to find its true vocation in the role of bomber-killer. In the final days of the war *Raidens* managed to bring considerable grief to American bomber crews in the skies over Japan.

Having taught a world infatuated with in-line engine fighters to respect radial-engined fighters, the Japanese now, for the first time since 1935, produced an in-line-engined fighter of their own. The Army's Kawasaki Ki-61 Type 3 *Hien*

BELOW LEFT: Type 97 Kate bomber takes off to attack Pearl Harbor.

BELOW: Kate torpedo bomber prepares for take-off.

BOTTOM: Kate leaves the deck of a carrier.

('Tony') was a beautifully streamlined plane powered by a 1100-hp engine based on the German DB601A, a powerplant of the Messerschmitt. There were several variants of the *Hien*, ranging in armament from two light and two heavy machine guns to two heavy machine guns and two 30mm cannon, but all versions were fast, maneuverable and formidable. *Hiens* first entered combat over New Guinea in April 1943, and thereafter fought in every theatre. Along with the Navy's *Shiden* and *Raiden*, and the Army's *Shoki* and *Toryu*, the *Hien* was one of the most important types operating with the Japanese Air Defense Forces in 1945. Its final variant was an astonishing eleventh-hour improvization (May 1945), involv-

ing the substitution of a Mitsubishi radial for the *Hien*'s original in-line engine. So successful was the result – the Ki-100 Type 5 Army fighter – that it might have become one of the world's greatest fighters, but in the event only 99 examples were produced.

Also in 1943, the Navy brought out its last – and in some ways, its best – land based bomber. The twin-engined Yoko-suka P1Y *Ginga* ('Frances') was originally intended as an aircraft capable of both level and dive bombing, after the fashion of Germany's Ju-88. In fact, this sleek, powerful light bomber proved so versatile that it was used as a torpedo bomber and a night fighter (the P1Y1-S *Kyokko*) as well. It was only when the Americans

approached close enough to the shores of Japan to be within the *Ginga's* 2700-mile range that the US Navy encountered the aircraft in significant numbers. It proved to be a dangerous opponent and is credited with sinking at least one American carrier; but by then the inevitable defeat of Japan was rapidly nearing and the intercession of the *Ginga* could make little difference.

Indeed, the besetting irony of Japanese military aviation was that after 1942 every advance in warplane design was matched by a corresponding decline in the ability of Japanese airpower to affect the outcome of the war. By mid-1944 this paradox had become acute. In terms of quality, the last Japanese warplanes were

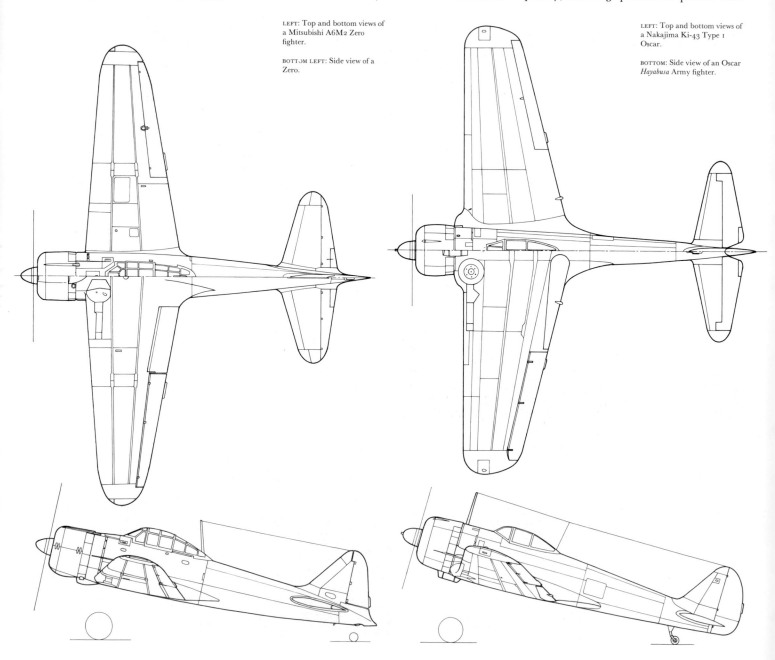

LEFT: Top and bottom views of a Mitsubishi A6M2 Zero fighter.

BOTTOM LEFT: Side view of a Zero.

LEFT: Top and bottom views of a Nakajima Ki-43 Type 1 Oscar.

BOTTOM: Side view of an Oscar *Hayabusa* Army fighter.

of unprecedented brilliance; in terms of efficacy, they were fast approaching irrelevance.

For example, in mid-1944 the Japanese Army at last received a plane fully worthy of replacing the now-antiquated 'Sally' of 1937; the splendid twin-engined Mitsubishi Ki-67 Type 4 Army heavy bomber *Hiryu* ('Peggy'). Had the well-defended *Hiryu*, with its 1764-lb bombload and its 334 mph top speed, entered service two years earlier, it might have done much to advance the Japanese cause. Instead, it was at best merely an irritant to the massive Allied forces now closing on Japan for the final kill.

Similarly, the best fighter to be used by either of the Japanese air forces in World War II appeared so late, in such inadequate numbers, and often so poorly piloted, that it contributed hardly more than a footnote to the history of the war. The Nakajima Ki-84 Type 4 Army fighter *Hayate* ('Frank') was a world-class machine. When the 22nd *Sentai* first introduced the *Hayate* into combat against the US 14th Air Force in China (in August 1944), the Americans correctly concluded that they were up against an antagonist that could be compared favorably to the most advanced versions of the Hellcats, Mustangs, and Thunderbolts (and therefore to such European superstars as the Spitfire, Tempest, FW-190D and La-7). The *Hayate* was a powerful, strongly constructed single-engined fighter possessed of a 388-mph top speed, a strong armament of two heavy machine guns and two 20mm cannon, and outstanding maneuverability. Its versatility was such that at various times it was employed as an air superiority fighter, an interceptor, a night fighter and a close air support fighter-bomber. It fought well in the Philippine and Okinawa campaigns and in the fight over the home islands, but once again, to no historically important purpose.

Japan's last generation of carrier-borne aircraft may be taken as the final illustration of the paradox of Japanese air power at the end of the war. In late 1944 two new Navy types began to trickle

off the production lines. The Aichi B7A *Ryusei* ('Grace') was arguably the world's best carrier torpedo bomber and the Nakajima C6N *Saiun* ('Myrt') was certainly the world's fastest carrier reconnaissance plane, able to outrun most Allied fighters. But by the time both types began to reach service units, the Japanese Navy had hardly any ships left to accommodate them. Landmarks in naval aircraft design, these fine planes were in other respects monuments to pointlessness.

Thus the 25-year enterprise of Japanese military aviation had followed its trajectory from promise to glory to futility. By the summer of 1945 it was all over: the great fleet carriers were at the bottom of the sea, most of the best pilots were dead and their once-famous *Sentais* and *Koku Sentais* were a shambles. Since October 1944, in a lunatic paroxysm of

desperation, the Japanese air forces had been immolating their own men and equipment in *kamikaze* suicide attacks on US warships. The list of aircraft used as *Kamikazes* – Zeros, Kates, Vals, *Suiseis*, *Shidens*, *Gingas*, and the rest – reads like a roster of Japan's most prestigious warplanes. The damage they caused would once have been sufficient to stop the Americans in their tracks; now it could not even slow them. Hordes of US war-

RIGHT: Captured Kate bomber in flight over Maryland in February 1943.

BELOW: A variety of Japanese aircraft at Yokosuka on 6 September 1945 after the surrender.

ships gathered off Japan's coasts and Superfortresses clouded the skies over her cities. While hundreds of *kamikaze* pilots were seeking fiery death at the hands of the enemy, hundreds of thousands of Japanese civilians could not avoid it. At last, like the final strokes of a surgeon's knife, the desolation of Hiroshima and Nagasaki cut short the death throes of the Greater East Asian Co-Prosperity Sphere.

BELOW: The Japanese air forces over Bataan in the Philippines.

BOTTOM: Val dive bomber shot down during the Pearl Harbor attack being salvaged by US naval forces.

兵徴募
海軍志願

# MASTERS OF THE PACIFIC

Japan's attack on Pearl Harbor was but one part of her offensive to neutralize European forces in East and Southeast Asia and create by force the Greater East Asia Co-Prosperity Sphere Japanese leaders had talked about only a year before. Even as the Japanese task force steamed toward the Hawaiian Islands, Japanese forces were poised and ready to occupy Burma, Hong Kong, Malaya, and the Philippines.

When news of the attack on Pearl Harbor reached the American command in Manila, a Japanese strike force was already off the Philippine coast. Although General Douglas MacArthur and Admiral Thomas Hart had been forewarned of the imminence of a Japanese attack by the War Department as early as 27 November 1941, defensive preparations were still incomplete when the Japanese struck at 0530 on the morning of 8 December. From air bases on Formosa, the Japanese attacked American installations throughout the Philippine archipelago, literally destroying Clark, Nichols,

and Iba air stations and neutralizing the United States Army Air Force just as effectively as the Pacific Fleet had been destroyed only hours before. The Asiatic Fleet, stationed in Manila, was also badly mauled, leaving the American government virtually powerless to prevent Japanese forces from overrunning the Islands despite the heroic defense put up by American forces and Filipino scouts.

Japanese forces were landed on Luzon on 10 December and in the weeks that followed, similar landings were made elsewhere on the island. Since American forces were powerless to prevent or hamper these amphibious operations, plans were hastily drawn up for a withdrawal of American and Filipino forces to Corregidor and the Bataan Peninsula. MacArthur and Hart hoped that such a strategic withdrawal would buy time until reinforcements were sent. Unfortunately for them, this proved impossible given Japan's almost complete control over the air and shipping lanes into and out of the Philippines.

BELOW LEFT: General Masaharu Homma comes ashore for the first time on Philippine soil at Santiago on Lingayen Gulf, 24 December 1941. Homma commanded the invading Japanese Army.

BELOW: General Sugiyama, Chief of Staff of the Japanese Army, arrives in the Philippines. MacArthur's defenses were ill-prepared for the assault, and the Japanese seized most of the archipelago within a few weeks of the initial attack, which coincided with the descent on Pearl Harbor.

BOTTOM: Japanese troops land at Lingayen Gulf, 22 December 1941.

RIGHT: Japanese field gun in action as the perimeter closed around Bataan. MacArthur's Philippine and American forces abandoned Manila to the Japanese and were beseiged in the Bataan Peninsula.

BELOW RIGHT: Nakajima G3M2 Nell naval bombers on a mission over Bataan. The peninsula could not hold out without reinforcements which, though promised, never came.

Although American and Filipino forces fought valiantly to preserve their positions, resistance proved hopeless. By 11 March 1942 MacArthur was forced to evacuate to Australia, leaving command of the garrison on the Bataan Peninsula to General Jonathan Wainwright. Wainwright and his men were able to hold on until 8 April when they evacuated the peninsula to the 'safety' of the Corregidor fortress. There, the American and Filipino survivors held out until 6 May when the American garrison surrendered to the Japanese. This was the worst defeat in the war to that date and marked the temporary end of American colonial rule in the Philippines. General MacArthur might vow to avenge this defeat and 'return' to the Islands, but as of June 1942, the Philippines had been added to the Japanese Empire.

The Japanese attack on the Philippines was mirrored by a similar attack on British Malaya which was launched on the same morning as the first Japanese air raids against Clark, Nichols and Iba fields. Unlike the Americans, who had little advance warning of the attack on Pearl Harbor and the Philippines, the British command in Malaya and Singapore had been aware of the imminence of a Japanese attack for weeks but had taken few measures to prepare for such an attack except to put the fleet at Singapore on full alert. The reason for this seemingly casual attitude reflected the confidence of the Royal Navy and Air Force that British naval and aerial forces were sufficiently strong to repel a Japanese offensive.

Preferring not to violate the Thai border, Air Marshal Sir Robert Brooke-Popham, commander of British forces in Malaya, waited for the Japanese to cross the border first, assuming that such a crossing could be blunted by deploying British forces in a line across the Kra Isthmus. He reasoned that such a defensive deployment would buy sufficient time for the British to rush reinforcements to the area, thus allowing them to cross the border and take the ports of Singora and Patani in Siam before Japanese ships landed. Failing in this, the British expected to be able to cut the railway line between Singora and the town of Jitra in Malaya, slowing the Japanese advance in the process and providing time for additional mobilization and deployment of forces in Malaya.

The failure of the British to make a preemptive strike across the Thai border was to cost dearly, for when the Japanese did cross the frontier on 8 December 1941 their numbers were such that the British had neither time nor sufficient manpower to strike toward Singora and Patani nor could they keep the Japanese from breaching their line across the Kra Isthmus. Within four days after they crossed the Malay border, Japanese forces had broken the British line, forcing the hasty evacuation of British forces to the south.

As British forces tried to prevent the southward movement of Japanese troops into Malaya, the British Navy suffered a significant setback when two capital ships, the Prince of Wales and the Repulse, were destroyed off the Malayan coast on 10 December. The loss of these two battle wagons ultimately crippled the defense of Singapore and Malaya. Thanks to the absence of effective naval resistance, the Japanese had no trouble landing troops along the Malayan coast, sealing the fate of the British in the process.

Within a month after launching their attack into Malaya, Japanese forces had reached Johore and were preparing to attack Singapore. By this time the seriousness of the Japanese threat was clear to all and the new commander of British forces in Malaya, General Sir Archibald Wavell ordered his forces to hold Johore at all costs until such time as reinforcements might be sent north and a counterattack launched. As Wavell understood, if Johore fell, then Singapore could not be defended. If Singapore fell, then the Dutch East Indies would be threatened. Thus, the defense of Malaya was not only important to the British; it was also a matter of vital concern to the Dutch.

In order to defend Johore, British forces north of Kuala Lumpur had to be diverted to the south. In so doing, however, the British surrendered control of much of their colony to the Japanese who were now free to move troops southward without fear of molestation. Because the Japanese were prepared for a rapid thrust south whereas the British were not, they were able to move their forces into Johore before British reinforcements from the Kuala Lumpur area arrived. The result was that British forces were overrun. By the end of the first week in February 1942, Johore was in Japanese hands and Japanese forces were ready to attack Singapore itself.

The Japanese attack on Singapore was launched on 8 February 1942, at which time two divisions crossed the straits from the mainland into Singapore. By the next day almost 15,000 Japanese troops had successfully penetrated Singapore, forcing the British to fall back to a defensive posture. Unfortunately for them, once the straits were crossed Singapore did not offer a natural barrier similar to that of Corregidor or the Bataan Peninsula. Thus, defense of the colony proved hopeless. Furthermore, since the Japanese attacked the British naval station in Singapore from the north instead of by sea from the south, the British could not defend even this enclave.

Singapore fell to the Japanese on 15 February 1942. Even more than the retreat of the Americans from the Philippines, the fall of Malaya and Singapore was a psychological defeat for the Allies of great importance. Conversely, for the Japanese this victory was sweet. Having neutralized the United States in Hawaii and the Philippines, they easily overran Malaya and Singapore whose British defenders had underestimated Japan's strength and relied too heavily on the protective cover of the United States.

Even as the battle raged in the Philippines and Malaya, Japanese forces seized the Crown Colony of Hong Kong. The first Japanese troops entered the colony on 8 December 1941. By the end of the month, the British had surrendered. The

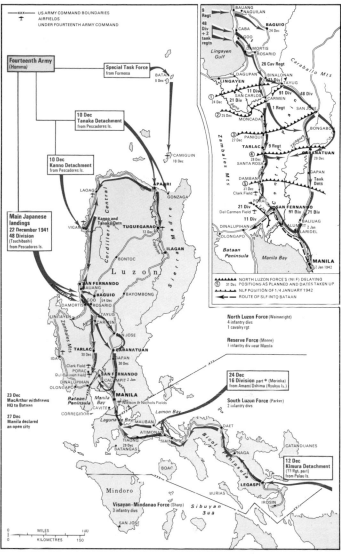

FAR LEFT: The Stars and Stripes is lowered for the last time on the island stronghold of Corregidor after its capture on 6 May, 1942.

CENTER LEFT: Lieutenant General Jonathan Wainwright broadcasts his announcement of the surrender of Corregidor.

LEFT AND BELOW: Japanese troops raise their arms and weapons in triumph. The forces of Imperial Japan had conquered the whole of Southeast Asia in 100 days.

relative ease with which the Japanese took Hong Kong reflected the isolation of the British garrison from command headquarters in Malaya. Whereas the Japanese had only to launch their offensive by moving troops across the Kwangtung border into Hong Kong and could bomb British installations from bases on Formosa, only 400 miles away, the nearest British reinforcements were in Malaya, almost 1500 miles away. Despite the importance of Hong Kong, the British garrison there was hardly more than a police force, which even with such reinforcements, namely Canadian, as could be rushed to bolster the colony's defenses,

Map labels:

Isthmus of Kra
Imperial Guards Div (from Bangkok)
SINGORA
5 and 18 Divisions
8 December 1941 Japanese Twenty-fifth Army (Yamashita)
PATANI
S I A M
KANGAR
12 Dec
CHANGLUN
JITRA
Kedah
ALOR STAR
The Ledge
Takumi Force (part 18 Div)
KOTA BHARU
SOUTH CHINA SEA
11 Ind Div
GURUN 15 Dec
KROH 14 Dec
GONG KEDAH
KUALA KRAI
GEORGE TOWN Penang 16 Dec
BUTTERWORTH
9 Ind Div
KUALA TRENGGANU
TAIPING 23 Dec
26 Dec
IPOH 28 Dec
M A L A Y A
KUALA DUNGUN
1 Jan
KAMPAR 2 Jan 1942
KUALA LIPIS
TELOK ANSON
IDOR
RONGKAI
TROLAK
R Slim
5 and 18 Divs
1 Jan 1942
KAMPONG SLIM
KUANTAN 30 Dec
2/3 Jan
SERANDAH
GOC Malaya Percival
KUALA SELANGOR
III Corps HQ (Heath)
10 Jan
KUALA LUMPUR 5 Jan
PORT SWETTENHAM 10 Jan
8 Aust Div
ENDAU 16 Jan
Imp Guards Div
GEMAS
BATU ANAM
SEGAMAT 19 Jan
MERSING
Strait of
PORT DICKSON
TAMPIN
Mt Ophir
YONG PENG
Malacca
Muar
MALACCA
MUAR 16 Jan
KLUANG 25 Jan
Sumatra
BAKRI
DUTCH EAST INDIES
BATU PAHAT
AYER HITAM
OVER 3000 FEET
0 MILES 100
0 KILOMETRES 160
31 January 1942 Last British and Commonwealth forces withdraw to Singapore
JOHORE BAHRU
SINGAPORE

RIGHT: Japanese troops invade Malaya on 8 December 1941 by landing on the Kra Isthmus at Singora.

FAR RIGHT: Japanese soldiers bicycled through the jungles and down the roads of the Malay peninsula, taking its British defenders by surprise.

BELOW: Japanese infantry pass abandoned British weapon carriers as they advance toward the 'impregnable' fortress island of Singapore.

BELOW RIGHT: British forces retreat through the Malayan jungle which had been thought to be impenetrable.

BOTTOM: Japanese soldiers enter Penang after having abandoned their bicycles.

proved helpless in holding the Japanese at bay. Indeed, the Japanese not only succeeded in taking the colony in less than a month; they captured over 12,000 of the British-Canadian defense forces, almost the entire reinforced garrison in the colony of Hong Kong.

With Malaya in their hands, the Japanese initiated an invasion of the Dutch East Indies. After their victory in the Battle of the Java Sea, 27–28 February 1942, Japanese forces landed on Java. Nine days later, the Dutch colonial regime capitulated. For the Japanese, the occupation of the Indies was the culmination of years of effort to gain access to and control over the oil fields and refineries in the Dutch colony. As an industrial power almost totally dependent upon petroleum imports, Japan had covetously eyed the Indies for over a decade. Fearing, however, that any precipitous action against the Dutch might inflame American opinion, the Japanese carefully avoided use or threat of force against the Dutch, preferring to try diplomacy. Thus, in 1940 and again in 1941, the Japanese tried to persuade the Dutch to raise the amount of petroleum products exported to Japan and to permit Japanese interests to ex-

plore and develop new oil fields in the Indies. Such suggestions fell on deaf ears, although some concessions of a minor nature were granted.

Although the Dutch were in no position to withstand a Japanese attack, they doggedly refused to knuckle under to diplomatic efforts to give Japan control over the petroleum industry in the Indies. Frustrated in two successive efforts to 'open up' the Indies, the Japanese laid plans for a more direct effort to incorporate the colony into the Greater East Asia Co-Prosperity Sphere. As early as October 1940, the Imperial Army and Navy were instructed to draw up contingency plans for an occupation of the islands. Furthermore, Japanese intelligence operatives were instructed to step up their program of assistance to Indonesian nationalist groups so that in the event of an armed attack, the Dutch would find themselves facing two enemies, one external and one internal.

Japanese–Dutch talks relative to the Indies came to an end in June 1941 when the Tokyo government withdrew its negotiators from Batavia after failing to secure meaningful concessions from the Dutch. Contingency plans for an invasion

of the Indies were now to be effected and coordinated with the overall grand strategy which had been approved at an Imperial Conference on 6 September 1941. Where diplomacy had failed, war would triumph.

The Japanese attack force which invaded the Indies in 1942 enjoyed an advantage not shared by similar task forces in Malaya and the Philippines, namely the support of the nationalist movements in the islands. In Indonesia the Japanese came not as conquerors but, rather, as liberators. Pro-Japanese sympathy, which had been strong even before the invasion, increased as the invaders made headway against the Dutch. Such support had been carefully cultivated before the war when Japanese operatives infiltrated Muslim and secular nationalist groups and it was enhanced by the relative ease with which the Japanese despatched Dutch forces. The psychological impact of Japan's humiliation of the Dutch was tremendous, dissipating what support existed for the Dutch from Indonesian leaders.

The Dutch authorities, for their part, did little to exploit what anti-Japanese sentiment existed in the Indies, even as

BELOW: Street fighting in
Kuala Lumpur, capital of the
FMS (Federated Malay
States), which fell to Japan in
short order.

the Japanese invasion was in progress. Unfortunately for them, colonial administrators had come to accept the propaganda emanating from the regime as reality, fully expecting the Indonesian masses to rally to their banner. To the contrary, the masses responded to the Japanese attack not with support of the Dutch but, rather, with violent attacks of their own against government and business leaders. Indeed, the Japanese had eventually to use considerable power of persuasion to restore order in Batavia and other urban centers. But now the Indies were under Japanese control, marking the culmination of a long cherished dream to bring this oil rich area into the Greater East Asia Co-Prosperity Sphere. After centuries of Dutch rule, the colonial system was suddenly destroyed. Although Indonesian nationalist leaders would soon find the Japanese more oppressive in their own way than the Dutch, for them the war and the Japanese occupation

were to be an unprecedented opportunity, a milestone on the road to independence.

With Japanese forces attacking and occupying the Dutch East Indies, Hong Kong, Malaya, and the Philippines, it was only a matter of time before they launched an invasion of Burma, the last stop in their game plan calling for the creation of the Greater East Asia Co-Prosperity Sphere. In some respects, Burma was of special importance to the Japanese, since it was through the port of Rangoon and over the Burma road that supplies were sent to the government of Generalissimo Chiang K'ai-shek, permitting that government to continue to resist Japanese entreaties for the negotiation of a diplomatic settlement of the China Incident. With almost a million men tied down in the occupation force in China, the Japanese would continue to be hamstrung in the conduct of the war in the Pacific. Hence, the occupation of

Burma and the subsequent closing of the Burma Road was a matter of considerable priority.

The Japanese launched their first attack against Burma on 23 December 1941. Unlike Japanese strikes against Malaya, the Philippines, and the Indies, the Japanese attack in Burma was initially limited to a series of air raids aimed at destroying warehouses and storage depots in Rangoon and other stops along the road into China. The results of these raids was devastating. Many of the dock facilities and warehouses were destroyed, and thousands of Burmese and Indian laborers were killed and/or injured. By January 1942 the city of Rangoon had been brought to a halt and thousands fled the city for the safety of the countryside. Fearing riots and pillaging British authorities were forced to impose martial law in Rangoon even before the new year.

Japanese air raids against Rangoon and other installations, including rail

BELOW: Japanese troops fight through the city center of Kuala Lumpur.

BOTTOM: Japanese infantry advance through the rubber plantations of Malaya. Malaya and the Dutch East Indies held about 90% of the world's rubber supply, which was denied to the Allies for the balance of the war.

heads and depots, were continued for three weeks in January 1942. Then, after aerial reconnaissance revealed the extent of the damage done and the havoc wreaked, Japanese land forces were sent across the Thai border on 20 January. It was Japan's purpose to cut the rail link between Rangoon and Kunming in China and then proceed south toward Rangoon.

The British were poorly equipped and ill-prepared to meet the Japanese advance. Once again, their disdain for the ability of the Japanese and exaggerated self-confidence was to prove a disaster. Not only did British commanders underestimate the fury and rapidity with which Japanese forces poured into and across Burma, they stubbornly refused to accept offers of assistance from the Chinese Nationalists, for whom the Burma Road was a vital lifeline, until it was too late. It was only after Japanese forces broke through British defenses in the vicinity

BELOW: Lieutenant General Yamashita interviews General Percival at the moment of the surrender of Singapore, 1900 hours, 15 February 1942.

BOTTOM LEFT: Japanese troops parade past the GPO in Singapore after its surrender. Singapore's lack of landward defenses and the lack of tenacity of its defenders shocked the British and the world and left the Dutch East Indies exposed to Japanese conquest.

BOTTOM RIGHT: The Japanese erect a field post office in Batavia, capital of the Dutch East Indies, after its capitulation on 9 March 1942.

RIGHT: Japanese tanks in Orchard Road, Singapore after its surrender.

BELOW RIGHT: The Rising Sun flag goes up over the Nicobar islands north of Sumatra, which had been held by the British Raj in India, as the Japanese Navy tried to establish their hegemony in the Indian Ocean.

of the Sittang Bridge that Chinese aid was accepted and by this time, it was impossible to move Chinese forces into a position in which they might help to defend Rangoon and the supply route into China.

Having successfully defeated British and Indian forces in the vicinity of Sittang, Japanese forces moved quickly toward Rangoon where the British were making hasty efforts to prepare for the defense of the city. As the Japanese moved closer to the city limits, lend-lease supplies destined for China were moved out as quickly as possible or jettisoned lest they fall into Japanese hands. By 1 March, the Japanese were poised around the city and five days later, on the 6th of the month, they captured Rangoon, taking countless supplies in the process. Despite their efforts to prevent the Japanese from capturing this cache of aid, the British could not destroy it before the Japanese took the city. Thus, the Japanese victory in Rangoon was doubly sweet. Not only had they closed the main port of entry for supplies destined for Free China, they had also captured intact weaponry and ammunition which would facilitate the rest of their offensive in Burma.

As the British evacuated Rangoon, Japanese forces regrouped in the city before heading north toward Prome and Toungoo. It was the hope of the British and their Chinese allies that they might prevent the Japanese from capturing the Yenaungyuan oil fields which lay just north of Prome and Toungoo. Since these fields constituted China's only source of crude oil, it was imperative that the line be held. Furthermore, if the Allies were able to hold the Japanese south of these cities, it might be possible to build a new supply route into China from Assam to Burma, linking the Indian ports of Calcutta and Chittagong to Yunnan, thus replacing the route from Rangoon. If this new line could not be held, the Japanese would easily overrun the rest of the colony.

Shortly after the middle of March 1942, Japanese forces marched northward from Rangoon. As they moved, they

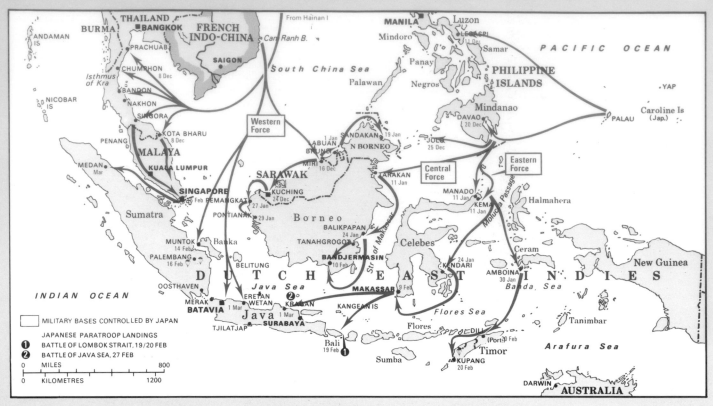

were harassed by air raids conducted by the RAF and Claire Chennault's American Volunteer Group, the Flying Tigers. Responding to these aerial attacks, the Japanese launched a series of massive air raids of their own, aimed at knocking out Anglo–American installations at Magwe and elsewhere. By the end of March, they had succeeded in forcing the evacuation of these bases and the destruction of Allied air strength in Burma.

Without air cover, British and Chinese forces were easy targets for the Japanese who had secured information relative to their whereabouts from aerial reconnaissance missions and Burmese nationalists. On 26 March Japanese forces took the city of Toungoo and shortly thereafter Prome as well. With Prome and Toungoo secured, the Japanese pushed on toward Lashio, the southern

terminus of the Burma Road, which they took by 29 April. With the capture of Lashio, the Burma Road was finally closed, isolating China from the outside world except for the aerial route 'over the hump'.

The defense of Lashio marked the final Allied effort to hold Burma. Following their defeat there, the remnants of the Sino–British defense force in Burma was hastily withdrawn to China. Before leaving Burma, Allied forces destroyed what equipment and supplies they could not carry and bombed the bridges across the Salween River after their evacuation across the Chinese border. By June of 1942 the Japanese were in full control of Burma. The fleshing out of the Greater East Asia Co-Prosperity Sphere had been completed.

As had been the case in Indonesia, the

Japanese occupation of Burma was aided and abetted by the co-operation of Burmese nationalist leaders who had been cultivated by the Japanese for at least a decade before their forces entered the colony. The British, on the other hand, had done little to rally nationalist leaders to their banner. Had they promised some measure of greater autonomy or independence at a later date, the Burmese might have stood with them after the outbreak of World War II. Failing to do this, the British could hardly expect their 'wards' to flock to their banner when the war reached Burma. Not only did the Burmese not aid the British in their effort to defend the colony, they fought against them with groups like the Burmese Independence Army facilitating the Japanese conquest.

By May 1942 the Japanese had success-

RIGHT: USS *West Virginia*, damaged at Pearl Harbor, approaches a drydock on the American West Coast in June 1942. The Japanese Navy had established its domination over the western Pacific.

RIGHT: Cover of a Japanese
wartime magazine showing a
helmet, rifle and American flag
abandoned by the surrendering
US forces in the Philippines.
Japan's victory was complete.

FAR RIGHT: Indonesian
nationalists sporting the
emblem of the Rising Sun
celebrate their liberation from
Dutch rule on the cover of
another issue of the same
magazine.

fully completed their offensive and had
they stuck to their original plan, they
would have turned to a defensive strategy
designed to consolidate and protect their
new empire in East and Southeast Asia
against an eventual Allied counterattack.
In light of the ease and speed of their
victories, however, Japanese leaders were
reluctant to give up the momentum they
had achieved following Pearl Harbor. In
particular, the Imperial Navy was eager
to finish the job they had started at Pearl
Harbor where they had destroyed or incapacitated the battleships of the Pacific
Fleet but missed the four aircraft carriers
of the fleet which were out at sea when the
attack took place. As long as these ships
remained, the United States would be in
a position to menace Japanese forces and
if they were augmented by the despatch
of other vessels, the Pacific Fleet might
once again constitute a serious challenge.
Such a possibility dictated a second and
decisive strike against the United States
Navy.

In March 1942 the Imperial Navy

ABOVE: Indonesian natives
at Palembang remove oil
drums and attempt to cap
the wells immediately prior to
the Japanese invasion. The
Dutch, British and American-
owned oil companies blew up a
few oil wells to deny them to
the Japanese, but most were
superficially destroyed, for the
oil companies calculated that
they would return to the area
with the victorious Allies by
the time the Japanese could
prepare the wells for their use.

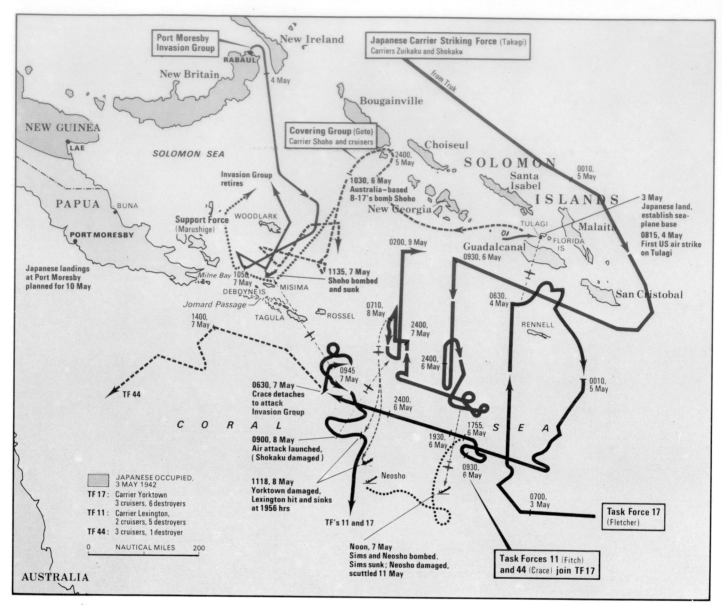

Port Moresby Invasion Group
RABAUL
4 May

Japanese Carrier Striking Force (Takagi)
Carriers Zuikaku and Shokaku
from Truk

New Ireland
New Britain
NEW GUINEA
LAE
SOLOMON SEA
Bougainville

Covering Group (Goto)
Carrier Shoho and cruisers

Choiseul
SOLOMON
Santa Isabel
0010, 5 May

PAPUA
BUNA
PORT MORESBY

Invasion Group retires
WOODLARK
Support Force (Marushige)

2400, 5 May
1030, 6 May
Australia-based B-17's bomb Shoho
New Georgia
ISLANDS
3 May Japanese land, establish seaplane base
0815, 4 May First US air strike on Tulagi
TULAGI
Malaita
FLORIDA IS

Japanese landings at Port Moresby planned for 10 May.
Milne Bay 1050, 7 May
DEBOYNE IS
1135, 7 May Shoho bombed and sunk
MISIMA
Guadalcanal
0930, 6 May
0630, 4 May
San Cristobal

Jomard Passage
TAGULA
ROSSEL
0710, 8 May
0200, 9 May
RENNELL
0010, 5 May

1400, 7 May
TF 44

0630, 7 May Crace detaches to attack Invasion Group

0945 7 May
2400, 7 May
2400, 6 May

0900, 8 May Air attack launched, (Shokaku damaged)
2400, 6 May
1755, 6 May
1930, 6 May
S E A

C O R A L

1118, 8 May Yorktown damaged, Lexington hit and sinks at 1956 hrs
Neosho
0930, 6 May

JAPANESE OCCUPIED, 3 MAY 1942
TF 17: Carrier Yorktown 3 cruisers, 6 destroyers
TF 11: Carrier Lexington 2 cruisers, 5 destroyers
TF 44: 3 cruisers, 1 destroyer
0    NAUTICAL MILES    200

TF's 11 and 17
0700, 3 May

Task Force 17 (Fletcher)

Noon, 7 May Sims and Neosho bombed. Sims sunk; Neosho damaged, scuttled 11 May

Task Forces 11 (Fitch) and 44 (Crace) join TF 17

AUSTRALIA

proposed to expand Japan's perimeter in the Pacific by initiating action in the area of the Coral Sea and Midway Island. It was hoped, at the same time, that what was left of the Pacific Fleet might be lured into a battle in the Aleutians and destroyed there. As envisaged by Japanese naval officers, the Battle of the Coral Sea would be a combined naval, aerial and land effort with Japanese forces assembling at Rabaul and off the island of Truk in the Carolinas and proceeding toward the Coral Sea and Midway. This plan was presented and approved at an Imperial Conference in April 1942.

At the beginning of May 1942, Japanese forces were landed in the Solomon Islands at Tulagi. Thanks to Allied intelligence, the Australian garrison on the island had been withdrawn before the Japanese landed in an effort to deceive the Japanese into thinking that their offensive might proceed without opposition. More important, Admiral Nimitz, alerted as to the plans of the Imperial Navy, ordered what was left of the Pacific Fleet to sail south from Pearl Harbor in anticipation of the arrival of the Japanese task force in the Coral Sea.

On 7 May 1942 the Japanese and American fleets converged in the Coral Sea. After Japanese search planes spotted the Americans, they opened fire, sinking a tanker and destroyer escort. In response, American planes were sent aloft in search of the Japanese. On the following day the Battle of the Coral Sea took place. This battle found both sides relatively evenly matched. The Japanese task force consisted of two carriers and 121 carrier aircraft while the American task force consisted of the same number of carriers and 122 carrier-based planes.

Although relatively brief, the Battle of the Coral Sea was significant in that it marked the first time in history that a naval battle was decided by aircraft and not artillery barrages or naval maneuvers. Neither fleet was close enough to their enemy to sight them; neither fleet fired upon their adversaries. Nevertheless, the toll of the battle was great. When the battle ended and the casualties were counted, both sides learned of the enormity of their losses. The Americans lost both of their carriers, one totally destroyed, the other incapacitated. The Japanese lost one of their carriers but al-

most all of their 121 planes were lost as compared to only 76 American aircraft.

Neither the Japanese nor the Americans won a clear cut victory in the Battle of the Coral Sea, but the United States had stopped Japan's effort to cut the supply route from Hawaii to Australia. Perhaps even more important was the psychological effect of the encounter. The Americans were in need of some sign that the Japanese were not invincible. The Battle of the Coral Sea provided such a sign, although it was not nearly as great a victory as some American propagandists would have led the public to believe. For the Japanese, conversely, the Battle of the Coral Sea was a sobering encounter which did much to dissipate the idea among some in Japan that the United States was merely a 'paper tiger' with insufficient will and unity of purpose to resist them.

If the Battle of the Coral Sea was significant, the Japanese effort to capture Midway and annihilate the American fleet was of even greater importance. Whereas the Battle of the Coral Sea involved relatively modest naval task forces on both sides, the encounter at Midway

LEFT: Battle of the Coral Sea.

BELOW: SBD Dauntlesses over
the burning Japanese
battleship *Mikuma* during the
Battle of Midway, 6 June 1942.
When the Japanese Navy was
stopped by the Americans at
Midway, the long march of
conquest was over.

BOTTOM: The sinking of the
aircraft carrier *Shoho* after
being torpedoed in the Battle
of the Coral Sea, 7 May 1942.
A US Navy plane veers off to
the right after dropping an
aerial torpedo splashing in the
foreground.

was an epic confrontation involving hundreds of ships and even more aircraft. It was to be one of the greatest naval confrontations of the Pacific war.

Even as the Battle of the Coral Sea was still raging, the Japanese were readying their strike against Midway. On 5 May 1942 the Midway task force was gathered off the coast of Japan and proceeded to steam toward Midway and the Aleutians. Japan's strategy called for a two-pronged effort. The larger part of the Japanese attack force, consisting of almost 200 ships including eight carriers, eleven battleships, and almost 600 carrier based planes, was to be dispatched. A smaller task force, consisting of two carriers and four battleships, was to head for the Aleutians where the Japanese hoped to lure the bulk of the American fleet while their main task force took Midway and then proceeded north to destroy what was left of the Pacific Fleet. Unfortunately for the Imperial Navy, this scheme did not work.

Thanks to the cracking of Japanese codes, Admiral Nimitz learned of Japan's plan of attack at Midway even before the Japanese task force reached the vicinity of the island and took appropriate measures to meet this threat. Thus, the Americans did not fall prey to the Japanese ruse in the Aleutians but, rather, gathered their resources and moved them toward Midway. For the Americans, the greatest obstacle to overcome in confronting the Japanese fleet off Midway was the sheer size of the Japanese fleet. With no battleships at his disposal and only three carriers available for the fray, Nimitz would have to face a Japanese force almost five times his size if not more. Unlike the Battle of the Coral Sea, which was an encounter between two foes of relatively equal strength, the Battle of Midway was more like the biblical contest between David and Goliath except for the fact that unlike David who had no prior knowledge of the intent of his giant, Nimitz, knowing the game plan of his adversary, could husband what resources he had and make appropriate preparations for the contest.

When the Japanese task force reached Midway on 4 June 1942, the American

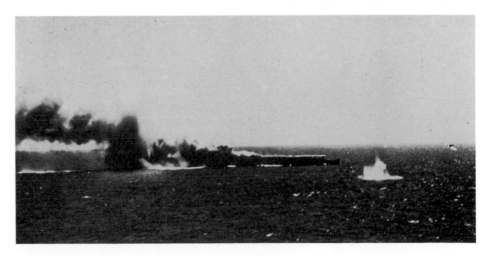

BELOW LEFT: The aircraft carrier *Kaga* veers off after it is pummeled by American aircraft during the Battle of Midway. All four Japanese carriers were sunk in the battle. The victory of Admiral Yamamoto at Pearl Harbor had been avenged.

BELOW RIGHT: The USS *Yorktown* under attack at Midway, 6 June 1942. The resuscitated aircraft carrier, which had been badly damaged in the Battle of the Coral Sea and which was sent back into action after being repaired in only three days, finally went down at Midway.

fleet was lying in waiting just north of the island and out of the range of Japanese carrier-based reconnaissance craft. Expecting that the Americans were steaming north toward the Aleutians, it did not occur to the Japanese naval command at Midway that they might encounter the Pacific Fleet there. It was only after Japanese pilots had flown two rounds of missions against land-based installations on the island that the Americans were spotted, and even then the Japanese assumed that the American force was limited to several cruisers and destroyers. Thus, no precautions were taken to protect the carriers of the Japanese task force nor were the sorties over Midway stopped.

When the first wave of American planes appeared over the Japanese fleet, almost all of Japan's carrier-based aircraft were aloft over Midway. Nevertheless, Japanese anti-aircraft gunners were able to down 35 of the initial 41 American planes sent against them. Not expecting that there might be more than one American aircraft carrier in the area, the Japanese command did not panic immediately nor were efforts made to recall Japanese pilots to their carriers and prepare for a strategic retreat. When a second wave of American planes arrived only minutes later, the Japanese were caught nearly totally off guard. During this second mission, American pilots hit Admiral Nagumo's flagship, the *Akagi*, as well as two other carriers, the *Kaga* and *Soryu*. By day's end, the Japanese fleet was badly mauled and prepared to leave the

RIGHT: The Battle of Midway.

BOTTOM: The burning *Yorktown* shortly before she sank.

vicinity of Midway. The Americans had lost only one major ship, the carrier *Yorktown*, in the fray.

The defeat of the Japanese effort to take Midway marked a major turning point in the Pacific War and was the first significant defeat inflicted by Allied forces on the Japanese. After Midway, the Japanese returned to a defensive posture, allowing American and Allied forces to seize the offensive in the Pacific. Although the battle against Japan would be a long one, the tide had definitely turned.

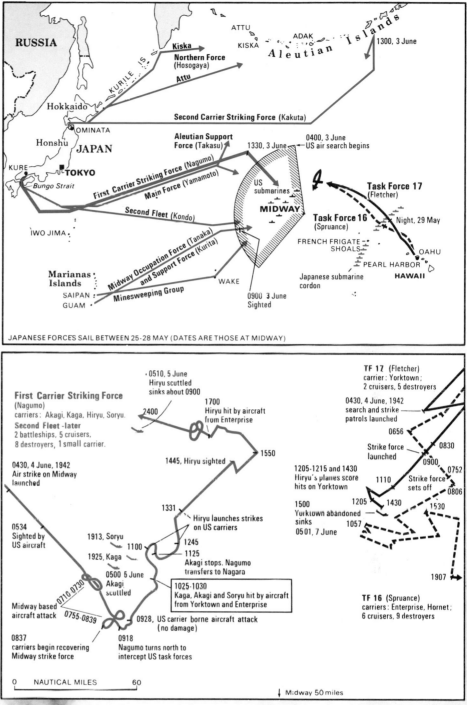

# THE LONG RETREAT

BELOW: US transports leave Tulagi on 10 August 1942. After Midway the Allies began to recover territory in the Pacific, but like the Japanese they were dependent on continued supplies of food and war matériel. The fight for domination of Pacific sealanes was on.

RIGHT: Occasional raiding ships crept into Japanese waters and caused damage. One was the USS *Nautilus*, which sank the destroyer *Yamakaze* off the Japanese coast on 25 June 1942.

The pressure of the original Japanese offensive which launched the war in December 1941 had overrun Southeast Asia and much of the Southwest Pacific within six months. In the latter area, energy had flagged when the chain of coral islands just to the north of Australia was only half occupied. The success of this first grand offensive with its negligible casualties and the demonstrated ineffectualness of American and British power determined Imperial General Headquarters to embark on a second grand offensive. Tulagi in the Solomon Islands and Port Moresby in Papua (Australian New Guinea) were to be seized to gain mastery of the Coral Sea. The Combined Fleet under Admiral Isoroku Yamamoto was to cross the Pacific, capture Midway Island and the western Aleutians, and annihilate the remains of the American Pacific Fleet, especially its four aircraft carriers. A 'ribbon defense' anchored at Attu, Midway, Wake, the Marshalls and the Gilberts would be set up, followed by the invasion of New Caledonia, the Fijis and Samoa to isolate Australia. The reasoning was that with the American Pacific fleet wiped out, the Japanese conquests could be organized and the ribbon defense made impregnable. Tiring of a futile war, the United States would negotiate a peace which would leave Japan master of the Pacific.

The second grand offensive was launched in May 1942 with a seaborne expedition against Port Moresby and the occupation of Tulagi. American naval

intelligence had broken the Japanese naval code, however, and was able to give Admiral Chester Nimitz the main threads of the Japanese plan in time to shift all available forces southward to meet the threat. The occupation of Tulagi took place uncontested on 3 May when the small Australian garrison prudently withdrew. The days of 5–8 May saw an American carrier force fight a drawn battle with a similar force in the Coral Sea which forced the Port Moresby invasion convoy to turn back. A month later, the failure of Admiral Yamamoto at Midway squandered the margin of naval strength he had gained for Japan at Pearl Harbor and restored the balance between the Japanese and American navies. Many of the Japanese generals believed that now the offensive should be limited, that overlong lines of communication should be avoided, that combat should be declined whenever possible, and that Japan should not be drawn into a debilitating contest for islands of marginal strategic use. But contrary to the views of its sister service and despite the fact that the loss of its carriers had condemned it to fight a defensive war, the Navy resolved to defend its heavy commitments in the Southwest Pacific, first by enlarging its position and subsequently by selling its territory inch by bloody inch in the hope that the United States would weary of the attack. Thus the initial occupation of Tulagi was to grow into the Guadalcanal campaign while a new assault against Port Moresby was launched overland.

The Japanese Navy was opposed in these objectives by an enemy with a command divided between a general and an admiral. Escaping by submarine after his defeat in the Philippines, General Douglas MacArthur had arrived in Australia in March to assume command of the Southwest Pacific Theater. MacArthur found his new command short of manpower, poorly equipped, and quite deficient in air power. He also found Australian morale shattered by the Allied débacle in Asia and especially by the fall of Singapore which had been regarded by the Australians as the keystone of their security. MacArthur made the reconquest of Papua his first priority, as it was from Papua that the Japanese posed the most immediate threat to Australia, the main American base in the South Pacific. Since a large part of New Guinea was Australian territory, a strong offensive there would do wonders for Australian morale. Perceived by both the Japanese

and their opponent as a primary objective, New Guinea was to result in a hard fought campaign lasting over a year.

The other Allied command sector was the Central Pacific Theater of Admiral Chester Nimitz, based in Hawaii. He was often in conflict with MacArthur over strategy and priorities. Nimitz represented the overall desire of the American Navy to fight a war of ships and planes in the vast expanses of the Pacific Ocean to the exclusion of the Army whenever possible. Although MacArthur was in conflict with the Army chiefs in Washington over the global priorities of the war, he did represent the interest of the Army against the Navy in this inter-service rivalry.

The sudden shift in the fortunes of the Japanese after Midway brought the same desire to both MacArthur and Nimitz – to go on the offensive as quickly as possible. The prospective offensive raised intense and indeed passionate debate about command arrangements, but a compromise was reached. Nimitz was to direct initial operations in the eastern Solomons, beginning with Tulagi and Guadalcanal. Subsequent operations by MacArthur were to clear the northern coast of New Guinea and capture Rabaul, the main Japanese base in the Southwest Pacific, and the remainder of the Bismarck Archipelago. 'Operation Watchtower' was the name given to the offensive.

Already in possession of the small island of Tulagi, the Japanese initiated their own plans in early July by moving forces to the neighboring island of Guadalcanal and beginning construction of an airfield. The threat of Japanese bombers operating from Guadalcanal forced an immediate change in Allied strategy. The capture of Guadalcanal was raised to a primary objective in itself and a landing by 7000 Marines was made on 7 August. The landing was uncontested and the nearly completed airfield captured the following day. Most of the Japanese forces in that area had been construction troops who had wisely decamped. Tulagi was invaded the same day as Guadalcanal by 6000 Marines who took two days to wipe out its fiercely resisting garrison of 1500. Grossly underestimating the size of the American landing force on Guadalcanal at 2000, the Japanese sent in inadequate reinforcements and a prolonged campaign developed.

The early fighting for Guadalcanal was marked by sharp night actions between

American naval units and the Japanese, who were running supplies and reinforcements down the middle passage of the Solomons, called 'the slot'. The Americans were initially beaten in this night fighting, suffering particularly heavy losses off Savo Island the night of the initial American landing on 7 August. Timely intelligence from Australian coast watchers cost the Japanese a severe setback ten days later in what was called the Battle of the Eastern Solomons. At the same time, the weak Japanese forces on the island made various strenuous but unsuccessful efforts to recapture the airfield, losing 1200 men on one night alone (13 September). The Japanese forces steadily increased as destroyers slipped in new units by night. A new directive from Imperial General Headquarters on 18 September gave the Guadalcanal campaign priority over the concurrent New Guinea operations against Port Moresby. Seaborne reinforcements precipitated another pitched battle off Cape Esperance on the night of 11/12 October. This time the action was more favorable to the American forces but even so, the Japanese still managed to

RIGHT: The Battle for Guadalcanal.

BELOW: The civilian vessel *Maizuru* was damaged off the Aleutians after it was sequestered by the Imperial Navy. Hit by USS *Growler* in July 1942, it returned to a friendly port for repairs.

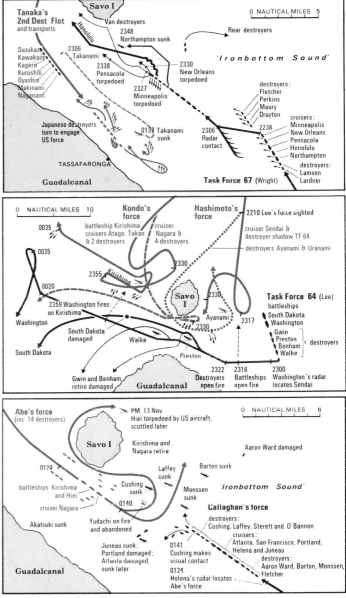

*Map 1 (top):*

Tanaka's 2nd Dest Flot and transports

Savo I

0 NAUTICAL MILES 5

Van destroyers

2348 Northampton sunk

Rear destroyers

'Ironbottom Sound'

Suzukaze
Kawakaze
Kagero
Kuroshio
Oyashio
Makinami
Naganami

2306 Takanami

2338 Pensacola torpedoed

2330 New Orleans torpedoed

2327 Minneapolis torpedoed

destroyers:
Fletcher
Perkins
Maury
Drayton

Japanese destroyers turn to engage US force

0137 Takanami sunk

2306 Radar contact

2238

cruisers:
Minneapolis
New Orleans
Pensacola
Honolulu
Northampton

TASSAFARONGA

Guadalcanal

destroyers:
Lamson
Lardner

Task Force 67 (Wright)

*Map 2 (middle):*

0 NAUTICAL MILES 10

Kondo's force

Hashimoto's force

2210 Lee's force sighted

battleship Kirishima cruisers Atago, Takao & 2 destroyers

cruiser Nagara & 4 destroyers

cruiser Sendai & destroyer shadow TF 64

0035

0035

destroyers Ayanami & Uranami

2330

2355 Kirishima

0020

Savo I

2330

Task Force 64 (Lee)
battleships
South Dakota
Washington

2359 Washington fires on Kirishima

Washington

South Dakota damaged

Ayanami

2317

2330

Gwin
Preston
Benham
Walke

destroyers

South Dakota

Walke

Preston

Gwin and Benham retire damaged

Guadalcanal

2322 Destroyers open fire

2316 Battleships open fire

2300 Washington's radar locates Sendai

*Map 3 (bottom):*

Abe's force (inc 14 destroyers)

PM, 13 Nov
Hiei torpedoed by US aircraft, scuttled later

0 NAUTICAL MILES 6

Savo I

Kirishima and Nagara retire

Aaron Ward damaged

0174

Laffey sunk

Barton sunk

battleships Kirishima and Hiei

Cushing sunk

Monssen sunk

'Ironbottom Sound'

cruiser Nagara

0140

Callaghan's force

Akatsuki sunk

Yudachi on fire and abandoned

destroyers:
Cushing, Laffey, Sterett and O'Bannon

cruisers:
Atlanta, San Francisco, Portland, Helena and Juneau

Juneau sunk;
Portland damaged;
Atlanta damaged,
sunk later

0141 Cushing makes visual contact

0124

destroyers:
Aaron Ward, Barton, Monssen, Fletcher

Guadalcanal

0124 Helena's radar locates Abe's force

bring their troop strength up to 22,000. They persisted, however, in underestimating American strength at 7500 when in reality they faced 23,000 and 4500 more on Tulagi.

After delays by heavy rain and dense jungle, the Japanese managed to launch a major land offensive on 24 October. Striking from the south, the attack met well dug-in American Marines with effective artillery support. Three days and 2000 dead later, the order for retreat was given. That same day, Admiral William Halsey marked his appointment as Commander of Allied naval forces in the Southwest Pacific by downing over 200 enemy planes in a clash with elements of the Combined Fleet under Yamamoto, who was in the vicinity waiting to hear that the airfield on Guadalcanal had been captured by Japanese troops. Each side continued to reinforce its position on the disputed island until a naval battle on 13/14 November caused heavy losses to each belligerent and destroyed the ability of the Japanese to supply and reinforce its position. Now with the advantage in supplies, the Americans went over to the offensive and began to expand their per-

imeter while the Japanese were reduced to supplying by submarine. Weakened by disease and hunger, 25,000 Japanese fought tenaciously against 50,000 Americans.

The Guadalcanal fighting had resulted in such severe losses for the Japanese Navy that its leaders advocated terminating the unhappy project, but the Army demurred, as it still hoped to be able to use 50,000 troops assembled at Rabaul to retrieve the situation. But by 4 January, even the Army was convinced of the hopelessness of continuing the wasteful struggle, and an order for gradual evacuation was sent. On three separate nights during the first week of February, 12,000 Japanese troops were taken off, as Allied forces cautiously advanced, unaware that the campaign was over.

Lasting from August 1942 to February 1943, the protracted struggle for Guadalcanal had produced seven major naval engagements, which had cost each adversary 24 ships and the Japanese over 600 planes. In a land campaign highlighted by ten pitched battles, there had been 25,000 Japanese casualties, including 9000 from hunger and disease.

Even as the first shots began to rattle in the Guadalcanal campaign, a Japanese force was advancing overland in a renewed attempt on Port Moresby. The Battle of the Coral Sea in May 1942 had aborted the seaborne assault on Port Moresby, but at the same time the Japanese had established a base at Lae on the north coast of New Guinea and on 21 July landed 2000 men near Buna. By the 29th, the Japanese had seized Kokoda halfway across the island and had 13,000 men driving on Port Moresby.

Most of the Australian divisions serving with the British Eighth Army in North Africa had now been brought back for the defense of their country and there were eight new divisions in training. Two American divisions and eight air groups were based in Australia as well. Two Australian brigades held Port Moresby while a third was based at Milne Bay on the eastern tip of the Papuan peninsula. Two battalions had been despatched over the Kokoda trail to establish a base at Buna to cover the planned Allied attack on New Guinea. These last had collided with the Japanese force moving over the same route from the opposite direction to at-

LEFT: An American fighter just fails to make it back to the USS *Enterprise* during the Battle of the Santa Cruz Islands late in 1942.

RIGHT: Imperial Navy G4M Betty bombers come in low through anti-aircraft fire to attack US naval units off Guadalcanal, 8 August 1942.

BOTTOM: D3A Val dive bomber makes a crash dive on the USS *Hornet* (CV.8) on 26 October 1942 during the Battle of the Santa Cruz Islands. A B5N Kate torpedo bomber is flying over the *Hornet* and another Val is off her bow. Note the anti-aircraft burst off the carrier's starboard side, with its shrapnel striking the water below.

tack Port Moresby. The Australians had been unable to halt the Japanese advance until the fighting reached the 8500 feet-high Owen Stanley Mountains. As the Japanese attacked in very difficult terrain with lengthening supply lines, they met stiffening Australian resistance and harassment from the air. The advance was finally halted only 30 miles from its objective by an Australian division which had won distinction at El Alamein. Meanwhile, 2000 Japanese Marines nearly succeeded in capturing the airstrip at Milne Bay after five days of fierce fighting but were finally forced to re-embark by Australian troops.

By mid-September MacArthur was ready to take the offensive in Papua with the Sixth and Seventh Australian Divisions and an American regiment. Operational command was in the hands of General Sir Thomas Blamey, the Australian Commander-in-Chief of Allied land forces in the Southwest Pacific. Roles were now reversed as the Allied forces tried to drive the Japanese back over the route they both so recently had contested. It was at this point that Imperial General Headquarters decided to de-emphasize operations in Papua and throw all resources into the struggle for Guadalcanal. Allied progress remained slow, however, as the Japanese put up fierce resistance. The Papuan campaign was also being waged with considerable acrimony on the Allied side. The slow advance of the Australians frustrated MacArthur who considered these troops inferior to his Americans. The American troops in return received criticism from the Australians, criticism which had more than a grain of truth in it.

The Allied offensive was renewed in October, but the advance was still painfully slow for MacArthur, even though the Australians had reopened the Kokoda airfield by November 2, which eased Allied supply problems and enabled better air support. A Japanese stand at the Kumasi River was overcome with the

assistance of air-dropped bridging materials and an airlift of troops to the north coast to threaten the Japanese flank. Falling back on Buna, the Japanese waged a prolonged stand in that area throughout December. MacArthur finally sent General Robert Eichelberger to command, ordering him to take Buna or 'don't come back alive'. Reinforced by a fresh Australian brigade, Eichelberger led his troops through the stinking malarial jungle and eliminated the last pocket of Japanese resistance on 21 January 1943. But the directive of 4 January from Imperial General Headquarters had ordered not only the abandonment of Guadalcanal but also of Papua, since control of the air and sea had passed to the Allies and it was no longer possible to supply and reinforce the Papuan operations.

The fighting in the Papuan campaign had consisted largely of savage hand to hand conflicts in the jungle and mountains. The Australians had borne the brunt of the campaign and showed it with 5700 battle casualties, while the Americans had 2800. But the Japanese forces had shown their true mettle and given the Allies an unpleasant taste of what was yet to come. Skilled in the arts of defensive warfare in difficult terrain, the Japanese soldiers were also possessed by a cult of death. All recruits to the Japanese Army received an intensive three-month indoctrination course to prepare them to die for their Emperor, their country and the honor of their regiment. Many officers and men in fact had their funeral rites performed before leaving for overseas service to signify their intention to die in action. The results spoke for themselves – of 13,000 Japanese battle casualties in the Papuan campaign, only 38 were prisoners of war.

The second grand offensive had failed. It cost the Japanese dearly in irreplaceable resources. Their losses in ships and planes at Midway and through the Guadalcanal and Papua campaigns now precluded any effective offensive action, thus Japan would now be forced to fight a static defensive war. Although the strategic initiative lay with enemy, the councils of the enemy were divided and a long lull in the action ensued.

MacArthur of the Army and Nimitz of the Navy were the two personalities who dominated not only the direction of operations but also the development of strategy in the Pacific. Early in the war, Roosevelt and Churchill had decided that the Pacific area including Australia should be under the direction of the American Joint Chiefs of Staff. The Pacific area was further divided between MacArthur's Southwest Pacific Command, comprising Australia, New Guinea, the Philippines and most of the Netherlands East Indies, and the Central Pacific Command of Nimitz. Such a clumsy arrangement, dictated as it was by inter-service rivalry, not surprisingly produced two divergent strategies for the Pacific.

LEFT: Young volunteers join the Japanese cause in Southeast Asia. Although Japan was first greeted as a liberator, feelings became mixed as the Japanese imposed regulations often far more stringent than the Europeans they replaced as imperialists.

BELOW: A Japanese machine gun nest holds off the enemy.

RIGHT: General Douglas MacArthur, in command of Allied Southwest Pacific forces, in his Australian redoubt, flanked by Major General Gill and Colonel Robert McBride, both of the 32nd Division, at Camp Cable in Queensland. MacArthur planned to drive the Japanese from New Guinea in the leap toward the Philippines.

The naval chiefs adamantly advocated a purely naval campaign westward from Hawaii via the Gilbert, Marshall, Caroline and Mariana Islands to Japan. Such a campaign would enable them to use their large and growing force of fast aircraft carriers to better advantage than in the crowded waters around New Guinea and to fulfill their concept of using carrier task forces to isolate and dominate a group of islands. There would also be no question of flank attacks on the Southwest Pacific from the Micronesian 'spider webs' which the Japanese had spread across the Pacific, since these would become the main objects of attack. Another factor was simply that the Navy did not want naval forces under Army command, especially the potent new fast carriers with all their possibilities. The Navy felt MacArthur should stay on the defensive in the Southwest Pacific and let Nimitz get on with defeating Japan.

Such a role was unacceptable to MacArthur, who determined to launch his own campaign north from Australia to Japan via New Guinea and the Philip-

pines. He wanted the entire Pacific fleet placed under his command to cover the advance along what he termed the 'New Guinea – Mindanao Axis'. The argument of the Navy was in fact strategically sound but MacArthur was taking other factors into consideration. The débacle of the colonial powers had cost them great prestige in Asian eyes. As the United States had been driven out of the Philippines by force of arms, MacArthur felt strongly that control of these islands had to be regained by the same means; otherwise the United States would never be able to reassert its prewar authority. In MacArthur's view, the only road to Tokyo which took account of American interests in Asia lay through the Philippine Islands.

Fond of this sort of confrontation, Roosevelt had approved the divided command in the Pacific in the hope that the inter-service rivalry would produce more rapid results. At the Trident Conference of May 1943 in Washington, the Combined Chiefs of Staff of the Allies had approved both strategies. Thus the Jap-

anese were to face one thrust from MacArthur through New Guinea, while a second thrust was delivered by Nimitz across the Pacific. The theory was that the Japanese would not be able to concentrate their forces to block either thrust successfully because of the continual threat of the other one. The reality was that inter-service politics prevented the Americans from achieving a unified command in the Pacific. Two relatively independent campaigns, however, required much larger forces and thus more time for preparations. Hence the Japanese were given a respite by their enemy until June 1943 when the new Allied offensive was scheduled to begin.

However much Allied councils may have been divided over strategy, so were the Japanese divided along the same inter-service lines. The differences were in fact so deep that the Japanese also initiated no action during this period. Both the Army and Navy agreed that all territory then held should be defended but there the agreement ceased. Naval leaders gave top priority to holding the

ABOVE: USAAF Liberator
bomber heads for home after
hitting Japanese-held Nauru
Island, as smoke rises from the
demolished installations

Bismarcks and the remainder of the Solomon Islands to protect their great naval base at Truk, 1000 miles to the north in the Carolines. Land operations in New Guinea were the aim of the army which considered these necessary for the security of army held territory in the Philippines and the Netherlands East Indies. As the stronger service, the views of the army prevailed. The line of defense was to run from Santa Isabel and New Georgia in the Solomons to Lae in New Guinea with the New Guinea area under army command and the Solomons under Navy direction. Command was centered at

Rabaul, from which the 17th Army in the Solomons and the 18th Army in New Guinea was controlled. The naval forces were light, consisting only of cruisers and destroyers, but capital ships were available from Truk. The Japanese forces were considerably inferior to those of the enemy as there were only 410 aircraft, 55,000 troops in New Guinea and about 40,000 in the Bismarcks and Solomons. A blocking strategy was, however, thought to be feasible, as ten to fifteen divisions and perhaps 850 planes could augment the defenses within six months. With over 40 Japanese divisions inactive in China and Manchuria, it was not that Imperial General Headquarters was deficient in manpower; the available manpower was maldistributed. With its defensive

strategy now set, the Army and the Navy prepared to meet the next offensive of the Allies.

The immediate goal of the Allies was to break the barrier formed by the Bismarck Archipelago and capture the Japanese headquarters at Rabaul in New Britain. MacArthur was to have strategic control of the New Guinea – Solomons operations with Admiral Halsey in tactical command. Each with a well deserved reputation for confident and aggressive leadership, these two commanders complemented each other well. In the first phase of the campaign, Halsey was to seize the Russell Islands west of Guadalcanal as air and naval bases and then occupy the Trobriand Islands for the same purpose. The second envisaged

LEFT: Japanese soldiers killed in the Battle of Raider's Ridge on Guadalcanal, 13–14 September 1942. The bitter fight for the island which went on for half a year at the cost of thousands of American and Japanese lives convinced MacArthur that island hopping and by-passing Japanese installations by attacking behind their front

lines of defense would save lives and shorten the war. The Japanese proved that they would not relinquish territory without a bitter struggle to the last man.

BELOW: Destroyer Squadron (Desron) 23 maneuvering in the Solomons in 1943.

BELOW: Japanese naval officer stands by a scoreboard of downed US aircraft on his carrier.

BOTTOM: Desron 21 in the Solomons in 1943. The Japanese were put to flight for the first time in the Solomons chain.

MacArthur advancing along the north coast of New Guinea to take the Japanese positions around Lae, while Halsey took points on New Georgia and Bougainville to complete the conquest of the Solomons. The third phase was an attack by MacArthur on New Britain as preparation for the last phase – the direct attack on Rabaul. The entire campaign was conceived as alternating strokes to keep the Japanese off balance over a period of eight months. The 30th of June was D-Day.

The Allies had ample strength to achieve their objectives. Under Mac-Arthur were four American and three Australian divisions, augmented by eight Australian divisions in training and the later arrival of two more American divi-

sions. Over 1000 planes were also available. To these forces were added 1800 planes and seven divisions under Halsey who also commanded six battleships and two carriers. Thus there was a comfortable margin of strength over the Japanese in all categories.

The landings in the Russells and Trobriands went uncontested while little initial resistance was encountered as the drive on Lae began. Soon, however, 6000 Japanese began to slow the Allied forces which did not reach Salamaua until mid-August. The attack by Halsey on New Georgia met immediate and heavy opposition as the 10,000-man garrison had been ordered by Imperial General Headquarters to hold as long as possible. Halsey had in fact received intelligence that

BELOW: US Navy Helldivers massed on the flight deck of a carrier while members of the crew place life rafts in readiness below a battery of 20mm machine guns ranged along the side of the carrier. By 1943 US Navy yards and shipbuilding plants were setting records in deliveries of new ships.

BOTTOM: Wrecked Japanese airfield at Wewak on New Guinea.

LEFT: Admiral Marc Mitscher commanded the aircraft carrier groups of the US Pacific Fleet in most of the later battles of the war.

BELOW: Antiaircraft lookouts and the talker who relays their messages to the guns and fire control center on a battleship during the Okinawa campaign when the Japanese Kamikaze operations were at their height.

LEFT: Marines advance on Tarawa, where the Japanese put up bitter resistance once again.

BELOW RIGHT: US soldiers inspect Japanese dead on Attu, one of the Aleutian islands taken by Japan in the spring offensive of 1942, and re-occupied by the Americans a few months later.

BOTTOM: Kate torpedo plane shot down during an attack on a US carrier in the Marshalls in December 1943.

Japanese reinforcements were landing in southern New Georgia and advanced his landings in that area to 21 June but no Japanese were discovered. Overall, the Japanese resistance on New Georgia was serious enough that the inexperienced American troops made little progress despite overwhelming artillery, naval gun and air support. A further division and a half were thrown into the fray but even so, the remains of the Japanese garrison did not retreat to the neighboring island of Kolombangara until 5 August. Japanese casualties were about 2500 killed and seventeen warships lost against 1000 Allied casualties and six warships.

But the New Georgia campaign brought about an important change in Allied tactics. MacArthur and Nimitz realized that 'island hopping' or methodically reducing each Japanese position in turn was not only costly and time-consuming but gave ample time to the enemy to strengthen the next position.

Island hopping was an ineffectual use of the air and naval superiority possessed by the Allies. 'Leap-frogging' was to be the new tactic, which meant by-passing the stronger Japanese positions, sealing them off by air and sea, and leaving them to 'wither on the vine', or as a baseball fan on MacArthur's staff described it, 'hittin' 'em where they ain't'. The first instance of leap-frogging was the by-passing of Kolombangara with its 10,000 defenders in favor of Vella Lavella with its 250-man garrison. The Japanese response in this case was to evacuate the garrison of Kolombangara to Bougainville as soon as the Allied tactic was evident. The development of leap-frogging as a tactic was to give new impetus to the lagging operations both in New Guinea and the Solomons.

MacArthur's drive on Lae was initially off-schedule, but a neat series of converging and flanking attacks forced the evacuation of Salamaua on 11 September and

of Lae on 15 September. Thus by mid-September the Allies were close to completion of the second phase of their offensive. All that remained was the capture of Bougainville by Halsey for the ring to begin closing around Rabaul.

September was a difficult month for Imperial General Staff in Tokyo. In that month, not only did the failure of the blocking strategy have to be acknowledged but also the implications of the failure for Japan's whole policy toward the United States. Recovering from their initial defeat and demoralization in a remarkably short time, the Americans now held uncontested mastery of the sea and air. The imposing forces of MacArthur were steadily driving in the southwest flank while Nimitz was assembling the largest flotilla of ships since the Grand Fleet of Admiral Jellicoe in World War I for a mortal thrust across the Pacific. Clearly Imperial General Headquarters had been over optimistic in its assessment of its own defensive and American offensive capabilities. A careful estimate was therefore made of the minimum area needed for the maintenance of Japan's basic war aims. Termed the 'zone of absolute national defense', this area extended from Burma through Malaya and the Netherlands East Indies to west New Guinea and thence through the Carolines and Marianas to the Kuriles. All else – even the Bismarcks and Rabaul – was to be held for six months and then abandoned. Within these six months, it was planned to develop the zone of absolute national defense into a firm defense line,

LEFT: A torpedoman checks the 21-inch torpedo tubes of a *Fletcher* Class destroyer before an operation in the Solomons in 1943.

BOTTOM: Under heavy bombardment US Marines hit the beach at Saipan in the Marianas in June 1944.

spring of 1943 when his plane was ambushed and shot down by American fighters. The other is that such was the secrecy maintained over the course of the war that even most of the Japanese military was unaware of the true situation and tended to be over-optimistic.

The real problem of Japan in 1943 was, however, of a much more fundamental nature. Having conquered a large empire with vast natural and economic resources, the Japanese had failed to organize their economy for all-out war production in the same manner as the United States and Britain. Planes and ships were needed to defend the far-flung maritime empire and yet by 1943, Japan was acutely short of both due to lack of planning. In 1943 alone, Japan produced only one-fifth as many planes as the United States and, equally important, had failed to undertake a program of training and mobilizing pilots. The quality of Japanese air pilots had dropped radically during 1942 and was an important factor in the rapid erosion of Japanese air strength. There were but three carriers under construction in Japan in 1943 as opposed to 22 in the United States. There had also been little provision made for building the merchant shipping necessary to hold a maritime empire together. American air and submarine attacks were taking a heavy toll, sinking over one million tons in 1942 alone. Much of the available merchant shipping had been squandered trying to support the wasteful operations in the Solomons which also had consumed over 3000 aircraft and their crews. Although Japan controlled the rich oil fields of the Netherlands East Indies, there was not enough shipping by 1943 to move the fuel. Thus

to treble Japanese aircraft production, and to build up the Combined Fleet to challenge once again the American Pacific Fleet in battle.

This plan was called the 'New Operational Policy' and only required that six Japanese divisions (none had ever been transferred from China and Manchuria) in the Southwest Pacific with little air and naval support hold off twenty-odd Allied divisions supported by 3000 aircraft. The element of unreality about the plan is accounted for by two factors. One is that Yamamoto, perhaps the only genius and surely the most realistic leader produced by Japan during the war, had died in the

---

RIGHT: The light cruiser *St. Louis* bombards Japanese positions on Guam, 21 July 1944.

an acute shortage of oil was curtailing operations of the Navy and grounding such aircraft as there were. The real weakness of Japan was organizational and economic.

MacArthur and Halsey were pushing their own operations at this point due to the impending start of the rival campaign in the central Pacific in November 1943. Halsey was under pressure as many of his ships had been on short loan from the Central Pacific Command and were now being recalled as was the Second Marine Division. Similarly, MacArthur knew that priority was being given to the new offensive by the Joint Chiefs of Staff who now considered that Rabaul should be by-passed.

Halsey accordingly attacked Bougainville, the most westerly of the Solomons, in October 1943, thereby initiating another protracted struggle which lasted until March 1944. Manned by 40,000 soldiers and 20,000 sailors, the main defences were in the south of this large island. To the surprise of the Japanese, the main American landings were shrewdly made on the weakly defended west coast. The Japanese made little response as over 60,000 Americans established a comfortable bridgehead over ten miles wide. The real contest began only at the end of February 1944 when the Japanese had finally traversed 50 miles of jungle. Hopelessly underestimating American strength at 20,000 combat troops, the Japanese commander attacked with 15,000 men in March. In a two week struggle, 8000 Japanese died assaulting the well dug in Americans who suffered only 300 losses. The remains of the shattered Japanese on Bougainville were then left to wither and die.

Pursuing his ultimate objective of isolating Rabaul, MacArthur was fighting his way up the New Guinea coast. Using his favorite tactics of converging, pincer attacks and leap-frogging, MacArthur forced Imperial General Headquarters to order a continuous series of withdrawals. By April 1944 the Japanese had been forced back to Wewak where the 18th Army dug in 50,000 troops in a strong position. The Joint Chiefs of Staff had already directed that Rabaul be isolated and left to wither, as it contained 100,000 defenders under a tough and resourceful leader with ample supplies stockpiled for previous expeditions which had come to nought. Even so, it was necessary to ensure that no flanking attack came from New Britain to menace the coastal drive in New Guinea, and MacArthur attacked Cape Gloucester across the straits from the New Guinea coast. The cape was held by 8000 Japanese troops recently arrived from China, but they were separated by 300 miles of rough terrain from any support from Rabaul. With little air support, their wisest course was to make the long retreat to Rabaul which they soon did. Several weeks of stiff resistance on the Admiralty Islands was overcome in early March, thus providing the Allies with another major air and naval base. This operation completed the breaking of the Bismarck Barrier and left Rabaul completely isolated.

The Japanese defense of New Guinea was now becoming chaotic and sporadic. The Central Pacific offensive meant that no support could be received from the Japanese forces in that sector. Troop convoys from China were suffering severe losses from attacks by American submarines while the forces already in New Guinea tended to be too dispersed for effective resistance. The 18th Army con-

BELOW: US Navy Avenger torpedo bombers in formation. They played a major role in repelling the Japanese at Midway as well as subsequently. Each one carried a 2000-pound torpedo, heavy armament, a crew of four, and they had a range of 1400 miles.

RIGHT: Motor torpedo boats (*MTB.224* and *244*) surge forward. These small 72½ foot long craft were invaluable in the South Pacific having the advantage of maneuverability and speed.

LEFT: An Avenger using four 330hp jet propulsion units for its take-off. These units, known as JATOs (jet-assisted take-offs) enabled heavy carrier-based planes to cut their take-off runs by more than half. This gave the flight deck more space for planes and allowed planes to get into the air more quickly and more heavily loaded when an attack came.

LEFT: An Avenger using four 330hp jet propulsion units for its take-off. These units, known as JATOs (jet-assisted take-offs) enabled heavy carrier-based planes to cut their take-off runs by more than half. This gave the flight deck more space for planes and allowed planes to get into the air more quickly and more heavily loaded when an attack came.

BOTTOM: With a 1000-pound bomb slung under its fuselage, a US Navy Dauntless gets the flag to take off from its carrier in an attack on Japanese positions on Wake Island in 1944.

centration at Wewak was now by-passed by MacArthur who planned to arrive at the northwest point of New Guinea in four operations. Supported by Halsey's Seventh Fleet, MacArthur's army aboard a flotilla of 215 LSTs and LCTs successively conquered Wakde, Biak, Noemfoor and Sansapoor. Biak was a particularly tough fight as the Japanese had prepared a skilled defense in depth. But on 30 July, the capture of Sansapoor completed Allied control of New Guinea and represented the last stop on that island on MacArthur's road back to the Philippines. There were still the remnants of five Japanese divisions in New Guinea, but Australian troops would welcome the opportunity to mop these up, leaving MacArthur to look across the Celebes Sea at Mindanao.

Although the offensive of his rival MacArthur had begun in earnest in July 1942, Nimitz had been forced to wait until November 1943 before launching the Navy's cherished sweep across the Pacific. The offensive was not aimed at Japan itself but was intended to mop up the Japanese island fortresses and converge on the Philippines with that of MacArthur. With the American position

in the Philippines restored, it was thought that American forces would establish large bases in China from which heavy bombers could hammer Japan into submission. The first attack in the Nimitz offensive was to be against the Gilbert Islands with Makin and Tarawa the main targets. Under the tactical command of Vice-Admiral Raymond Spruance, the victor of Midway, 7000 troops were to assault Makin while 18,000 attempted Tarawa. Over 1000 aircraft, six fleet carriers, five light carriers, and six new battleships were in support. A service fleet intended to supply and service the battle fleet in all its needs made Spruance virtually independent in terms of logistics.

The assault began on 20 November against a force of 800 defenders on Makin and 3000 on Tarawa. The defense was not as strong as planned because the reinforcements envisaged under the New Operational Policy had not yet arrived. An inexperienced American army division needed four days to overrun Makin, but the defenses of Tarawa proved a different matter. The three-day battle opened with a massive naval (3000 tons of shells in two and one half hours) and air bombardment, after which 5000 men of the Second Marine Division set out for the beaches in landing craft. A third had never reached the beach under the murderous Japanese fire but the remainder slowly forced the dogged Japanese back into two fortified points midway on the island. Surrounded, the defenders annihilated themselves in a series of suicidal counterattacks on the night of the 22nd. The costly assault on the Gilberts set off instant controversy in the United

States but proved an invaluable testing ground and led to refinements in the assault techniques later used.

The next target was the Marshall Islands, but here Nimitz modified his strategy. Instead of striking at the easternmost islands, he chose to by-pass them in favor of Kwajalein 400 miles beyond. Once Kwajalein was secured, Spruance was to be sent to seize Eniwetok at the far end of the chain. The arrangements were the same as the campaign in the Gilberts except that the preparatory bombardment was to be four times as heavy. This new tactic of leap-frogging had an added benefit, as the Japanese reinforcements had been sent to the eastern Marshalls in anticipation of an attack in that quarter.

The fast carrier forces of Admiral Mark Mitscher neutralized any Japanese air and sea intervention and destroyed 150 enemy planes in the process as the main attack on Kwajalein opened on 1 February 1944. The 8000 defenders destroyed themselves by repeated 'banzai' charges which cost the Americans only 370 casualties, a far cry from the slaughter on Tarawa. Eniwetok subsequently succumbed after a three-day fight.

Construction of new airfields was begun immediately as American forces were now only 700 miles from the big Japanese base at Truk and 1000 miles from the Mariana Islands. In fact, to prevent any intervention from Truk during operations against Eniwetok, a fast carrier force had blasted it with three heavy raids which destroyed 32 ships and 250 planes, thus demonstrating plainly Japan's fatal weakness in air power. The

Gilberts and Marshalls had fallen within a two-month period, dashing the hope of the New Operational Policy that they could hold out for six months. The next American objective was the Marianas, a key segment of the absolute zone of national defense. The coming battle for the Marianas was to have profound effects on the course of the war in Asia.

The most important island in the Marianas was Saipan, lying only 1350 miles from Tokyo. The loss of Saipan would not only breach Japan's inner defenses but enable the Americans to bomb the home islands and disrupt the communications of the remaining forward areas with Japan. The presence of airfields on Tinian and Guam made these two islands of significance as well. So strongly fortified it was thought to be impregnable, Saipan was held by 32,000 men, while Tinian and Guam were garrisoned by 9000 and 18,000 respectively. Because Saipan was so vital to Japanese defense, the American threat was to be countered with as much force as Japan could muster. The naval forces under Admiral Ozawa comprised a main battle fleet of four battleships, three light carriers, and cruisers and destroyers; a main carrier force of three fleet carriers with supporting cruisers and destroyers; and a reserve carrier force of two fleet carriers, a battleship and cruisers and destroyers. The plan prepared by the Naval Commander-in-Chief, Admiral Toyoda, was to trap the American carrier forces between Ozawa's powerful force and land-based planes from the Marianas. Facing Ozawa's force was Spruance's mighty Fifth Fleet, with its seven battleships and 21 cruisers

LEFT: The heavy cruiser *Minneapolis* seen in April 1943. The *Minneapolis* had been badly damaged during the Guadalcanal fighting in 1942.

BELOW: From left, Admiral Chester Nimitz, Admiral Ernest King and Admiral Raymond Spruance seen aboard the cruiser *Indianapolis* in 1944. King was Chief of Staff of the US Navy, Nimitz commanded the Pacific Fleet and Spruance led the Fifth Fleet.

BOTTOM: Flight deck operations aboard the carrier *Cowpens* during the Marshall Islands campaign.

and the fifteen carriers and 950 planes of Mitscher, brought together to protect and support the three Marine and one Army divisions intended for the assault on the Marianas.

The bombardment of Saipan, Tinian and Guam began on 11 June with the first landings occurring four days later against heavy opposition. Receiving news of Ozawa's force in the Philippine Sea, Spruance moved his ships 180 miles west of Tinian and waited in exactly the position for which Toyoda had hoped. Half of the trap was missing, however, as the carrier planes of Mitscher had already annihilated Japanese air power in the Marianas; hence it was to be fleet against fleet in a classic carrier confrontation. The first strikes were put in the air by Ozawa on 19 June. By the following day 480 Japanese planes had

LEFT: Crewmen aboard an aircraft carrier in Task Force 58 rush away as a Helldiver warms up prior to take-off. By August 1944 Helldivers had hammered away at Saipan, Guam and Tinian as Allied forces penetrated Japan's inner defense zone.

LEFT: An F6F about to take off from the deck of USS *Yorktown (CV.10)* on 19 June 1944. This new carrier replaced its namesake which was sunk in the Battle of Midway.

RIGHT: Dauntless dive bombers attack Japanese bases in the western Carolines in preparation for the final assault on the Philippines in mid-May 1944.

LEFT AND BELOW: Curtiss SB2C-4 Helldiver with wings folded.

RIGHT: Avenger torpedo bomber is flagged off the deck of a carrier. With their range of 1400 miles they were able to attack the home islands.

BELOW: Sailors man the
20mm antiaircraft guns on
the quarterdeck of the
destroyer *O'Bannon* while in
the background the ship's
main armament of 5-inch
guns can be seen. A picture
taken in 1943.

BOTTOM: First American plane to land on Peleliu in the Palaus after it was captured from the Japanese in September 1944. A few Japanese held out nearby and continued to attack the airfield for some time after its capture.

been downed in what American pilots called the 'Great Marianas Turkey Shoot'. Added to the three fleet carriers sunk, this was a smashing defeat from which the Japanese naval air force never recovered, as so many pilots had been lost. Saipan was cleared by 5 July and Tinian and Guam had both fallen by early August. The road to the Philippines from the Central Pacific was now open.

The fall of Saipan was such a disaster for Japan that it could not be hidden in the same manner as earlier disasters like Midway. The disquiet was so intense that the government of Hideki Tojo fell, to be replaced by that of General Koiso Kuniacki. Despite its desperate situation, the Japanese military still hoped to fight the war to a drawn peace and thus maintained their warlike posture while secretly trying to open negotiations with the United States.

In the meantime, in a radical shift in strategy, the United States gave up its plan to use China as a base for the bombing of Japan and shifted its new super bomber – the B-29 – to its newly-won bases in the Marianas. November 1944 saw the beginning of a heavy bombing offensive from the Marianas against the home islands of Japan. The MacArthur and Nimitz offensives converged on the Philippines with landings at Leyte Gulf in October 1944, landings which signaled the beginning of MacArthur's long cherished reconquest of the Philippines. Nimitz was ordered to occupy Iwo Jima and Okinawa, lying midway between the Marianas and the Japanese islands, as close-up bases to support the air bombardment of Japan. The preparatory bombing of Iwo Jima began in early December and continued until landings actually were made on 19 February. The 25,000 defenders did not expand themselves in suicide charges as had other Japanese island garrisons but remained in a heavily fortified complex of caves and tunnels which the attackers had to take one by one. For the first time, American casualties were higher than Japanese at 26,000 versus 25,000. By the end of March, however, Iwo Jima was in use as an emergency base for B-29s on the Tokyo run.

Okinawa was a large island in the Ryukyus, lying only 340 miles from Japan, which the Allies wanted as a staging base for an invasion of Japan. The Japanese High Command was naturally determined to defend Okinawa to limit of its resources, and 100,000 troops manned an in-depth defense of the type that had proved so costly to the attackers on Iwo Jima. The Allies committed 170,000 combat troops to the landings made on 1 April. The invaders were able to overrun most of the island quickly as only the southern portion was heavily defended. From April 6, however, a series of heavy *kamikaze* attacks began, including a suicide run by the giant battleship *Yamato*, which took a toll of Allied ships. Little progress was made against the southern defenses until the Japanese, tiring of the defensive, launched an ill-fated counter-attack and suffered heavy losses. Slowly the tenacious defense was pressed back until by early May the last defenders were burned out of their caves with flame throwers. The Japanese loss was around 100,000 men against 49,000 American casualties. Okinawa was a costly victory.

With the brilliant exception of Admiral Yamamoto, Japan had suffered from a lack of military and political leadership throughout a war which she was never really prepared to fight. Her adversaries had been fortunate to have two aggressive and able leaders in MacArthur and Nimitz, but in the end, it was the economic and organizational weaknesses of Japan which prevented her from holding out long enough to achieve the negotiated peace on which she had rested her hopes from the beginning.

# KAMIKAZE

RIGHT: Group of early *kamikaze* pilots receive a ceremonial cup of sake from Vice Admiral Takajiho Ohnishi, founder of the *kamikaze* corps.

FAR RIGHT: USS *Gambier Bay* during the Battle of Samar, 25 October 1944, under heavy attack from Japanese ships and aircraft.

BELOW: *Kamikaze* pilot with the rank of first lieutenant salutes as he receives orders which will send him to almost certain death.

The Battle of Midway in June 1942 marked the end of Japan's offensive in the Pacific and the beginning of an Allied counter-attack which was to eventually lead to an occupation of the Japanese islands. Having established themselves in Southeast Asia, the Japanese dug in for a war of attrition which would last another two and one-half years. Since their resources were limited and manpower finite, the Japanese were ill-equipped to fight a protracted war and paid a heavy penalty for continuing the effort. By 1944 the situation had become so acute for the Japanese that they were increasingly forced to resort to desperate measures, including the use of suicide or *kamikaze* missions.

*Kamikaze* pilots made their first appearance during the Battle for Leyte in the fall of 1944. By that time, American forces had secured the Solomons, New Guinea, and Saipan and were preparing to avenge their earlier defeat in the Philippines. Japanese losses in the epic battles of 1943 and 1944 had been heavy. They were short of equipment and even shorter of trained personnel. The Allies, on the other hand, were in peak condition with more supplies and personnel arriving daily. This being the case, when the Japanese determined that Leyte was going to be their Waterloo, their decisive battle for survival, they were forced to adopt unconventional means to hold their position in the Philippines.

The American plan for the re-occupation of the Philippines called for landings on Leyte and Luzon. In preparing for the invasion of Leyte, the Allies concentrated the largest naval force yet seen in the Pacific War. The combined fleets of Admirals Halsey and Kincaid numbered well over 700 ships, including more than a dozen aircraft carriers and scores of battleships and cruisers. To meet this threat, the Japanese amassed what was left of their Combined Fleet and prepared to engage the Allies on the waters off the Philippines.

For the Japanese, the defense of Leyte and the Philippines was crucial. If the Allies succeeded in their offensive, Japanese forces would be isolated in the Philippines and the Imperial Navy cut off from its fuel supplies in the Indies and elsewhere. In preparing to counter the American offensive, the Japanese hoped to surprise the Allied armada as it debouched its forces in the Leyte Gulf. The plans adopted by Admirals Kurita, Shima, and Nishimura, called

LEFT: A young Korean bids good-bye to his friends and family as he sets out on a mission in mid-1944. In the first stages of the war Koreans and Formosans, though under Japanese colonial rule, were not allowed to join the Japanese forces. By 1943, however, lack of manpower obliged Japan to accept them, and many fought heroically.

BELOW: General Kuribayashi, whose stout defense of Iwo Jima cost thousands of Japanese and American lives. He was one of the few score Japanese left on the island, and committed *hara-kiri* before he was captured.

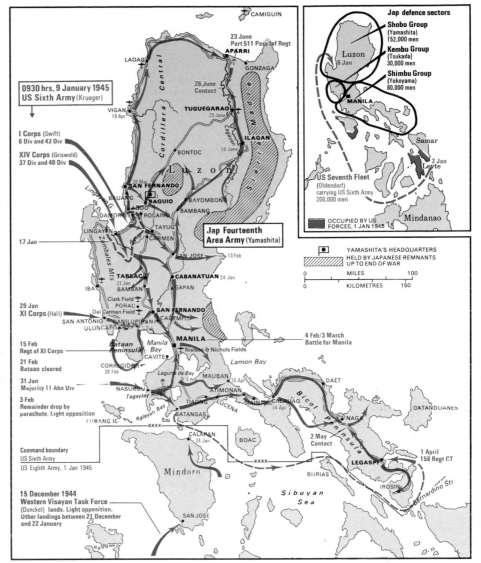

for Kurita's Center Force to sail into the Leyte Gulf through the San Bernardino Straits and attack American transports, while the Southern Force under command of Shima and Nishimura advanced into Leyte Gulf from the Surigao Strait to the south. A third force, under the command of Admiral Ozawa, was to lure Admiral Halsey's Third Fleet up north and out of the way. This force was to be made up of carriers without planes and would, thus, be undertaking what amounted to a suicide mission to divert American attention from the Leyte Gulf. It should also be noted that the Japanese plan called, for the first time, for suicide raids against the American aircraft carriers off Leyte.

On 20 October 1944 American Forces were landed on Leyte, but it was not until the 23rd that American and Japanese forces met off the island. On that day American submarines located Admiral Kurita's Center Force, sinking three Japanese cruisers in this first engagement. On the following day, 24 October, American carrier based planes destroyed the battleship *Musashi* and damaged several other Japanese ships, forcing Kurita to withdraw his task force.

Admirals Shima and Nishimura fared no better than Kurita. On 25 October

their Southern Task Force was spotted moving toward the Surigao Strait and the United States Seventh Fleet was quickly moved into a position in front of the Strait where it emptied into Leyte Gulf. When the Japanese tried to sail through this bottleneck, they suffered the loss of many ships, forcing the joint task force commanders to abort their mission and beat a hasty retreat from the Surigao Strait.

Having disposed of the Japanese task forces in the vicinity of Leyte, or so he thought, Admiral Halsey ordered his forces north to annihilate Ozawa's task force. While his fleet headed north, leaving the area of the San Bernardino Strait unprotected, Admiral Kurita launched an attack against the unprotected escort carriers of the Seventh Fleet, sinking one carrier and two destroyers in the process. Fortunately for the Americans, Kurita did not have any significant air power to use against them or their losses would have been greater. The Americans, however, did have large numbers of planes available and used them effectively to attack Kurita's force and send it into retreat.

With Kurita in retreat and Admiral Ozawa's task force under attack and finally eliminated as a potent force, the defense of the Philippines fell to the

Imperial Army and Air Force. Between October and December 1944 Japanese reinforcements were rushed to Leyte from the other Philippine Islands, 45,000 troops eventually being landed on Leyte. Despite regular Allied attacks on Japanese transports headed for Leyte, the Japanese succeeded in reinforcing their garrison on the island and dug in for one of the bloodiest battles of the Pacific war.

Having lost the bulk of their fleet in the various encounters with Allied forces in Leyte Gulf, the Japanese had to depend increasingly on suicide missions flown by Japanese pilots, the *kamikazes*, to neutralize the American fleet. The *kamikazes* conducted suicide missions from land based fields against the American fleet, particularly the carriers, from November 1944 through the beginning of the new year. They operated as a kind of guided missile with human control. Locked into their planes which were filled with bombs, *kamikaze* pilots tried to crash their planes into enemy ships and were very difficult to defend against as Admiral Halsey was to find out.

The term *kamikaze* meant 'divine wind' and derived from a legendary Japanese victory over invading Mongol forces in the 13th century. At that time a typhoon or *kamikaze* wind destroyed the Mongol

THE FIGHTING FILIPINOS
WE WILL ALWAYS FIGHT FOR *FREEDOM!*

LEFT: Poster produced by the Americans urging Filipinos to join them to throw off the Japanese yoke. Actually many Filipinos co-operated with the Japanese, since they were given their 'independence' by Japan under the Presidency of Jose P. Laurel. But most, if not all, Filipinos answered the appeal.

BELOW: Captured Japanese pilots aboard a US aircraft carrier during the Battle of Leyte Gulf.

an Allied victory and occupation in the 20th century.

*Kamikaze* units were originally formed in 1944 to compensate for the critical shortage of Japanese aircraft and the desperate situation of the Japanese air forces which had virtually been wiped out after the Battle of the Philippine Sea. A combination of improved American fighter planes and the introduction of the proximity armed fuses for anti-aircraft shells had created a new tactical situation in the air war in the Pacific which, when combined with the absolute superiority of Allied forces in numbers of planes and pilots, had led the Japanese to implement plans calling for suicide missions.

Admiral Arima, the architect of the *kamikaze* concept, had little trouble in recruiting pilots for his suicide missions. Thousands of young Japanese volunteered for such missions. *Kamikaze* squadrons were to constitute an élite corps which captivated the popular mind in Japan and struck fear in the hearts of the Allies. Using antiquated aircraft, including biplanes with non-retractable gear, the *kamikaze* missions wreaked havoc on Allied shipping without strapping Japan's resources.

The first *kamikaze* missions were flown during the Battle for Leyte. The toll of these missions was modestly impressive. Between November 1944 and January 1945 at least half a dozen major Allied ships were sunk and/or damaged by *kamikaze* raids with a loss of hundreds of lives. But it was not until the Lingayen landings in January 1945 that the *kamikazes* unleashed their full fury. By that time, Leyte was nearly secured and Allied forces were preparing to land on Luzon.

With the loss of Leyte, there was little the Japanese could do to stop the American advance in the Philippines. However, General Yamashita and his colleagues had determined to make the Luzon campaign a costly one for their adversaries. Husbanding all of the resources at his disposal, including the *kamikaze* squadrons, Yamashita dug in for a long fight.

As Allied naval forces entered the Lingayen Gulf, they encountered heavy Japanese resistance. During the landing of American forces on Luzon, *kamikaze* pilots constantly harassed the American fleet. Since *kamikaze* pilots flew close to the ground, Allied radar often failed to pick them up. Although Allied intelligence estimated that three out of every four *kamikaze* planes were destroyed, one out of every four found his target and one out of every 33 *kamikaze* attacks sank a ship. *Kamikaze* attacks were sufficiently successful during the first weeks of January 1945, that Allied leaders decided to take definitive action against them. Since it was impossible to detect the whereabouts of these suicide missions once in the air, it was decided to destroy the Japanese air stations on Luzon, from which the *kamikazes* were sent aloft. By 14 January 1945 this mission was accomplished and Allied forces were able to continue their progress in Luzon without further Japanese harassment.

With the elimination of Japanese air power in the Philippines, the drive toward Manila continued. As American

Fleet as it lay off Japan in preparation for invasion. The Japanese had long believed that this natural calamity or *kamikaze* was a divine intervention, and over many centuries had come to accept the proposition that Japan was shielded from calamity by a supernatural force much greater than any man might assemble. It was, perhaps, apt that the suicide pilots first sent aloft against the Allies in November 1944 were called *kamikazes*. Like the divine wind which had spared the Japanese a Mongol conquest seven centuries earlier, it was hoped that these men would spare Japan

RIGHT: The Battle of Leyte
Gulf, the biggest naval battle
and arguably the most
complicated in history.

BOTTOM: US flotilla bombards
Leyte, 20 October 1944.

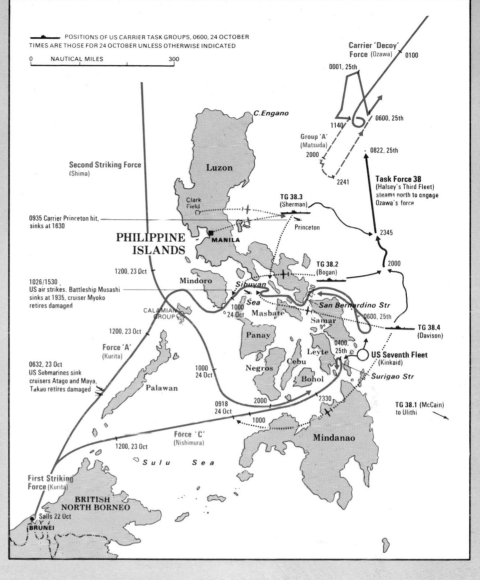

POSITIONS OF US CARRIER TASK GROUPS, 0600, 24 OCTOBER
TIMES ARE THOSE FOR 24 OCTOBER UNLESS OTHERWISE INDICATED

forces pressed toward the Philippine capital, Japanese forces were evacuated to the mountains and deployed around Clark Field. Although Manila was liberated in February 1945, it was not until July that General MacArthur was able to declare Luzon secured. By that time, the major confrontation between the Japanese and Allied forces had moved to Iwo Jima and the Ryukyu islands.

As the campaign in the Philippines was winding down, the Allies prepared to take Iwo Jima. Iwo Jima, a relative small and obscure island in the Bonin group, was needed by the Allies as an air base to provide for emergency landings of B-29s on bombing missions against Japan launched from the Marianas. Such an air station would also be used as a base for fighters escorting the B-29s to and from Japan. Since these smaller planes did not have the range of the larger craft and could not make the round-trip run between the Marianas and Tokyo without refueling, escort units might be permanently stationed on Iwo Jima and meet the heavy bombers over the island for the final run to and from Japan.

It was originally the intention of the American command to land troops on Iwo Jima in October 1944, but the unexpectedly bitter and prolonged action in the Philippines forced a postponement of the invasion of Iwo Jima until after the new year. However, beginning as early as October 1944 and accelerating in tempo in November and December 1944, Allied aircraft regularly attacked Japanese installations on the island. In January 1945 such attacks became daily affairs. By the beginning of February 1945, Iwo Jima had witnessed the heaviest bombardment of the Pacific war.

Unfortunately for the Allies, the Japanese defenses on Iwo Jima were virtually unaffected by the massive air raids against them. The Japanese had constructed an elaborate series of subterranean defenses on the island and had built gun emplacements on Mount Sura-

bachi which were impossible to knock out by air raids. Under the command of Lieutenant General Kuribayashi Tadamichi, the island of Iwo Jima had been turned into an armed fortress which could not be taken without a costly amphibious invasion. Since the Japanese were prepared to defend the island to the last man if necessary, the Battle for Iwo Jima was to be one of the most brutal campaigns of the entire war.

It was not until the middle of February that Allied forces were ready to launch their attack on Iwo Jima. As their task force steamed toward the island, it was attacked by Japanese submarines using a new weapon, *kaiten*, or human guided torpedos. Guided by swimmers launched from I-boats, the *kaiten* were used against the Allied fleet but with little effect. Still, the use of the *kaiten* was another example of the extent to which the Japanese were

RIGHT: *Kamikaze* nicknamed
'Ginga' crashes his bomber into
US aircraft carrier in
December 1944. Over 6000
Japanese pilots died in *kamikaze*
raids over the Philippines and
Okinawa.

BELOW: The ceremonial
drinking of water by Navy
*kamikaze* pilots before their final
flights.

FAR RIGHT: Patriotic song to
the sea chanted by soldiers in
Hokkaido in 1944. As the Allies
pressed closer to Japan,
fanaticism grew more intense.

BELOW RIGHT: US carrier
*Intrepid* is attacked by
*kamikazes*, 25 November 1944
off Luzon.

BOTTOM RIGHT: The deck of the
*Intrepid* after the attack, which
killed over 60 men on the ship.

willing to go to protect their interests and resist the American advance.

On 19 February the first American forces were landed on Iwo Jima, accompanied by a huge aerial bombardment of Japanese defenses on the island. From the first moment they stepped onto the volcanic soil of the island, American troops were subject to incessant Japanese strafing, pinning them down on their beachheads in a manner reminiscent of the landings on Omaha Beach months before. It was only after the ships of the Allied task force opened fire on Japanese installations that the Marines were able to dig in, awaiting the protection of nightfall to move forward to more advantageous positions. On this first day of battle some 30,000 troops were landed, but not before some 2500 men were wounded or killed. This grim statistic was a barometer of things to come.

From the first day of the Iwo Jima campaign until its conclusion almost a month later, the battle proceeded on a yard by yard basis. Contrary to Allied assumptions, the Japanese did not counterattack but held their manpower in reserve, knowing full well that with the Allies in control of the sea and air lanes, there was no chance that Japan's garrison on Iwo Jima might be reinforced.

On the other hand, the Japanese were prepared to contest the Marines for every meter. Enjoying an initial advantage because of their subterranean positions, the Japanese would extract heavy casualties.

American forces slowly moved toward Mount Surabachi protected as much as was possible by naval artillery barrages and air strikes launched from off-shore carriers against Japanese positions. Because of the distance between Iwo Jima and the nearest Japanese air bases, the Americans enjoyed virtual aerial supremacy and encountered relatively few *kamikaze* attacks. Nevertheless, the *kamikazes* found their mark during the course of the battle for Iwo Jima, damaging the carrier *Saratoga* and destroying some four dozen of her planes. The escort carrier *Bismarck Sea* was also hit by *kamikaze* pilots.

On 23 February United States Marines successfully scaled Mount Surabachi, raising the American flag atop the mountain in a scene immortalized by an Associated Press photographer. By the beginning of March the Japanese had retreated to the northern part of the island. By 4 March, even as the Marines were mopping up the campaign, Allied bombers were using Japanese air strips

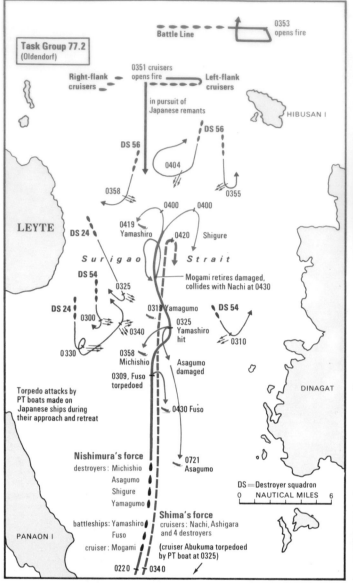

Task Group 77.2 (Oldendorf)

Battle Line — 0353 opens fire

Right-flank cruisers · 0351 cruisers opens fire · Left-flank cruisers

in pursuit of Japanese remnants

HIBUSAN I

DS 56 · DS 56

0404

0358 · 0355

0400 · 0400

0419 Yamashiro · 0420 Shigure

LEYTE

*Surigao Strait*

DS 24

DS 54

0325

Mogami retires damaged, collides with Nachi at 0430

0318 Yamagumo · DS 54

0325 Yamashiro hit

0300 · 0340 · 0310

0330 · 0358 Michishio

Asagumo damaged

0309, Fuso torpedoed

DINAGAT

0430 Fuso

Torpedo attacks by PT boats made on Japanese ships during their approach and retreat

0721 Asagumo

DS = Destroyer squadron
0 NAUTICAL MILES 6

**Nishimura's force**
destroyers: Michishio, Asagumo, Shigure, Yamagumo
battleships: Yamashiro, Fuso
cruiser: Mogami

**Shima's force**
cruisers: Nachi, Ashigara and 4 destroyers
(cruiser Abukuma torpedoed by PT boat at 0325)

PANAON I

0220 — 0340

LEFT AND FAR RIGHT BOTTOM: Stages in the Battle of Leyte Gulf.

BELOW: Vice Admiral Ohnishi, founder of the *Kamikaze* Special Attack Force.

BOTTOM: *PT.321* picks up Japanese survivor from the Battle of the Surigao Strait during the Leyte Gulf actions in October 1944.

BOTTOM: General Tomoyuki Yamashita, who was called the 'Tiger of Malaya' because of his sudden victory in 1941–42, commanded Japanese troops in Luzon who fought the Allies for months, refusing to surrender despite their hopeless situation. He was executed after the war.

BELOW: Wreckage of a Japanese truck and its victim on a road in the Philippines during its liberation.

on Iwo Jima which had been hastily expanded by American seabees. By the end of the month the island was taken.

The American victory on Iwo Jima was achieved only after a major bloodletting on both sides. When the campaign ended on 27 March 1945, the Allies had suffered over 25,000 deaths and casualties. The Japanese lost an approximately equal number of men. Well might it be said by the official historian of the United States Marine Corps that the Battle for

Iwo Jima was 'the most savage and costly battle in the history of the Marine Corps'.

Even as the Battle for Iwo Jima was still in progress, Allied leaders were preparing to invade Okinawa, the largest of the Ryukyu Islands. Located midway between Japan and Formosa, some 360 miles from the China mainland, Okinawa was even more strategically important than Iwo Jima. If Okinawa was captured, the Allies would be in a position to advance on Japan itself. If they failed

to take Okinawa, their plans for an occupation of Japan might have to be postponed indefinitely.

Given the relatively large size of Okinawa, approximately 480 square miles, and the size of the Japanese garrison on the island, estimated to number well over 100,000 men, the Battle for Okinawa would demand a huge concentration of Allied forces and dwarf the action on Iwo Jima. Furthermore, since the Japanese had considerably more air power avail-

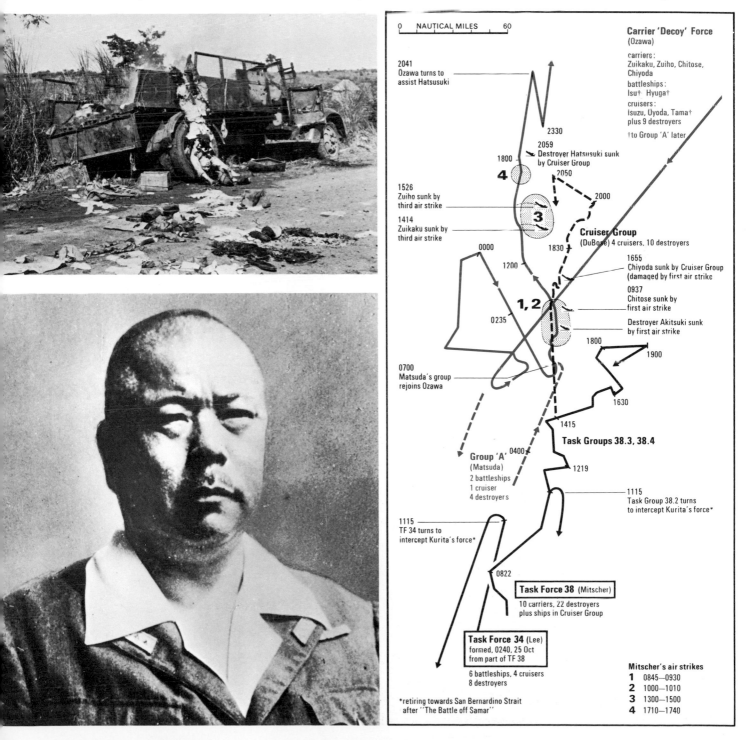

**Carrier 'Decoy' Force** (Ozawa)

carriers: Zuikaku, Zuiho, Chitose, Chiyoda
battleships: Ise†  Hyuga†
cruisers: Isuzu, Oyoda, Tama†
plus 9 destroyers
†to Group 'A' later

2041 Ozawa turns to assist Hatsusuki

2330

2059 Destroyer Hatsusuki sunk by Cruiser Group
2050

1526 Zuiho sunk by third air strike
2000

1414 Zuikaku sunk by third air strike

**Cruiser Group** (DuBose) 4 cruisers, 10 destroyers

1655 Chiyoda sunk by Cruiser Group (damaged by first air strike

0937 Chitose sunk by first air strike

Destroyer Akitsuki sunk by first air strike

**Task Groups 38.3, 38.4**

1115 Task Group 38.2 turns to intercept Kurita's force*

**Group 'A'** (Matsuda) 2 battleships 1 cruiser 4 destroyers

1115 TF 34 turns to intercept Kurita's force*

0700 Matsuda's group rejoins Ozawa

**Task Force 38** (Mitscher)
10 carriers, 22 destroyers plus ships in Cruiser Group

**Task Force 34** (Lee) formed, 0240, 25 Oct from part of TF 38
6 battleships, 4 cruisers 8 destroyers

*retiring towards San Bernardino Strait after ''The Battle off Samar''

Mitscher's air strikes
1  0845–0930
2  1000–1010
3  1300–1500
4  1710–1740

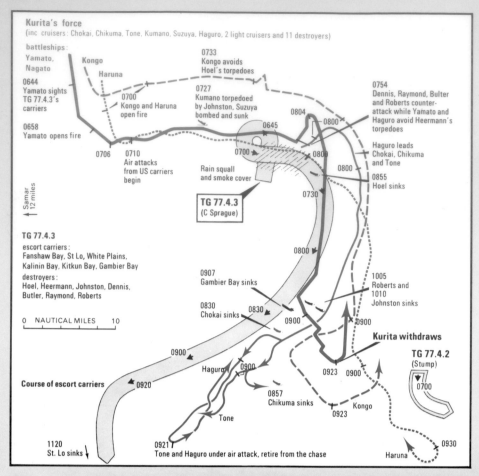

**Kurita's force**
(inc cruisers: Chokai, Chikuma, Tone, Kumano, Suzuya, Haguro, 2 light cruisers and 11 destroyers)

battleships:
Yamato,
Nagato

Kongo
Haruna

**0644**
Yamato sights
TG 77.4.3's
carriers

**0658**
Yamato opens fire

**0733**
Kongo avoids
Hoel's torpedoes

**0700**
Kongo and Haruna
open fire

**0727**
Kumano torpedoed
by Johnston, Suzuya
bombed and sunk

**0804**

**0800**

**0754**
Dennis, Raymond, Butler
and Roberts counter-
attack while Yamato and
Haguro avoid Heermann's
torpedoes

**0706**
**0710**
Air attacks
from US carriers
begin

**0645**

**0700**

Rain squall
and smoke cover

**TG 77.4.3**
(C Sprague)

**0800**

**0800**

**0730**

Haguro leads
Chokai, Chikuma
and Tone

**0855**
Hoel sinks

Samar
12 miles

**TG 77.4.3**
escort carriers:
Fanshaw Bay, St Lo, White Plains,
Kalinin Bay, Kitkun Bay, Gambier Bay
destroyers:
Hoel, Heermann, Johnston, Dennis,
Butler, Raymond, Roberts

0  NAUTICAL MILES  10

**0907**
Gambier Bay sinks

**0800**

**1005**
Roberts and
**1010**
Johnston sinks

**0830**
Chokai sinks

**0830**

**0900**

**Kurita withdraws**

**TG 77.4.2**
(Stump)

**Course of escort carriers**

**0920**

**0900**

Haguro

**0900**

**0857**
Chikuma sinks

**0923**  **0900**

**0923**  Kongo

**0700**

**0900**

Tone

**1120**
St. Lo sinks

**0921**
Tone and Haguro under air attack, retire from the chase

Haruna

**0930**

LEFT: Final stage of Leyte battle.

BELOW: The battleship *Missouri* as a Zero fighter is about to crash into the ship. In the Battle of Okinawa 1809 planes were committed to *kamikaze* attack, and few pilots survived.

able to them in the Ryukyus than on Iwo Jima, Allied forces could not expect to escape *kamikaze* attacks or more orthodox air strikes against their naval and land forces.

Operation Iceberg, as the Allied plan for invading Okinawa was called, was to become the most audacious and complex amphibious operation of the Pacific war. In preparation for the assault almost 300,000 troops were gathered and transported to Okinawa by a vast armada of transports, supply ships, and tankers accompanied by an Anglo–American force of several battleships, aircraft carriers, cruisers, and other vessels. Never had the Allies massed a larger task force in support of an amphibious operation.

If the Allies gave their all for the coming battle, the Japanese command on Okinawa was equally prepared to engage their enemies. As had been the case on Iwo Jima, the Japanese constructed

BELOW RIGHT: Crew members cheering 'banzai' after the lowering of the Naval Ensign on the sinking aircraft carrier *Zuikaku*, 25 October 1944, during the Leyte Gulf action.

BOTTOM: The battleship *Musashi* and other Japanese units under air attack during the Leyte Gulf battle.

RIGHT: A Yokosuka D4Y Judy makes a *kamikaze* dive on the USS *Essex (CV.9)* off the Philippines, 25 November 1944.

an elaborate series of subterranean fortifications on Okinawa. These sturdy defenses were supplemented by hundreds of gun emplacements. Furthermore, the Japanese command on Okinawa had over 2000 planes available for use against the Allies, with hundreds more no more than an hour or two away at Japanese air stations in Formosa, Kyushu, and southern Honshu. Never before had the Allies encountered such a formidable array of Japanese force.

American forces made their first landings on Okinawa on the morning of 1 April 1945. Unlike Iwo Jima, where the Marines had encountered heavy resistance from the moment of their first landing, Allied forces were not overtly resisted as they established their first beach-heads. Indeed, it was not until three days later that Japanese forces were first sighted and even then, the Japanese did not engage the Americans except for

*kamikaze* strikes against the Allied task force off Okinawa.

*Kamikaze* pilots systematically attacked the Allied task force off Okinawa during the first weeks of the battle for the island, sinking more than a dozen ships and damaging many others. In addition, the Japanese employed a new weapon, floating suicide squads made up of old battle wagons, against the Allied armada. The battleship *Yamato* accompanied by a small escort force had been sent to Okinawa with only enough fuel for a one-way voyage. Her magazines, however, were loaded with explosives and incendiaries, and it was hoped that she could be sent careering into the midst of the Allied fleet in a manner reminiscent of the *kamikaze* crashes onto the decks of Allied ships. The use of the *Yamato* for a floating *kamikaze* mission was a measure of the desperation of the Japanese and their determination to combat their enemies by any means.

Unfortunately for the Japanese, Allied reconnaissance planes spotted the *Yamato* before she reached the Allied fleet. When she arrived off Okinawa on 7 April 1945, she was attacked by almost 300 planes and sent to the bottom. With the sinking of the *Yamato*, the Allied fleet reigned supreme, but there was still hard going ahead before Okinawa was taken.

The destruction of the *Yamato* did not spare the Allied fleet from further attack. Indeed, from the very first day of the Battle for Okinawa until the end of the campaign, *kamikazes* regularly attacked the Allies. Furthermore such attacks were not limited to individual efforts to crash onto enemy ships but also included, for the first time in the war, use of massed *kamikaze* raids. These *kikusui* or 'floating chrysanthemum' raids, as the Japanese called them, were far more devestating than single *kamikaze* attacks and took a heavy toll of Allied ships. In some *kikusui*

LEFT: Battleship *Ise* fires on attacking planes during the Battle off Cape Engano, 25 October 1944. The ship was finally sunk in late July 1945.

BOTTOM LEFT: Three Japanese survivors of the Battle of Iwo Jima. Only 212 Japanese surrendered to the Americans, out of 23,000 men stationed on the island.

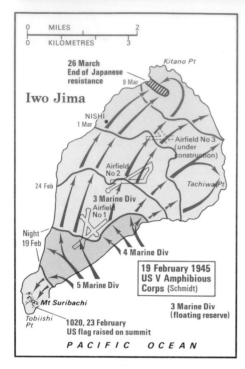

Iwo Jima

MILES 2

KILOMETRES 3

26 March
End of Japanese
resistance

9 Mar

*Kitano Pt*

NISHI
1 Mar

Airfield No 3
(under
construction)

Airfield
No 2

24 Feb

*Tachiwa Pt*

3 Marine Div
Airfield
No 1

Night
19 Feb

4 Marine Div

5 Marine Div

**19 February 1945
US V Amphibious
Corps** (Schmidt)

*Mt Suribachi*

3 Marine Div
(floating reserve)

*Tobiishi
Pt*

1020, 23 February
US flag raised on summit

PACIFIC OCEAN

planes. The toll of these raids was impressive. According to official histories of the United States Navy during the Second World War, the Japanese sunk at least 36 ships as a result of individual or massed suicide attacks and damaged at least 400 more ships, of which only 23 could be repaired and used during the remainder of the war.

If the Allies sustained considerable losses as a consequence of *kamikaze* attacks, Japanese losses were even more staggering. By the time the Battle for Okinawa was over late in June 1945, at least 1450 *kamikaze* pilots had given their lives for the glory of country and Emperor, and several hundred regular pilots were also lost in the skies over Okinawa. Their efforts, however, were in vain, for the Allies continued to press their campaign on Okinawa despite the *kamikazes* and the counterattack launched by Japanese land forces on the island.

On land, the battle for Okinawa involved some of the most bitter fighting of the Pacific war. Only Iwo Jima rivaled the Okinawa ordeal in sheer brutality and bloodletting. Given the cave and dug-out fortifications which dotted the island, Allied forces proceeded very slowly, supported by tanks, artillery, close air support, and naval bombardment. As had been the case on Iwo Jima, Japanese forces resisted this march every step of the way, launching counterattacks against the Americans and extracting exceptionally heavy casualties.

attacks as many as 350 planes were sent against enemy ships, and often these suicide missions were supplemented by conventional aerial attacks against the Allied task force.

Between 6 April and 22 June 1945 the Japanese flew over 3000 sacrificial *kamikaze* raids against Allied naval forces off Okinawa. In addition, Japanese pilots flying from Formosa and Japan flew hundreds of regular sorties using conventional dive-bombers and torpedo

BELOW: Kanoya airfield in southern Kyushu prior to the departure of Lt. Commander Goro Nonaka's *Ohka*-bomb carrying bombing group on a mission to attack US carrier forces operating off Japan, 21 March 1945. Almost all these bombers were shot down and no *Ohka* hits were made.

RIGHT: The Battle of Okinawa.

BOTTOM: Japanese cruiser *Kashii* sinking off the Indo-Chinese coast after being attacked by SB2Cs from Task Force 38. The cruiser was convoying a fleet of tankers and transports on 12 January 1945.

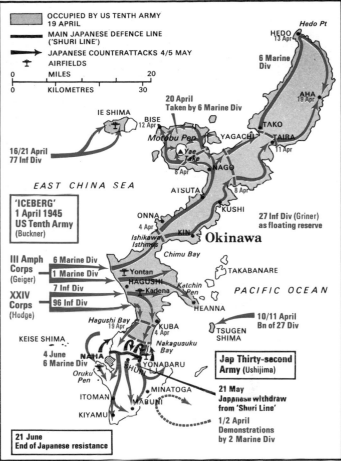

BELOW: Judy *kamikaze* carrier
dive bomber burning after
being hit by anti-aircraft fire
from the USS *Wasp (CV.18)*
off the Ryukyus, 18 March
1945.

BELOW: Japanese bodies on Okinawa. The cost in Japanese lives was high: 109,629. Okinawan civilians suffered losses of up to 100,000 more, but over 11,500 American lives were lost as well.

As American forces pressed their attack, the Japanese withdrew to successive series of caves and entrenchments. Each defense line was held until the last minute, at which time Japanese forces would retreat. As a result of this pattern, Okinawa was the most prolonged of any battle in the Pacific war save for Guadalcanal in 1943, and the cost of victory was the largest of any battle in the Pacific. By the time American forces finally achieved victory on 22 June 1945, losses had already amounted to more than 49,000 men, including 12,500 killed, while the Japanese had sacrificed more than 100,000 men in their effort to stop Allied progress toward Japan. If one adds to this the loss of equipment, the cost for victory on Okinawa staggers the imagination. It certainly made an indelible impression on Allied leaders contemplating the occupation of Japan. If the Japanese were willing to sacrifice more than 100,000 men for the defense of Okinawa, how many Japanese would die in the defense of their home land?

The Battle for Okinawa was the last major land battle of the Pacific war. Following their victory on Okinawa, Allied leaders began to prepare for an invasion of Japan proper, which was scheduled for 1946. Since the Japanese government still

BELOW: Japanese bodies on Okinawa. The cost in Japanese lives was high: 109,629. Okinawan civilians suffered losses of up to 100,000 more, but over 11,500 American lives were lost as well.

showed no sign of being willing to surrender and the Allies were not yet ready to launch their attack, the months between June and August 1945 saw Allied forces prepare for their invasion of Japan by escalating the strategic bombing of Japanese cities and industrial sites and by tightening the blockade they had established around Japan.

Since the Japanese depended upon imports for a good portion of their foodstuffs, Allied attacks on Japanese merchant shipping had a particularly devastating impact. Japanese merchant shipping had barely enough tonnage at the start of the war to handle Japan's needs. By 1945 the Japanese merchant fleet was a skeleton of its former self. Since Japanese shipyards had been virtually destroyed by Allied bombing raids, each time a merchant ship was sunk, the noose was tightened a

FAR LEFT: *Kamikaze* pilot on Kyushu before his final flight to Okinawa. He drew characters on his own back indicating that he planned to sink an American ship on his suicide mission.

LEFT: Japanese air defense organization collects scrap metal from civilians as vital supplies ran out in 1945.

BELOW: Ohka human-piloted rocket bomb is fixed to a Betty bomber as *kamikaze* pilots prepare for their mission.

BELOW CENTER: George fighter of the Japanese Army is waved farewell on Chiran airfield in Kyushu in April 1945.

BOTTOM: Japanese ship goes down after being hit by the USS *Aspro* in January 1945.

little more around the neck of the government in Tokyo. As General Tojo said after the war, the successful submarine war conducted by the United States Navy against Japanese merchant shipping was one of the main causes of Japan's defeat.

If the Allied blockade did not immediately break the back of Japan's resistance, the escalation of the strategic bombing of Japan's cities was no more successful in bringing the Japanese to the conference table. Despite the fact that between March and July 1945 strategic bombing raids against Japan had destroyed virtually all of her industrial facilities and left millions homeless and dead in their wake, the Japanese showed no sign of immediate capitulation. On the contrary, the Japanese appeared to be husbanding their resources in anticipation of the final Allied attack on

208

BELOW: War matériel was not
the only thing in short supply
towards the end of the war.
Food became increasingly
scarce, and parks were dug up
for the planting of rice, as in
this former pond in Tokyo's
city center.

RIGHT: The Ohka, a rocket powered suicide craft. It was nicknamed Baka (stupid in Japanese) by the Americans. It was piloted by one man and directed in *kamikaze* missions against US ships. It was carried by a bomber to its ultimate target.

BELOW RIGHT: Baka flying bomb in its storage bunker on Okinawa.

BOTTOM: The mangled body of a Japanese soldier, a member of an airborne unit that attempted a commando raid on Yontan airfield, Okinawa. He lies pinned under the wing of an attacking plane.

OVERLEAF: Over 35,000 university students enter military service in a rally called by the Japanese military in Tokyo near the Meiji Shrine.

their homeland. Whatever losses they had suffered, they were still, according to Allied intelligence, able to inflict monumental losses on any army of occupation.

In assessing the cost in life, limb, and matériel of an invasion of Japan, Allied leaders were obsessed by the specter of the *kamikaze*. If several thousand of these suicide pilots could wreak so much havoc on Allied forces in Leyte, Iwo Jima, and Okinawa, what might one expect when Japan was invaded? Would Allied troops encounter an armed nation of 90 million *kamikazes*? Such thoughts, however exaggerated, were commonly discussed and contributed, no doubt, to the ultimate decision to shorten the war by use of the new atomic weapons which were now available.

海軍志願
兵徴募

# CHINA-BURMA-INDIA

BELOW: Japanese seamen are decorated for valor in South China. As morale weakened when the final breakthrough against the Nationalists did not come, ceremonies of this kind became ever more frequent.

RIGHT: Japanese sharpshooters in their advance on Kuomintang positions in southwest China. The Japanese hoped that the Chiang régime would collapse after the fall of coastal China and all the major cities and industrial centers by 1939, but thanks to American support the Nationalists maintained their positions in southwest China.

As the Japanese onslaught against the Western colonial powers in Asia began to wind down in the spring of 1942, the Fifteenth Army under General Shojiro Iida found itself firmly in control of the British colony of Burma. British command in India had officially abandoned the country at the end of April, leaving only a portion of the far north held by Chin and Kachin tribesmen out of Japanese hands. As the British had made no particular provision for the defense of Burma, Iida's troops, aided by a population largely hostile to British rule, had had an easy campaign. Yet Burma was not to be quickly overrun and then forgotten – a backwater on the periphery of the war – but was instead to remain an area of intense combat throughout the war years.

A transit area between China and India, Burma had been invaded primarily to secure the southwest flank of China. After seizing the main population areas of China in 1937–38, the Japanese had not deemed it wise to attempt to pursue the forces of the Kuomintang leader Chiang Kai-shek into the mountainous interior of the country. The immediate strategy was to cut the routes over which foreign supplies reached Chiang at his base of Chungking. The 1941 non-aggression pact between Japan and the Soviet Union ended Soviet aid to China, while the occupation of French Indochina in 1940

closed the road and rail route from Hanoi to Kunming. A marginal amount of supplies had come in via the British colony of Hong Kong which fell in December 1941, but the most important route was the road between Kunming in Yunnan in southwest China and Lashio in northern Burma, hewed by hand by 100,000 Chinese coolies in 1937 and 1938. Supplies were docked in Rangoon, shipped up the Irrawaddy River to Lashio, and thence to China over what came to be known as the Burma Road. This supply route was so important to China that Chiang volunteered his best troops, the German-trained Fifth and Sixth Armies, for the defense of Burma in 1942. This move did not forestall the loss of Burma and the closing of the Burma Road, but it did cost Chiang his armies which were virtually shattered in the campaign.

Japan also had no designs on India at this time but had wished to include the important rice exporting country of Burma within the new 'Greater East Asia Co-prosperity Sphere'. The modest British and Indian forces in India were demoralized and ill-equipped and were considered to present little threat. The pestilential border area between Burma and India was thought to constitute a natural barrier as it had few communications. Posting troops to guard the several possible approaches from India, the Japanese in Burma were content to remain on the defensive after the spring of 1942, even shifting some of their air power from Burma to the campaigns in the Pacific.

The Japanese in Burma had little to fear in 1942 as the war priorities of the Allies had placed Europe first, the Pacific second, and what was termed the 'China–Burma–India Theater' or CBI last. China was now completely isolated and no longer taking an active part in the war. Having born the brunt of the war with Japan since 1937, the Kuomintang under Chiang Kai-shek believed that China had already done its share and that the war would be won elsewhere by China's new allies, Britain and the United States. Prime Minister Winston Churchill had little respect for the corrupt government of Chiang or for China's military capacity and, once Burma had fallen, had no other interest beyond regaining Burma and Malaya. The British were therefore quite unsympathetic with the American determination to break the blockade of China and ultimately to use China as a base against Japan. Thus

British aims in the CBI were much more limited than those of their American allies. While the immediate efforts of the Americans were directed toward opening an air supply route from northeast India to China, the immediate British interest was to strike in Burma as quickly as possible.

Whether it was launching the air supply route over the 'hump' or launching however limited an offensive against Burma, India was a difficult base from which to attempt either. An agricultural land with a population of over 400 million already on the verge of famine, India had no surplus capacity for military effort and could not be an important source of supplies. India also lay 12,000 miles from the main source of supplies, which was the United States. After over two months in transit from America, supplies had to be docked at Bombay and Karachi on the west coast of India and trans-shipped 1500 miles to eastern India and Assam where the forward Allied air bases and defenses lay. Heat, dust, disease and bad food made India and Assam an extremely difficult and debilitating environment for occidental troops. Accepting the opportunity offered by the war, the Indian nationalist movement under Mohandas K. Gandhi was undertaking a campaign

LEFT: Japanese infantry rest during the gruelling campaign against the Kuomintang. The difficult terrain of southwest China worked against the Japanese to an even greater extent than the opposition of the Nationalist armies, which was sporadic and listless in the initial years of the campaign.

RIGHT: Japanese machine gunners take up a position above a town in northwest China. The Japanese were fighting both the Communists in the northwest and the Nationalists in the southwest.

BELOW RIGHT: Japanese 75mm gun fires a salvo in the mountainous terrain of southwest China in 1942.

of civil disobedience which led to widespread strife and sabotage.

The most formidable problem faced by the Allies in India was the fact that the Indian transportation system was wholly inadequate for moving large quantities of supplies from western India to Assam. The road system was simply undeveloped. Motor transport could not seriously be considered, even if there had been a sufficient number of trucks. The burden, therefore, fell on the rail system which was subject to numerous delays and breakdowns under the new wartime requirements. The initial problem was somewhat alleviated by a trans-India air cargo service, and by 1943 it was possible to bring in supplies through Calcutta on the eastern coast of India as the Japanese naval threat in the Bay of Bengal had receded. A large program to construct pipelines and improve the Assam-Bengal Railway up the Brahmaputra Valley had to be launched with all the attendant difficulties of any wartime project in India. Until these logistic improvements could be made, the flow of supplies over the hump to China would be a trickle and the British ability to strike at Burma would remain limited. The overall question was that although the Allies paid lip service to the importance of China and Burma, the CBI in practice enjoyed the lowest priority of all the Allied theaters of the war in the allocation of resources, a fact which meant that CBI remained starved for men and matériel throughout the war.

CBI was primarily a British and Chinese theater. For the United States, it was almost entirely an air rather than a ground theater as there were never more than a few thousand American tactical ground troops in CBI, mainly OSS and commando units such as Merrill's Marauders. The theater came under the command of General Joseph 'Vinegar Joe' Stilwell, a tough and able fighter who never quite grasped the nature of his mission in CBI. The American units under his command were the Tenth American Air Force in India and the China Air Task Force at Kunming under Claire Chennault. Chennault had left the U.S. Air Force in 1937 to serve as an adviser to the air force of Chiang Kai-shek. He had subsequently been asked to form a group of mercenary pilots for the air defense of China. The new American Volunteer Group saw its first action in the defense of Burma. In conjunction with a few British squadrons, the AVG had fought well

LEFT: Vinegar Joe Stilwell
enjoys his C rations on
Christmas morning 1943 in
northern Burma during the
Allied advance which he
pressed upon Chiang Kai-shek.
Chiang was more interested in
attacking Burma than in
liberating coastal China, a
point which Stilwell took badly.

BELOW: Sgts. Mocklin and
Freeman of the USAAF talk to
a Chinese pilot they helped to
train beside an American
fighter given to the Nationalists
in 1943. The Kuomintang air
force eventually became a
formidable weapon, and with
the 14th Air Force began to
drive the Japanese from key
airfields in South China in 1944.

against overwhelming opposition, downing four and five Japanese planes for each AVG plane lost. After the fall of Burma, the AVG had moved to Kunming where it constituted China's only air defense against the Japanese. In July 1942 the AVG was incorporated into the US Air Force as the China Air Task Force and subsequently became the US Fourteenth Air Force.

As Chief of Staff of the Nationalist Chinese Armies, Stilwell also had control of the Chinese troops who had escaped from Burma to India. These were now being retrained and re-equipped at Ramgarh while more Chinese troops were being assembled in Yunnan for the same purpose.

British headquarters in India had fifteen divisions available after the end of the Burma retreat, but most were newly formed and lacked equipment, training and experienced officers. Only three divisions were actually in condition to undertake operations. In April 1942 the British commander, General Sir Archibald Wavell, organized his forces into three regional commands, with Eastern Command under General Noel Irwin the operational one. The Allied position was improving in at least one respect, however, as a flow of new aircraft was redressing the Japanese superiority in air power. Fortunately for the Allies, the Japanese were never motivated to launch a sustained air offensive against Assam and northeast India but made only a few sporadic raids in 1942 which went virtually unopposed.

In October 1942 Chiang put forward a plan for the reconquest of Burma. Chinese, British and Indian forces would strike from Assam while other Chinese forces advanced from Yunnan in a pincer movement. A seaborne attack was also to be made on Rangoon. The plan was much beyond British capabilities in air and manpower, but when Wavell pointed out his limitations, Chiang angrily withdrew. Under pressure from Churchill to take some action, Wavell attempted to recover part of the coast of Arakan with an advance by the Fourteenth Indian Division. A neat Japanese counterstroke turned the effort into a dismal and costly failure.

The next British effort against Burma was led by Brigadier Orde Wingate, a brilliant and unorthodox soldier who advocated guerrilla warfare on the model of T. E. Lawrence and the Arab Revolt of

FAR LEFT: Japanese infantry advance over difficult terrain in South China. These advances became increasingly sporadic as troops were diverted to the Pacific in 1942-43.

CENTER LEFT: Japanese troops cross a river in Chekiang south of Shanghai as they consolidate positions in South China.

LEFT: Lieutenant General Stilwell, flanked by Major General Sun Li-jen and Lieutenant General Lo Choying, inspect Chinese troops at the Ramgarh Training Center in India.

BELOW: Chinese Nationalist troops move through a village east of Tuyun in South China in 1944 during their offensive. The Chinese people often feared the Nationalists as much as the Japanese.

World War I. Wavell approved a long range penetration by 3000 commandos, known as 'Chindits', to disrupt the enemy lines of communication. In a two-month operation of no strategic significance, Wingate temporarily put a Burmese railway out of action and lost a third of his men. Wingate was killed in a plane crash at the beginning of a second and larger operation. As he had provided a model of exciting warfare with an emphasis on individual performance, the British propaganda machine overnight turned him into a hero. One of the more important results of the first Chindit operation, however, was that it made General Kawabe, the Japanese commander in Burma, aware that the Burma–India frontier was not impenetrable and that a British offensive was in the making.

Although various other operations for Burma were considered for the dry season of 1943, the logistic and administrative difficulties were much too great and all plans were shelved. Stilwell continued to train his Chinese troops in India and Yunnan while the US Air Force continued to build air fields and pipelines in India and Assam in an effort to get more supplies to China where Chennault was proposing an air offensive against the Japanese. Combined British and American efforts continued to improve the logistics between India and Assam. Guerrilla operations by tribesmen in North Burma were beginning while Allied intelligence became aware for the first time that the Burmese nationalists were disenchanted with their Japanese liberators and were organizing their own resistance movement. In military terms, however, the most important trend was that the RAF and the US Tenth Air Force were beginning to contest Japanese air superiority over Burma. Throughout 1943 and into 1944 the struggle for the air increased in vigor. The continuing Allied build-up in India now made it evident that the Japanese forces in Burma could now no longer safely remain on the defensive.

The Allies had now agreed that the conquest of North Burma must be a primary objective in order to reopen the Burma Road. The aim was to build up Chinese forces for an effort against the Japanese and to supply an offensive by the Fourteenth Air Force. Although not explicitly stated in Allied policy, it was expected that all of Burma would be cleared in the process. The CBI Theater had been reorganized with the Southeast

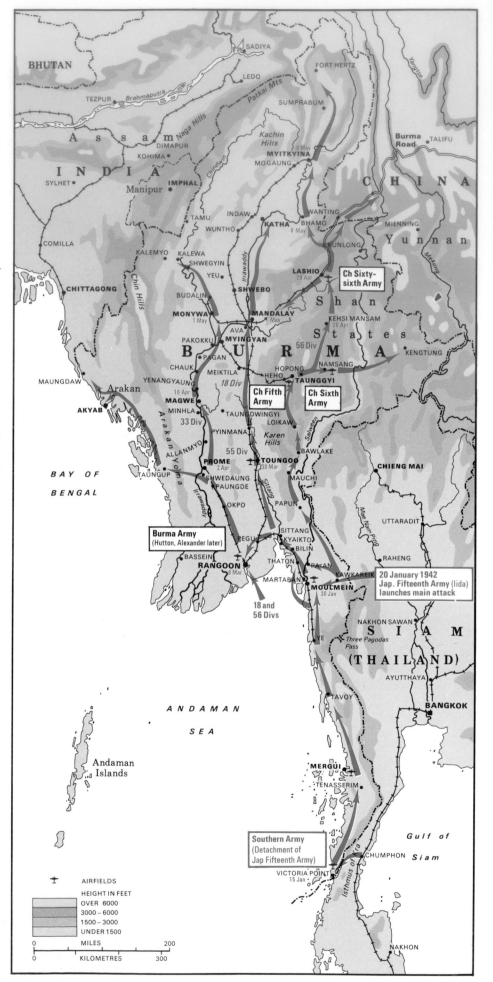

Asia Command or SEAC under Admiral Lord Louis Mountbatten as the operational body. Stilwell now served as deputy to Mountbatten but also as Chinese Chief of Staff. Wavell was made Viceroy of India while the duties of Commander-in-Chief in India fell to Sir Claude Auchinleck. The newly-formed Fourteenth Army

BELOW: P-40A fighter of the Nationalist air force flown by the Flying Tigers of the AVG (American Volunteer Group) prepares for take-off from Burma in 1941.

BELOW CENTER: General Renya Mutaguchi chats with a Japanese soldier in Burma during the 1942 offensive which brought the whole of the British colony under Japanese rule.

BOTTOM LEFT: Lieutenant General Masakazu Kawabe, Commander of the Japanese Burma Area Army.

BELOW RIGHT: An early photograph of Mutaguchi, who was C-in-C of the Japanese 15th Army in Burma.

under General William Slim intended a limited offensive in Arakan as preparation for a subsequent and larger offensive to clear Burma. Slim's idea was to move into the jungle, create strongholds supplied from the air, and then crush the counter-attacking enemy between these and his subsequent all-out drive. The air power to support this tactic was now available with 48 British and 19 American squadrons totalling around 850 planes. There were also now enough cargo planes for airborn supply operations while more could be borrowed from the India–China airlift. Operations were to begin in the dry season of 1944, concurrently with a pincer movement from Assam and Yunnan by Chinese troops under Stilwell.

The Allied offensive which was so obviously in preparation caused the Japanese to undertake a spoiling operation of their own. Realizing that they faced potential attack from fourteen divisions in China and from up to six in India, the Japanese planned to occupy the Imphal plain and thus deprive the Allies of their staging bases for attack on Burma and for support of China. Such a move would also cut Stilwell's operations off from supplies and reinforcements. Although this offensive was mainly preventive in its inspiration, there was a considerable propaganda fanfare about a 'march on Delhi' which stemmed from the presence of the Indian National Army. Led by a 46-year old former Mayor of Calcutta named Subhas Chandra Bose, the INA was the military arm of the Azad Hind or Free India movement among the overseas Indians in Southeast Asia (there were 800,000 Indians in Malaya alone). Bose dreamed of marching on Delhi at the head of his forces to liberate India from British rule, but the Japanese Army only wanted his men as guides, spies and liaison troops. In the end, the INA was allowed three fighting divisions of 2000 men each with the rest of its forces as auxiliary troops. The Japanese Army reserved for itself the right of gaining the first victory on Indian soil, however, and intended to offer the capture of Imphal as a birthday present to the Emperor.

At the top of the Japanese command structure was General Kawabe, under whom were three armies: the 33rd under General Honda in the northeast, the 28th under General Sakurai on the Arakan front, and the 15th under General Mutaguchi on the central front. Each of these armies was roughly equivalent to a British army corps. After preparatory

FAR LEFT: Japanese troops parade before the Governor's House in Rangoon after its capture in 1942.

LEFT: Poster in Burma in the early days of the Anti-Fascist Peoples Freedom League (the AFPFL), organized by Burmese nationalists to help Britain liberate the colony in return for independence after the war. It was led by Aung San, who was assassinated a few months before Burma became independent in January 1948.

BELOW: Japanese forces advance in South China in a renewed effort to overwhelm Chiang's armies.

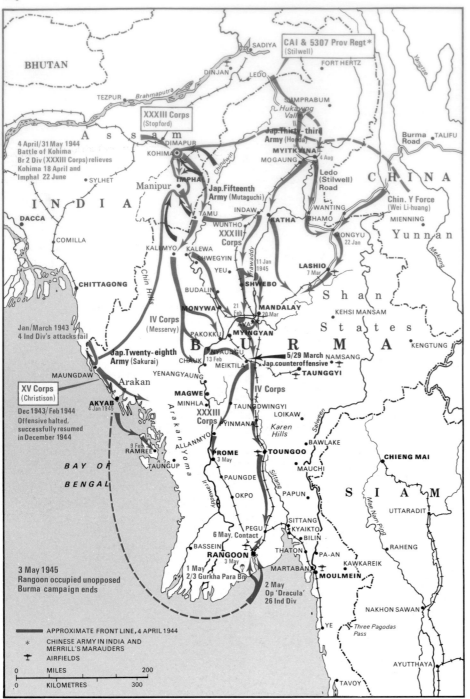

BHUTAN

ASSAM

INDIA

XXXIII Corps
(Stopford)

4 April/31 May 1944
Battle of Kohima
Br 2 Div (XXXIII Corps) relieves
Kohima 18 April and
Imphal 22 June

SADIYA
DINJAN
TEZPUR
DIMAPUR
KOHIMA
SYLHET
Manipur
IMPHAL
Jap. Fifteenth
Army (Mutaguchi)

CAI & 5307 Prov Regt *
(Stilwell)

FORT HERTZ

SUMPRABUM
Hukawng
Valley
Jap. Thirty-third
Army (Honda)
MYITKYINA
MOGAUNG      4 Aug
Ledo
(Stilwell)
Road
WANTING

LEDO

Burma
Road      TALIFU

CHINA

Chin. Y Force
(Wei Li-huang)

Yunnan

MIENNING
BHAMO
TONGYU
22 Jan

Mekong

DACCA
COMILLA

TAMU
WUNTHO
INDAW
KATHA
XXXIII
Corps
YEU
SHWEGYIN
BUDALIN

LASHIO
7 Mar

Shan

CHITTAGONG

Jan/March 1943
4 Ind Div's attacks fail

Chin Hills
KALEMYO KALEWA

Chindwin

11 Jan
1945
SHWEBO
21
Feb
MONYWA
IV Corps
(Messervy)
PAKOKKU

MANDALAY
20 Mar
AVA
MYINGYAN

KEHSI MANSAM

States

MAUNGDAW
Jap. Twenty-eighth
Army (Sakurai)
CHAUK
13 Feb
NYAUNGU
MEIKTILA

5/29 March NAMSANG
Jap. counteroffensive
TAUNGGYI

KENGTUNG

Arakan
YENANGYAUNG

XV Corps
(Christison)
AKYAB
4 Jan 1945

MAGWE
MINHLA

IV Corps

Dec 1943/Feb 1944
Offensive halted,
successfully resumed
in December 1944

Arakan Yoma

TAUNGDWINGYI
LOIKAW

XXXIII
Corps
YINMANA

Karen
Hills

BAWLAKE

Salween

CHIENG MAI

9 Feb
RAMREE
ALLANMYO
PROME
3 May

BAY OF
BENGAL

Irrawaddy

TAUNGUP

PAUNGDE
OKPO

Sittang

TOUNGOO
MAUCHI
PAPUN

SIAM

UTTARADIT

3 May 1945
Rangoon occupied unopposed
Burma campaign ends

BASSEIN
6 May. Contact
PEGU
RANGOON
3 May
1 May
2/3 Gurkha Para Bn

SITTANG
KYAIKTO
BILIN
THATON
MARTABAN

2 May
Op 'Dracula'
26 Ind Div

PA-AN
MOULMEIN

KAWKAREIK

Mae Nam Ping

RAHENG

NAKHON SAWAN

YE
Three Pagodas
Pass

AYUTTHAYA

TAVOY

——— APPROXIMATE FRONT LINE, 4 APRIL 1944
*    CHINESE ARMY IN INDIA AND
     MERRILL'S MARAUDERS
✈    AIRFIELDS

0        MILES        200
0      KILOMETRES     300

attacks against Arakan and Yunnan, the drive on Imphal was to be launched the forces of Mutaguchi.

In mid-March three Japanese divisions began their drive on Imphal, unaffected by ·a second and larger Chindit penetration into the valley of the Irrawaddy River. The Fourth Corps of General Sir Geoffrey Scoones had already begun Allied operations by slowly moving southward from Imphal in three columns, but on receiving intelligence of the possibility of a Japanese offensive, it halted and took up defensive positions. The Japanese move actually cut off one of Scoones' divisions while a flanking advance from the Chindwin area was also forcing a British withdrawal in the north. A deep flanking movement then cut the Imphal-Kohima Road at the end of March and required the British to move up three fresh divisions from India. Four divisions were then deployed in defensive positions on

the Imphal Plain, but Kohima to the north was held by only 1500 men. The Dimapur-Kohima area was assigned to Lieutenant General Montagu Stopford and his 33rd Corps, but the Japanese began their attack on Kohima on 4 April before the bulk of the corps had arrived from India.

The Kohima garrison suddenly found itself cut off from its reinforcements which in turn were cut off from their base at Dimapur. A general counteroffensive in the area was ordered by General Slim on 10 April. After heavy fighting two relieving brigades rescued the exhausted troops defending Kohima and began operations to clear the Japanese from the surrounding area.

The fighting around Kohima had been fierce but the struggle for Imphal surpassed it. The operations of the Third Tactical Air Force under Air Marshal Sir John Baldwin which were annihilating

Japanese air strength in Burma became a key factor. For their Imphal campaign to have any chance of real success the Japanese had to throw the bulk of their air power into support. Here the issue was decided as the 576 fighters and 149 bombers of the Allies destroyed 117 planes over Imphal and forced the Japanese air force into essentially defensive actions. Within two months another 85 Japanese planes had been downed, and Allied control of the air over Burma could no longer be challenged. This development meant that the Allies could make unrestricted use of air supply, first to keep the Imphal garrison alive during the Japanese siege, and subsequently to supply virtually their entire offensive in Burma as land communications were so execrable. As an added bonus, the hump airlift was now free from Japanese air harassment and greatly expanded its supply capacity for China.

Thus 28,000 British and 30,000 Indian troops endured a heavy siege at Imphal supplied entirely by air. The fighting at Imphal was characterized by hand to hand combat of such savagery that a Japanese journalist likened it to Verdun in World War I. Stopford's forces were pushing down the Imphal-Kohima Road in May, however, while Scoones' men were pressing from the south. At this point Mutaguchi could withdraw in good order and for good reasons. His troops were short of supplies and no longer had hope of receiving more as his makeshift lines of communication were long and ran through very difficult country. As the Japanese no longer had any air cover, the supply lines had been cut by Allied air attacks in any event. Yet despite the deterioration in his position, Mutaguchi clung on to the siege of Imphal in spite of fierce dissent from his subordinates. He was soon driven to relieve all three of his divisional commanders in his obstinacy. The siege had been broken by late May and a general counterattack begun by Slim's forces. Starving and disease ridden, the remnants of the Japanese invading force were saved only by retreating into the monsoonal rains.

General Kawabe had sent 85,000 men against India, but only 32,000 returned. The campaign had been so severe that for the first time in the war, Japanese morale cracked and some troops actually surrendered. Even measured against 16,700 British and Indian casualties, Imphal was the worst disaster suffered by the Jap-

RIGHT: Subhas Chandra Bose, leader of the Indian National Army, a Japanese puppet who purported to liberate India from the British, makes a speech in Malaya under Japanese auspices.

BELOW RIGHT: Japanese infantrymen pause before a Buddhist shrine in Burma.

anese Army in World War II. A number of factors had contributed to create this debacle. The loss of complete air superiority to the Allies was decisive. There had also been poor staff work on the part of an army not familiar with campaigning in the tropics. The only large scale tropical campaign fought by the Japanese Army had been in Malaya. Most training was still geared to temperate climates. The favored tactic of forcing the enemy to retreat by hooking movements around his flanks had failed for the first time after its brilliant use in the Burma and Malaya campaigns of 1942. Slim's tactics were not to retreat but, relying on air supply, to stand and fight. On the basis of the British and Indian performance in Malaya, a gross underestimation of the fighting ability of the enemy had led to supreme over-confidence on the part of the Japanese. Incidentally, the INA had mostly deserted when the shooting began. Bose was discredited and subsequently died in a plane crash while trying to escape to the Soviet Union.

On 3 June 1944 the Combined Chiefs of Staff ordered Mountbatten to improve the air link with China and re-open the Burma Road. With high hopes Stilwell had opened a limited offensive in North Burma with Chinese troops in February. One force was slowly pushing into the Hukawng Valley from Ledo in Assam, building a road as it proceeded. Another force was reluctantly advancing from Yunnan and making slow progress. Under the new Combined Chiefs of Staff directive, Stilwell's mission was to clear North Burma while Slim's forces seized Rangoon to force a Japanese evacuation of North Burma. The overall role of the China Theater was now to support the coming Allied offensives in the Pacific. This could only be accomplished by Chennault's Fourteenth Air Force, which needed an augmented airlift and the re-opening of the Burma Road. Stilwell's forces managed to capture the key airfield at Myitkyina in May but failed to conquer the town itself until August. The capture of the airfield assisted the airlift greatly as Myitkyina could now be used as a base as well as the southern and easier route over the hump to China. The Burma Road never did regain its place as the primary supply route for China, however, since Lashio was not recaptured until January 1945 and after that, the road was only used for the one-way delivery of vehicles and artillery to China. The Ledo Road was used to supply the Myitkyina

LEFT: Japanese bombers over Rangoon in 1942.

BELOW LEFT: Japanese troops advance down a road in Burma on a captured British Bren gun carrier. The trucks behind were also sequestered from the retreating British forces.

area, and that town was quickly turned into a major supply depot for the campaign to clear to the remainder of Burma.

Following the Japanese defeat at Imphal, two plans were developed by Mountbatten and Slim to destroy the Japanese hold on Burma. 'Dracula' was an amphibious operation against southern Burma, but since it required outside supplies such as landing craft, it was given lower priority than 'Capital', an overland drive into north-central Burma. The plan was that once on the central plain of Burma, Slim's tanks, artillery and air power could be used to maximum effect against the enemy. Operations could not begin until the dry season recommenced in October 1944. The intervening period was used to reorganize for the coming operations. Because the land communications of Burma were so poor, all operations depended on

RIGHT: The 15th Army moves down a narrow trail toward Imphal, where the toughest battle of the Burmese campaign was fought.

air supply; thus this key function was centralized under a command designated as the Combat Cargo Task Force. The 'Special Force' units were disbanded while the intelligence services were better coordinated. Some changes in command were made as well. General Sir Oliver Leese was made Commander-in-Chief of Allied Land Forces, Southeast Asia, under Mountbatten.

The most significant change in command came in the month that the new operations were to begin. Stilwell had been a controversial figure in CBI and in the Allied councils of war since his appointment as theater commander in 1942. Through no fault of Stilwell's the Japanese had shattered his Chinese forces in the invasion of Burma in that year. He was a soldier's soldier who wanted desperately to fight to redeem himself, but there was little fighting to be done. Stilwell never accepted the fact that what the Allies required of China was not offensives against the enemy but only survival. His relationship with Chiang was acrimonious largely because of his frustration at Chiang's refusal to fight more than when it was absolutely necessary. Stilwell was in conflict with Chennault over the allocation of the modest tonnage flown at great cost over the hump. The former wanted equipment for his Yunnan force to invade Burma while the latter needed gasoline and bombs for the planes of his Fourteenth Air Force. Allied strategists tended to favor Chennault's proposals for air offensives against Japan over Stilwell's costly and myopic plans to clear North Burma, reopen the Burma Road, and build up the Chinese armies to drive Japan from China. The politics surrounding the blunt personality of Stilwell finally angered Chiang to the point of demanding his recall. General Albert Wedemeyer, a man of more diplomatic mien, replaced Stilwell as Chief of Staff to Chiang and subsequently achieved some more tangible results through better working relationships with the Chinese and the British.

When the rains let up in October 1944, the Burma Area Army under General Kimura was ordered to block the Allied offensive to prevent the reopening of the Burma Road for an attack from Burma on Malaya. With General MacArthur and Admiral Nimitz attacking Leyte in the Philippines that same month, there were, of course, to be no reinforcements for Burma. Japanese strength in Burma had been shattered by the debacle at Imphal.

There was only one division in southern Burma to cover Rangoon while four divisions of the Fifteenth Army, a total of 21,000 men, faced nine strong British and Indian divisions. Other Japanese forces were attempting to hold the Chinese troops under Wedemeyer moving south from Myitkyina toward Lashio and the Burma Road. There was no air cover for the Japanese forces. In all, Kimura realized how poor his prospects were and knew that the Japanese position in North Burma was probably untenable, but he still hoped to hold a line across Mandalay and the Yenangyaung oil fields.

In mid-November the 33rd Corps of Stopford and the Fourth Corps of Messervy were over the Chindwin River, hoping to encircle the Japanese forces defending the Shwebo Plain. The Japanese withdrew on Mandalay, hence Slim sent Messervy due south to cut their communications with Rangoon and block their retreat. By March the Japanese were under serious pressure at Mandalay and had abandoned North Burma to Wedemeyer's advance. It was at Mandalay that the Japanese suffered their first attack from disenchanted Burmese nationalist forces, which at this point were also prepared to fight the returning British. The troops at Mandalay fought doggedly, repulsing repeated British attacks, while a counteroffensive was launched against Messervy around Meiktila. But the counteroffensive failed and Mandalay fell to Stopford's troops on 20 March. What was left of the Fifteenth Army retreated to the south as best it could, leaving central Burma to the victorious British and the road to Rangoon open.

Slim now decreed that Messervy's corps was to drive on Rangoon along the main road and rail route while Stopford did the same along both banks of the Irrawaddy. The former would continue to be supplied by air while the latter was to be sustained by riverine transport. Time was pressing, however, as the monsoon was due in May and would curtail the air supply on which the entire campaign had thus far depended. China was also in crisis, hence many of the cargo planes on which Slim depended were due to be shifted there in June. It was imperative, therefore, that Rangoon be secured before the monsoon broke. Operation Dracula thus was put into effect as insurance on 1 May by a British division, a tank regiment and a Gurkha parachute battalion. The Japanese had evacuated

LEFT: Chiang Kai-shek poses with Albert Wedemeyer after he replaced Stilwell in 1944. Chiang looks pleased, since he urged Roosevelt to sack Stilwell.

BELOW: Japan's puppet rulers pose with General Tojo in Tokyo. From left to right: U Ba Maw of Burma, Chou Kei-kai of Manchuria, Wang Ching-wei of Japan's Nationalist rival of Chiang in Nanking, Tojo, Prime Minister Phibul Songgram of Thailand, José P. Laurel of the Philippines, which was given nominal independence in 1943, and Subhas Chandra Bose of the Indian National Army.

RIGHT: Japanese troops use elephants to carry supplies during their retreat in Burma.

Rangoon during the last week of April, enabling the British to enter the city on 2 May unopposed. The city was in fact already under the control of Burmese nationalist troops under then Colonel Ne Win. Four days later, the troops of Operation Dracula met advance units of Messervy's force moving south.

The Burma campaign was essentially completed with the recapture of Rangoon. General William Slim had gained a complete and decisive victory, destroying three Japanese armies in the field during a brilliantly executed campaign. The Japanese generals and their men had fought tenaciously, but lacking air cover and supply, they were no match for the well-equipped and supplied Allied troops. The Japanese had also had to contend with the mainline Burmese resistance (as opposed to the guerrillas of the hill areas). Frustrated with the Japanese failure to allow true independence, the mainline Burmese nationalists had been cooperating with the British Force 136 since late 1943 and had launched a full scale offensive against the Japanese in March 1945. The nationalist leader Aung San had reached an accommodation with Slim and Mountbatten which prevented hostilities between the returning British and the well organized and armed nationalists. Burma subsequently achieved her long sought independence through negotiation rather than armed struggle.

Well before the Burma campaign got underway in the fall of 1944, the other combat area of CBI suddenly flared up with major offensives by the Japanese in China. After halting major operations against Chiang Kai-shek in 1938, the Japanese had been largely quiescent, preferring to blockade China and trying to draw Chiang into a separate peace to take China out of the war. It was thought that the constant strain of war and of the confrontation with the Communist forces of Mao Tse-tung in north, China would sooner or later bring Chiang to the negotiating table. And indeed, between 1938 and 1944, there were steady defections to the Japanese and the collaborationist government of Wang Ching-wei. The Chinese Communists, for example, estimated that no fewer than 27 Kuomintang generals changed sides. China not only had to cope with over a million Japanese troops but also with the continuing civil war between Chiang's Nationalists and Mao's Communists. Chiang employed 200,000 of his best troops to cordon off the Communist area around Yenan and blocked any American aid to Mao. The Communists for their part were eventually able to carry out some limited guerrilla warfare and to restrict the Japanese in their area increasingly to the towns while slowly bringing more and more of the countryside under their control.

Thus, from 1938 to 1944 the war in China was characterized by sporadic small-scale actions of minor military consequence. Occupying the cities and major towns, the Japanese were harassed by guerrilla activity and in many places could only venture into the countryside in great force. In return, the Japanese carried out sporadic raids and did much damage to the countryside. In some parts of the country, there was no fighting and the opponents reached a profitable modus vivendi through small scale trade. The Japanese Navy in particular was noted for its trafficking with the Chinese. Little territory had changed hands since 1938 in this stalemated war.

It was neither the Chinese nor the Japanese but the Americans who caused the stalemate in China to end. As the amount of supplies that could be flown over the hump increased, the Fourteenth Air Force had been intensifying its operations. Gasoline and bombs were always in short supply but even so, the successors of the Flying Tigers were destroying 50,000 tons of Japanese shipping per month. With sufficient supplies and planes, Chennault had hoped that his force could be the agent for the aerial destruction of Japan. He had also maintained that his planes could thwart a Japanese land offensive in China if need be. One source of the conflict between Chennault and Stilwell was the latter's doubt about the value of air power against ground troops and his firm conviction that the Japanese would attack the east China bases of the Fourteenth Air Force if it became more than a nuisance. The new Allied strategy of February 1944 was to build up the Fourteenth Air Force to support the Pacific offensives against Japan, which explains the need to clear north Burma for supply purposes. With an improved flow of supplies coming over the hump in late 1943, Chennault then undertook an air offensive which swept the China coasts of Japanese shipping, thus severely interdicting Japanese sea communications with Southeast Asia. But Chennault was soon severely handicapped by a new shortage of supplies as he now had a competitor in China in Project Matterhorn.

The new and untried American super bomber – the B-29 – was sent to China in early 1944 to fulfill the long cherished American ambition of bombing Japan from Chinese bases and as part of the political price paid to Chiang Kai-shek for his participation in the Burma campaign. This decision unwisely placed a voracious new consumer of supplies in a theater which had always been a logistic nightmare. Four B-29 bases were established around Chengtu and their defense given to the 312th Fighter Wing as its sole responsibility. This new operation ran the Fourteenth Air Force acutely short of gasoline in particular and indeed, the B-29s themselves were used to haul gasoline when not on tactical missions. Yet all told, the B-29s flew only twenty

missions from Chengtu – nine to Japan, ten to Manchuria, and one to Formosa. The official American postwar assessment stated that these missions 'did little to hasten the Japanese surrender or justify the lavish expenditures poured out on their behalf through a fantastically uneconomic and barely workable supply system'. Wedemeyer finally prevailed on the Joint Chiefs of Staff to withdraw the last of the B-29s by January 1945. Only after the new bombers were flying from bases in the Marianas did the effective air bombardment of Japan really commence and the B-29 fulfill its potential.

Even before the B-29s arrived in China to menace Japan, however, the Fourteenth Air Force had in fact hurt the Japanese enough for them to undertake an offensive and thus fulfill Stilwell's prophecy. The last straw for the Japanese was a brilliant Fourteenth Air Force raid on the Shinchiku Aerodrome on Formosa on 25 November 1943. The success of this raid and the ease with which it had penetrated Japanese air defenses on Formosa demonstrated the necessity of destroying American air power in China. The subsequent presence of the B-29s was an added incentive. In December 1943 General Hata of the China Expeditionary Army ordered an immediate air offensive against American air installations to be followed by a massive army offensive against east China. As plans progressed, the scope of the offensive was enlarged to 'forestall the bombing of the homeland by American B-29s based at Kweilin and Liuchow' and to 'destroy the backbone of the Chinese army and force increased deterioration of the political regime'. It was also intended to establish a corridor between Manchuria/North China and Hanoi in French Indochina as an interior line of communication which would be relatively safe from air attack. The Fourteenth Air Force bases in East China were also to be eliminated. Code named 'Ichigo', this offensive was the largest Japanese land operation of the war and ultimately involved 620,000 Japanese troops. If Ichigo was successful, the next step was to be a drive up the Yangtze valley on the Chinese capital of Chungking, whose fall would have decisively taken China out of the war.

As the massive preparations for the offensive clearly indicated what was to come, the Allied forces in China found themselves in a desperate plight. Over 200,000 of the best troops were committed to the Burma campaign. Stock-

piling for the B-29 project had left the Fourteenth Air Force generally short of supplies and acutely short of fuel at the threatened bases in East China; 200 of the 400 operational planes were also supporting the Burma campaign. Chennault was refused use of either the B-29s or the B-29 stockpiles and in April was even ordered to divert planes to the protection of a B-29 base at Chungking. Poorly led and equipped, the Chinese were incapable of halting the offensive which began in April 1944 without the support of the Fourteenth Air Force.

The Japanese offensive roiled forward quickly and on 18 June took Changsha, a major rail center and gateway to the

Fourteenth Air Force bases in east China. The drive then stalled for 49 days before the key city of Henyang, center of the Hankow-Hanoi axis. Despite the heroic defense put up by the Chinese General Hsueh Yueh, Henyang fell and by October the Manchuria-Hanoi corridor was completed. East China was isolated and the political prestige of Chiang's regime had suffered a disastrous blow. For the Japanese, Ichigo had been a most satisfactory operation. The drive on Chungking was to open in the new year.

It was obvious that the crisis created by Ichigo required that the Chinese troops in Burma and Yunnan be returned to defend east China posthaste. The cargo

BELOW LEFT: The long retreat through Burmese jungles was arduous for the 15th Army. Supplies had run thin to the point of non-existence, and Mutaguchi's men were left to fight on against an Allied force which was well supplied and growing in strength and morale in 1944–45.

BELOW: British and Indian troops return to Rangoon in May 1945. Paratroop assaults followed by seaborne landings supported by the Royal Navy freed the Burmese capital from Japanese rule.

planes of the hump run were initially used to transport the 25,000 men and 2200 horses of the Chinese Sixth Army to assist in the defense of Chihkiang, a key city controlling the approaches to Chungking. Organizing the defenses of Chungking, Wedemeyer soon requested that most of the remaining Chinese troops in Burma be returned. Thus a further 25,000 well-equipped and battle-tested troops were airlifted to Chungking. These forces became the nucleus of a larger force organized by Wedemeyer to counter the expected renewal of the Japanese offensive. In April 1945 the Japanese did renew their attack on Chihkiang but, supported by the full might of the Fourteenth Air Force, the American-trained and equipped Chinese troops had decisively defeated the Japanese and caused the beginning of a general enemy withdrawal by mid-May. Wedemeyer had demonstrated what Stilwell had denied – that a coordinated ground and air defense could defeat a superior enemy.

As a theater of operations, CBI was central neither to the Japanese nor to the Allies. The Japanese preferred to make peace rather than war in China, while both Chiang and the Allies believed that the war would be won elsewhere. The real function of China in the war was not to launch great offensives against Japan but simply to occupy the attention of over a million Japanese soldiers, soldiers who might have made a significant contribution to the defense of the Pacific had the leaders of the Japanese Army not been so enthralled with their China adventure. Burma was of marginal importance to the Japanese, serving mainly to protect the flank of Malaya and politically as a puppet state. The Americans thought Burma was important because through it lay the only line of land communication with China. The British concern with Burma stemmed partly from a desire to restore the military prestige lost in the débâcle of 1942, but mainly from a desire to restore their imperial position after the war both in Burma and in Malaya.

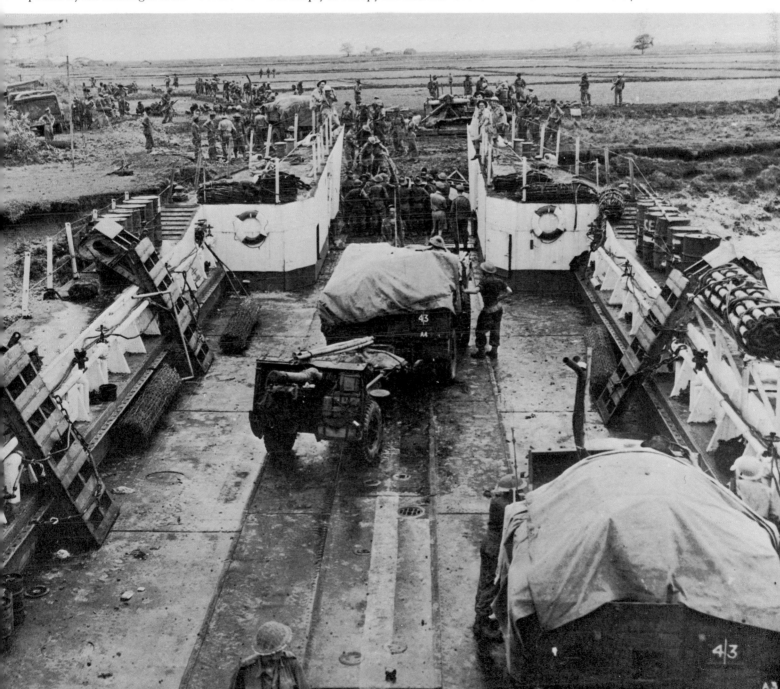

# BEHIND BARBED WIRE

BELOW LEFT: British Prisoner of War is held by a rope in a Japanese compound. In many instances treatment of POWs was petty and tyrannical to the point of absurdity.

Soldiers of the Imperial Japanese Army are remembered for their bravery and endurance – qualities which all men respect. But the Japanese are also remembered for their maltreatment of prisoners of war – behavior which the Occidental mind abhors. War is a savage business; yet it is difficult for the Westerner to relate the callous neglect and degradation of Japan's wretched prisoners of war with the creed which fostered the chivalrous spirit of the old samurai. Nevertheless the two were related. The Emperor's soldiers, born and nurtured in a system which revered heroism and the noble calling of the warrior, were taught that military honor dictated suicide rather than surrender. If they died bravely in battle, they were told, they would be rewarded; but if they were taken prisoner they would be severely punished. Japanese training manuals warned that 'those becoming prisoners of war will suffer the death penalty.' Thus it was only to be expected that the attitude of many Japanese troops towards their enemies reflected this philosophy. According to the penalties and social taboos attaching to their own survival as prisoners of war, many Japanese soldiers tended to regard their captives as men who were virtually dead anyway; consequently their living conditions were of no importance. Moreover, as British, Dutch and American prisoners of war were members of the white race that in the past had bullied and patronized Asiatics, they felt that their prisoners' loss of face should be made apparent to themselves and to the peoples which Japan was supposed to be liberating. Thus the beatings, the mass punishments, the tortures, beheadings, callous neglect and murder of Allied prisoners of war could be explained away in terms of the military code, *Bushido*. Unfortunately the sadistic complexes of individual guards also often played a part, and the circumstances of some of the bayonetings and beheadings of recaptured prisoners suggest that those who took part in these dastardly crimes were motivated by something more than a sense of duty.

In the first six months of the war – before the Imperial Army drove the British and American forces out of all their possessions in the Far East, occupied the Philippines and Singapore and penetrated the frontier of India – strict Imperial Army discipline governed the running of Japanese POW camps. Precise instructions were issued covering all aspects of camp routine and offences were usually punished on the spot by the culprit having his face slapped or being beaten for a length of time which depended on the culprit's so-called crime. Most Allied prisoners suffered face slapping at some time or other, and although some men's eardrums suffered damage the punishment lay rather in humiliation than in physical injury. Once a man had been thoroughly humiliated, however, further instances became relative and unimportant and the Japanese guards found it necessary to impose more brutal punishment.

Attempting to escape – something which the Geneva Convention specifically accepts as a POW's duty – was regarded by the Japanese as a crime which merited death. However, in an attempt to deter would-be escapers after the capture of Hong Kong, the Japanese authorities in Shamshuipo camp insisted that all prisoners there should sign a pledge not to escape. All the inmates of the camp were paraded for a mass signing of the pledge, and the Japanese guards mounted machine guns for the occasion. British troops could not sign such an undertaking, the senior British officer said at the outset. But he was compelled to change his mind and the majority of the camp eventually signed the form 'under duress'. The few brave, determined or headstrong individuals who continued to refuse were taken away to the Kempeitai barracks, where tortures and deprivations persuaded most of them to change their minds and sign. When they returned to Shamshuipo they were physical wrecks. And of those who are presumed to have held out, nothing more was ever heard.

A similar attempt was made to extract an understanding not to escape from POWs in Singapore. When General Percival accepted the Japanese surrender terms in February 1942, the British troops were ordered to assemble at Changi, and 50,000 weary captives trudged along the winding road from Singapore city to the concentration area. At first the Japanese placed no restrictions on movement within the area designated as a POW camp, and the prisoners were allowed to roam over the whole eastern end of Singapore island. On 12 March 1942, however, prisoners were ordered to wire themselves in, and a No-Man's land, separating the POW camps from the mainland, was established. This area was patroled by Japanese soldiers and turn-

BELOW: British and Australian POWs in a lumber camp in Thailand. Conditions were harsh, the weather brutally hot and the food scarce. The prisoners here were cutting wood for ties on the infamous Burma-Siam railroad.

BOTTOM: Members of the dreaded Kempeitai and British POWs after the fall of Singapore. Some of the men went to Changi Prison. Others found their way to the Burma-Siam railway. Many never returned from the war.

LEFT: An Australian prisoner paints a bridge. The Japanese were not ashamed of their treatment of prisoners. This one appeared on the cover of a fortnightly Japanese magazine published during the war.

BELOW: American troops display the white flag as they go into Japanese captivity after the fall of Corregidor in 1942. Many never made it to POW camp thanks to the infamous 'death march'.

coat Sikhs. With the passage of time the attitude of these guards hardened, and the Sikhs in particular took advantage of their position to make increasingly absurd demands on the POWs.

In August 1942 General Percival and most of the other senior British and Australian officers were taken away to Japan, and Major-General Fukuye and a large administrative staff began to establish a proper POW camp regime at Changi. Hardly had Fukuye arrived than four escaped prisoners were brought in. Two of these had got away from Bukit Timah five months previously and had rowed 200 miles in a small boat before re-arrest. The Japanese reaction was an announcement that all prisoners in Changi would be given an opportunity to sign a statement: 'I, the undersigned, hereby solemnly swear on my honor that I will not, under any circumstances, attempt to escape'. As at Shamshuipo, the senior British Officer pointed out that POWs were not allowed to give their parole and he and his fellow officers refused to sign. To a man the other ranks followed suit.

Two days passed, with no sign of the next Japanese move. Then, on the morning of 2 September, the senior commanders were ordered to witness the execution of the men who had tried to escape. The victims were dragged to Selarang Beach and ordered to dig their own graves. Corporal Breavington, one of the two Australians from Bukit Timah, pleaded that his comrade should be spared, saying that he ordered him to escape with him. His plea was rejected, and the Japanese followed up this cold-blooded execution with an order that all the British and Australian prisoners apart from those in hospital were to assemble on Selarang Barrack square. This assembly, ordered at midday, had to be finished in five hours, and that night 15,400 men were crammed on the square with only two water taps and totally inadequate latrine facilities. There they were kept for three days until the British and Australian commanders ordered their men to sign the undertaking not to escape.

In the event very few Allied prisoners of war ever attempted to escape; a European's color, appearance and language distinguishes him from the local population in Eastern countries, and practically all of those who succeeded in getting away from Japanese prison camps were recaptured and executed. Three British officers escaped from the Shamshuipo (Hong Kong) camp in 1942, swimming across Laichikoh Bay. After an adventurous tramp through Japanese occupied territory – during which they were attacked and robbed by Chinese bandits – they eventually reached a unit of the Nationalist Chinese and eight weeks after their escape from Shamshuipo they arrived in India. But for the great majority there was no alternative but to accept and try to endure captivity. Not that everyone even got as far as a prison camp. Many Americans captured by General Homma's forces in the Bataan

RIGHT: British soldiers go into internment after the fall of Hong Kong on Christmas Day, 1941.

OVERLEAF: Chinese prisoner is blindfolded and lashed to a post prior to his summary execution. Note the lines drawn across the picture. The Japanese, who were particularly brutal in their treatment of Chinese loyal to the Nationalist or Communist cause, suppressed photographs of this type during the war. They were only released decades afterwards.

Peninsula and at Corregidor perished on their way to the camps which the Japanese had designated for their occupation. Following their surrender these men were compelled to march 135 miles in tropical heat, and it took them 11 days to do so. For five days they were given no food at all, and then only a handful of rice on the days that followed. During short rest periods they were made to sit on the road under the full glare of the tropical sun and were not allowed to seek shade. When they marched through occupied villages, Japanese troops would line the route and beat the prisoners with sticks as they marched by.

Prisoners shipped from one region to another in Japanese freighters suffered equally as much. Battened down in the ships' holds in tropical heat, or packed together on the decks, unprotected from heavy tropical rain, they traveled in appalling conditions. On these 'hellship' moves only meager rations of rice and fish were provided, sometimes not properly cooked, and there was rarely enough water to go round. Diarrhoea and dysentery spread because the prisoners had to eat below decks, and the points from which the food was distributed were usually sited near what served as latrines. Most accounts speak of the filth, foul smells, lice and other vermin among which the prisoners were forced to live, sometimes for journeys lasting a month. On one voyage from Ambon to Java 21 died in a draft of 217, and it is a wonder that the mortality rate was not higher on some of the longer passages. Many of the prisoners did manage to keep an outward show of cheerfulness, but the revolting conditions, the intense heat, the endless waiting for food and water, and the nervous strain when Allied aircraft passed overhead made the voyages seem like prolonged nightmares to those who experienced them.

By 1942 the Japanese had a huge reserve of POW labor and they decided to use it to build the notorious Siam railway connecting Moulmein with Bangkok. Small advance parties of prisoners were sent from Singapore to Bampong in June 1942 to build transit camps to receive the main labor parties which followed. These were formed mainly in Singapore as battalions, each about 600 strong, from prisoners in the Changi POW camps.

After a week of travel in a steel goods wagon the prisoners were in poor shape. Herded 32 or more in a wagon, they could not lie down, and the intense tropical heat turned the wagons into ovens. Many of them were therefore not fit for the marches that followed. Eleven to thirteen miles a day over muddy jungle tracks through torrential rain caused most of the prisoners considerable distress. Stragglers were beaten up, food was poor, and some of the men – who were at first thought fortunate in being taken part of the way by barge up the Kwei Noi River – received no food at all while on board. The combination of poor food and physical exhaustion during these northward treks was the beginning of much illness that ended fatally for many of the men concerned.

They now found themselves in areas where the monsoon rains which had been pouring down for five or six months had converted jungle clearings into quagmires knee-deep in stinking mud. The camp-site clearings were on the east bank of the Kwei Noi River where the Japanese planned to lay the railway. Exhausted as they were from the march the prisoners were set to work to build coolie-type huts. These were bamboo structures about 100 yards long and eight yards wide roofed with attap palm leaves and fitted on each side for the length of the hut with 6-foot wide sleeping platforms of lashed bamboo. The task of building such a camp, making it habitable for 1000 – 2000 men and ensuring sufficient cookhouse and latrine accomodation, was a big one. But the majority of prisoners in these parties were put on to road and railway construction work long before proper living accommodation was completed. Water came from the river, and because much that was drunk could not be filtered and boiled, men fell victim to infections carried down from camps further upstream. Rations were nearly always below official Japanese scales. Vegetables arrived in a rotting condition; most of the rice was magotty and mixed with all kinds of fish. Supplies of fish, meat, oil, salt and sugar were meager and men sometimes had to live months on end on little more than an ounce and a half of rice per day. The rice, the vegetables, and whatever else could be found to go with them, had to be cooked over bamboo fires in shallow 12-gallon containers. But there were not enough of these to go round. Nor were there enough cooks to do the work, because the Japanese would only permit one or two men to cook for a hundred prisoners.

On this diet the prisoners were required to clear the jungle, fell trees, make embankments, lay rails, and bridge rivers and torrents. To complete their 'norm' the Japanese railway engineer drove the prisoners from dawn till dusk – demanding from each camp a certain percentage of its strength irrespective of the numbers of sick. To make up the quotas men quite unfit for work were driven out, sometimes even carried out to work. The line, boasted some of the Japanese engineers, would be laid over the dead bodies of the prisoners.

During the first two or three months officers went out with the working parties in an effort to safeguard the men's interests. But they were consistently ignored by the Japanese in charge of the work, and if they had occasion to remonstrate with the latter, were often made the object of especially spiteful treatment. By December 1942 the Japanese had decided that officer prisoners should also work on the railway, and within a month parties of officers were laboring alongside the men and being treated as part of the POW labor force.

For those whose health broke down under these conditions of work there were only the most inadequate medical facilities. The region through which the Burma-Siam railway passes is generally regarded as one of the most unhealthy in the world. Yet there were very few Japanese doctors, and medical arrangements were left in the hands of Japanese soldiers who knew nothing of the hazards of the disease and sickness that ravaged the wretched prisoners. A hospital was created merely by setting aside one of the jungle huts and POW medical personnel with the labor force had to rely on whatever equipment they happened to have been able to retain and bring with them. Epidemics of malaria, dysentery and cholera could not be controlled because there were no drugs – or rather the Japanese would not provide the drugs. A great deal of essential medical equipment

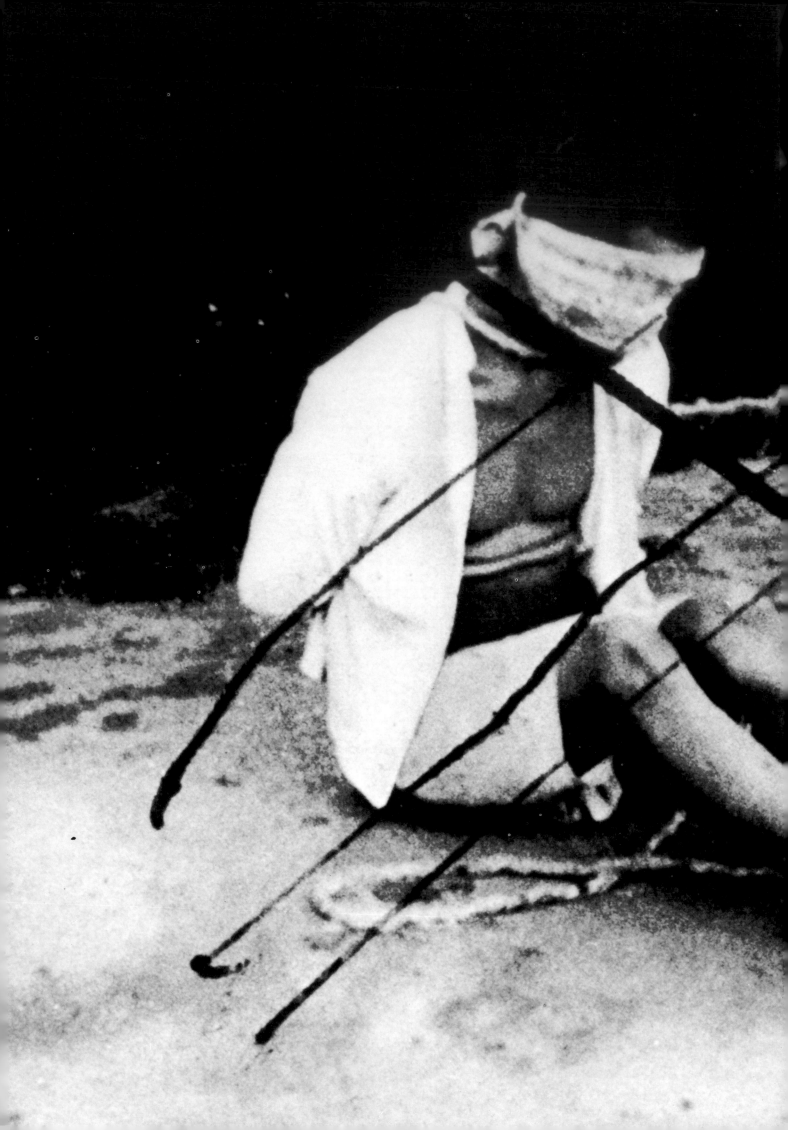

RIGHT: Members of the Kempeitai bandage a captured soldier's leg before he goes into confinement. There were many cases of humane treatment on the part of the Japanese captors as well.

OVERLEAF: But, particularly for the Chinese, this was the more common treatment. Chinese collaborators with the Nationalists are rounded up, beaten, and then executed. This photograph bears the marks of suppression by the Japanese military authorities.

was improvized, but it was not enough to save many thousands of lives.

Early in 1943 the Japanese decided that the railway was not being built fast enough and 10,000 more prisoners were ordered up from Singapore. More were sent up from the Dutch East Indies, and tens of thousands of Tamils, Chinese and Malays – men and women – were pressed into service as laborers. In addition to bringing up more workers, the Japanese increased their pressure on the whole labour force. From April until November 1943, the 'speedo' period, the Japanese engineers drove the Allied labor force mercilessly in an effort to complete the railway by the date set by their masters in Tokyo. In April conditions on the railway were hot and dry, with thick layers of dust everywhere; but May saw the onset of the monsoon, which continued until October. Ceaseless rain and thick mud soon made conditions for the workers doubly hard and turned their pitiful encampments of huts and tents into evil-smelling quagmires. Little account seems to have been taken of this in the demands of the Japanese: the daily task for one man could rise as high as moving three cubic yards of soil a distance of 300 yards through mud and then up an embankment 25 feet high. Tools and equipment were of poor quality and the earth had to be carried in bags or baskets or on stretchers. Work went on in some places until 11.30 at night, and for two or three months, some working teams hardly saw their camps in daylight. After roll-call at dawn they were marched off to work, and they did not return to camp until dark.

In June 1943 a senior Japanese officer in charge of POWs in Siam expressed the general attitude of the captors toward the sick of their work force: 'Those who fail in charge by lack of health is regarded as most shameful deed'. During the 'speedo' period, owing to exhaustion from overwork and semi-starvation, few of the workers were free from some kind of sickness. But as the sickness rate grew the Japanese increased their pressure. The threat to turn out all sick from the camp hospitals led to only those being admitted who were seriously ill. Men were forced to limp out to work on sticks and some were even carried on stretchers. Those who fell sick during work were liable to be severely and savagely punished. A prisoner stricken with a sudden attack of malaria might be stood up to his neck in a cold river; those who collapsed might be kicked or beaten; men with festering feet might be forced to work in the thorny jungle. Not until the railway was nearing completion were any of the seriously ill allowed to be evacuated to the so-called 'base-hospitals' in Siam and Burma. There, in hopelessly overcrowded conditions and what was described as 'pools of infection and gangrene', only the devotion, skill and enterprise of the POW medical staffs saved the lives of thousands of sufferers.

Reckless disregard of the health of the POWs by the Japanese decimated the labor force for the railway so quickly that only a small fraction of its original strength remained at the time of its completion. In the space of a year deaths among Allied prisoners on the railway amounted to something like a third of their number – or some 20,000 men out of a force of 60,000 or more. Groups working under particularly bad conditions had an even higher death rate than this. In addition large numbers of men were permanently disabled as a result of amputations or the after-effects of disease.

The Siam railway was Japan's biggest POW work project. But elsewhere in Japan's 'Co-Prosperity Sphere', prisoners were used to construct airfields. Many of these were on small islands in the Dutch Indies and no arrangements were made to accomodate or feed the POWs before they actually arrived. The treatment of a party of about 2000 officers and men which left Soerabaya in mid-April and spent 15 months in Haruku at Ambon takes its place with the worst examples of treatment in Burma and Siam. Many of the men were unfit before they left Java, and after a 2-week voyage in a 'hell-ship' they were totally unfitted to the heavy work of unloading the bombs and petrol to which they were set when their ships docked in the islands. Long hours of work on Haruku, inadequate food and no medical supplies rocketed the sick rate. By mid-May there were 700 patients in the improvized hospital on Haruku, mainly with dysentery and beri-beri. Besides reducing the rations for the sick the Japanese periodically drove out to work all those who were just able to stagger from the hospital and a policy of general intimidation was carried out with great brutality by some of the guards. In a little over seven months some 400 of the prisoners were dead.

Elsewhere in the Dutch East Indies all who could crawl out of the gates of the POW camps were made to work seven days a week from dawn to dusk. The tasks usually involved heavy manual labor, constructing airfield runways, building air-raid shelters, making roads, work in the sawmills and carpentry. Some of the few 'rest' days were filled in by compulsory labor in the camp gardens. Men who were considered to be idle were beaten, made to stand at attention in the hot sun for hours on end, hold heavy weights above their heads, or subjected to whatever other brutish punishment that sprang to the guards' minds.

Women POWs were interned in Sumatra, and although they were not compelled to do any work over and above that which the Japanese considered was related to their own maintenance and welfare, the latter was more than enough. It is also interesting to relate what the women had to do, with what could be expected of them under the terms of the Geneva Convention. The employment of POWs, the Convention provides, should be limited to those who are physically fit, and the work they do should be of a nature to maintain them 'in a good state of physical and mental health'. Age, sex and physical aptitudes of the individual prisoner are supposed to be taken into consideration when determining what job should be carried out by whom. Women, for example, should not be required to lift and move heavy loads. At Palembang a group of Australian Army nursing sisters captured on Banka Island soon found that the Japanese made few concessions for their sex, when they were ordered to unload and stack sacks of rice while the Japanese guards sat and smoked the cigarettes they had confiscated from Red Cross parcels intended for the nurses.

POWs transported to Japan were employed in shipyards and steelworks. In the Mitsubishi naval and shipbuilding yard at Yokohama the men worked from 7 am until 5 pm on all the heavy manual tasks connected with the building and overhauling of ships. In the Muoran Steel Works at Hakodate in the south of Hokkaido Island they worked similar hours for 13 days out of 14 shovelling coal and iron ore or in a repair shop for railway engines. Prisoners in a group of camps round Osaka in the South of Honshu Island were put to work constructing a dock. At Fukuoka other POWs were employed eleven hours a day in a factory making green carborundum, often working alongside high-temperature furnaces. At Zentsuji, on the island of Shikoku, the first batches of prisoners were employed

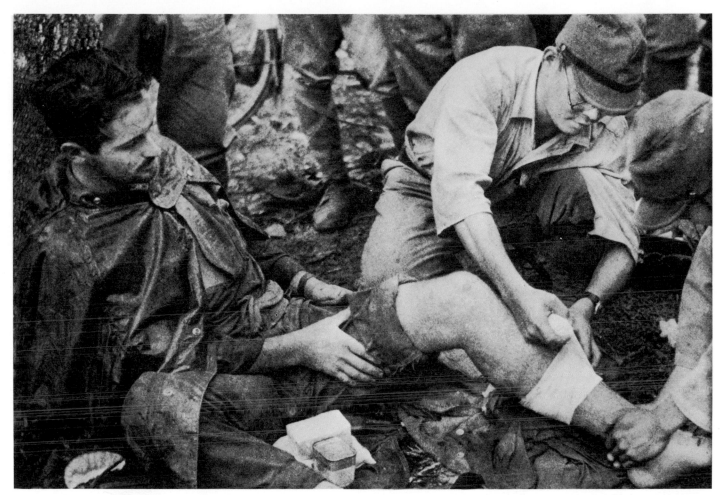

on agricultural projects, but in 1942 they were switched to railway yards and docks, loading grain and heavy military supplies – the latter being work specifically prohibited by the Geneva Convention.

Toward the end of the war some relaxation in the work program was permitted at a few of the larger camps, but other POWs were compelled to slog on up to the very day of Japan's capitulation. Few of the guards softened their treatment until news reached them of the Emperor's decision to stop the war, and the food everywhere did not improve until Allied aircraft were able to drop supplies on the camps. Apart from the fact that transport systems in Japan and Japanese occupied territories were in a state of complete chaos by August 1945, the Japanese had precious little food to distribute among themselves. In any event many of the wretched prisoners were past caring about work or food. Their physical condition had deteriorated to a state in which they no longer had the will to live. In the last two months of the war the death rate soared and working parties were busier than ever before burying their comrades.

To such men the news that two devastating bombs had been dropped on Hiroshima and Nagasaki and that Japan had capitulated was like a shot of adrenalin. To the majority of their guards, however, the Imperial Proclamation ordering the Japanese forces to lay down their arms came as a terrible shock. In

common with every other Japanese citizen they had been brought up to believe that nothing was more disgraceful than to surrender – either as an individual, as a group or as a country. It had also been impressed upon them that slavery in the service of the Allies would follow surrender. Despite all the setbacks in the field, the devastation and the disruption of communications, the morale of the troops away from where the battles were raging – the three million on the Japanese mainland in particular – was generally high up to this point. They believed that an Allied invasion of Japan would be repelled and enormous casualties inflicted on the enemy.

The future for Japan's POWs if the war had continued to the bitter end would unquestionably have been bleak. In the first place most of the Japanese guards had an indefinable fear of their captives. They had never understood how it was that such men, who in Japanese eyes were beneath contempt, could manage to retain shreds of dignity in the conditions to which they were subjected. No doubt more than a few of the guards who had been responsible for the death of prisoners by brutal treatment or sheer neglect, or who had degraded those who were still alive also wondered what their own future would be when the tables were turned and the captives became the captors. Of more general concern, however, was the fact that if the Allies had been forced to invade Japan, the Japanese

would have found it convenient to massacre the POWs – if for no other reason than that to guard and feed them would have interfered with the task of defending the 'sacred soil of Nippon'. Thus the Emperor's decision, provoked as it was by the terrible cremation of tens of thousands of Japanese at Hiroshima and Nagasaki, undoubtedly saved the lives of tens of thousands of POWs, just as it saved the lives of hundreds of thousands of Allied soldiers and almost certainly millions of Japanese – because if the Emperor had decided to fight on it is quite certain Japan would literally have fought to the last man.

In conclusion there must be some mention of the state of Japan's POWs when they were released from captivity. Generalization in such matters usually tends to be misleading because of individual circumstances and the enormous variety of conditions in the different camps. But the physical condition of almost every POW repatriated from the Far East was deplorable. Apart from the effects of malnutrition, many were suffering from tropical diseases such as malaria, dysentery and beri-beri. Many found that their eyesight had suffered; some had contracted physical handicaps; some others had aches and pains from which they are still suffering. The war has been over for many years now; the world has changed and Japan has changed. But such men find it difficult to forget their experiences of Japan and the Japanese.

# NUCLEAR HOLOCAUST

BELOW LEFT: Allied troops are welcomed into Shanghai during its liberation in September 1945. The posters over the street bear the likeness of Generalissimo Chiang Kai-shek, whose forces were flown in to re-occupy Shanghai by the Americans.

RIGHT: Japanese civilians crouch in doorways, ditches and along the sides of buildings as Allied planes begin their blanket bombardment of Tokyo.

FAR RIGHT: B-29s over Tokyo. The fire raids which the heavy bombing brought razed most of the city to the ground. More people died in these air strikes than in the two atomic attacks on Hiroshima and Nagasaki.

BOTTOM RIGHT: Firemen attempt to stop a blaze on the Ginza in the heart of Tokyo.

OVERLEAF: Piles of Japanese dead and rubble in the Honjo district of Tokyo. In this particular raid on 10 March 1945 which lasted two hours and 40 minutes, 334 B-29s dropped 190,000 bombs, leaving 85,000 dead in their wake.

By 1945 Allied forces were steadily pushing their way toward Japan, but victory was not yet in sight. Despite the continued success of Allied offensives across the Pacific, Japanese resistance was fierce and heavy casualties were suffered by American, Australian, British and Canadian forces fighting under the commands of MacArthur and Nimitz. The appearance of *kamikaze* units and their accelerated use against Allied forces not only increased such casualties but had a psychological impact on Allied leaders and strategists far exceeding the toll that such units extracted on the battle field.

American concern with regard to the toll in life and limb which would have to be sacrificed in obtaining victory over Japan was clearly in evidence when Allied leaders met in Yalta in February 1945. Although the agenda of the Yalta Conference was hardly limited to a discussion of the situation in the Pacific and the Far East, this was a major topic. The American Joint Chiefs had made it abundantly clear to President Roosevelt that a Russian commitment to enter the war against Japan was not only desirable but necessary if a victory over the Japanese was to be achieved without the greatest bloodletting of the war. This argument seemed to be confirmed by the reports of the Battle for Iwo Jima which was taking place even as the Yalta summit was in progress.

The Soviets had made a vague commitment to join the war against Japan as early as 1943 but only after victory over Germany was achieved or appeared imminent. Faced with intelligence estimates that an Allied effort to attack and occupy Japan might cost as many as a million casualties, Roosevelt and his advisors wished to have this vague commitment translated into reality and pressed hard to achieve this at Yalta. Stalin finally did agree to Soviet participation in the occupation of Japan but only on the condition that the Kuriles and southern Sakhalin be restored to Russian sovereignty and that Soviet commercial and strategic interests in Manchuria be recognized. For his part, Stalin promised to recognize the sovereignty of the Chinese Nationalists in Manchuria and to join in the war against Japan no later than three months after the surrender of Germany.

Although Roosevelt had succeeded in obtaining a pledge of Russian intervention against Japan, Allied military leaders were still concerned about the cost of final victory. Their concern and fear

was heightened by the terrible bloodbaths on Iwo Jima and Okinawa where the price of victory was over 75,000 men. If the Japanese were willing to sacrifice more than twice these numbers in defense of Iwo Jima and Okinawa, what might one expect them to do in defense of their homeland? Not even the intervention of the Soviets served to allay the fears of Allied leaders. The specter of the occupation of Japan remained a bleak one.

Since Allied leaders were committed to the proposition of an unconditional victory over Japan, they chose not to respond to Japanese peace feelers made in April 1945 after the resignation of Prime Minister Tojo Hideki. Rather, they continued to plan for the final victory over the Japanese Empire. In so doing, all efforts were focused on achieving a final victory at the minimal possible cost, using whatever strategy and/or weaponry which might facilitate this victory. It was in this light that consideration of the use of the atomic weapon against the Japanese took place.

American scientists, assisted by refugees from Hitler's Germany and Mussolini's Italy, had long been laboring on development of the ultimate weapon – the atomic bomb. Although the race to develop atomic weapons had not been initiated with an eye toward using such weapons in the Pacific War, the fact was that the Manhattan Project was not completed until after the end of the European War. Indeed, it was when President Truman was at the Potsdam Conference that American scientists informed Secretary of War Stimson that their 'ultimate weapon' might be ready for use. Truman suggested as much to Churchill and Stalin, without going into great detail, at the Potsdam Conference.

The availability of the atomic bomb injected a new element into the discussion of how to obtain the final victory over Japan. American military leaders were nearly unanimous in supporting the use of these new weapons against Japan if the war could be brought to a speedier conclusion than had been anticipated at the start of 1945 when Allied strategy called for an all-out attack on the Japanese Islands in 1946. Considering the horrendous battlefield casualties suffered in Iwo Jima and Okinawa, such a position was not hard to understand. On the other hand, there were those who opposed the use of this new weapon, arguing that victory could be obtained without unleashing a nuclear holocaust if Japanese peace

feelers were responded to and if the Allies were willing to settle for less than unconditional surrender.

Debate over use of the atomic bomb against Japan continued from mid-April to 1 June 1945, at which time a special commission recommended use of the weapon to President Truman. Despite the protest and warnings of some of the men who had worked on the Manhattan Project, the President chose to accept the recommendation of his commission that the new weapon be used against Japan as opposed to some demonstration of its power elsewhere in the Pacific. He shared this view with Churchill in July. Writing after the war, Churchill summed up his reaction to Truman's revelation in a manner typical of the general reaction to this new opportunity:

> We seemed suddenly to have become possessed of a merciful abridgement of the slaughter in the Far East. . . . To bring the war to an end, to avoid indefinite butchery, to give peace to the world, to lay a healing hand upon its people by a manifestation of overwhelming power at the cost of a few explosions, seemed, after all our toils and perils, a miracle of deliverance.

While President Truman was discussing the atomic bomb with his advisors, Japanese leaders stepped up their effort to find a diplomatic solution to the war. The new government, headed by Admiral Kantaro Suzuki, a man who was privately known to favor an end to the war, attempted to ask the Soviet Ambassador in Tokyo to convey a message to his government in Moscow asking Stalin to mediate an end to the Pacific War. This effort followed a similar but short-lived attempt to have the Swedish government play a similar role. Although the Soviets seemed to show no particular enthusiasm for this suggestion, some Japanese leaders

persisted to hope the Russians would carry their message to the other Allies. Other Japanese leaders steadfastly opposed this effort, preferring to fight to the death without surrender to Allied forces.

On 26 July 1945, even as Japan's frantic search for some way of effecting a cease-fire was in progress, Allied leaders issued the Potsdam Declaration which defined the terms under which the war might be ended. The Potsdam Declaration called for nothing less than an unconditional surrender of Japanese forces, an Allied occupation of Japan, and the dismantling of the Japanese Empire. For the Japanese, even those of a somewhat moderate persuasion, the terms demanded by the Allies as the price for peace were unacceptable. Indeed, the Potsdam Declaration strengthened the hands of the hawks in Tokyo who wished to go down fighting and brought an end, at least for the moment, to further effort to find a diplomatic solution to the war.

Since the Imperial Japanese Government did not respond affirmatively to the Potsdam Declaration, Allied leaders continued to prepare for the final strike against Japan. There seems to be little indication that the Soviets had passed along clear knowledge about the feeble effort of Suzuki to make peace but even if they had, it is doubtful that the Allies would have accepted anything less than an unconditional surrender from their foes. With their forces poised for the attack, the Soviets promising to join the fray, and the atom bomb ready for possible use against Japan, there appeared to be no reason to accept anything less than total victory.

After considerable discussion, President Truman approved plans to use atomic weapons against Japan. On 6 August 1945, the first atomic weapon ever to be used in modern warfare was

FAR LEFT: A Japanese painting of the terror of a strategic bombing attack. An air raid warden tries to direct civilians to a shelter.

LEFT: Wrecked aircraft on an airfield in the Japanese Home Islands demonstrate the ascendacy achieved by the Allied air forces by the time of the Japanese surrender.

BELOW: Marines of the Soviet Fleet hoist their flag over Port Arthur which was captured by the Soviets in their brief war against Japan in Manchuria in August 1945.

BOTTOM: The American battleship *Missouri* at anchor in 1944. The Japanese surrender was signed aboard the *Missouri* in 1945.

BELOW: Japanese air raid warden scans the skies before announcing the all clear signal in Tokyo.

RIGHT: Casualties are aided in an underground bunker during the air raids.

LEFT: Life goes on underground, as primitive cooking units were set up to feed civilians in the bunkers.

BOTTOM: Wreckage of the aircraft carrier *Amagi*, sunk at Kure harbor on 24 July 1945.

dropped on the city of Hiroshima, destroying the city and killing over 80,000 people. Three days later, on 9 August, a second atom bomb was dropped on Nagasaki with an equally devastating impact. Speaking to the American public shortly after the first bomb was dropped, President Truman justified its use in the following manner:

> Having found the bomb, we have used it. We have used it against those who attacked us without warning at Pearl Harbor. . . . We have used it in order to shorten the agony of war, in order to save thousands and thousands of Americans. *We shall continue to use it until we completely destroy Japan's capacity to make war. Only a Japanese surrender will stop us.*

Although the atomic bombings of Hiroshima and Nagasaki had resulted in horrendous casualties, they had not resulted in a mentality of surrender in Tokyo. Although the Emperor's advisors understood the need to end the war, they were divided as to whether to accept the conditions for surrender described in the Potsdam Declaration or to fight on until

LEFT: Japanese weep openly as they hear the capitulation broadcast of the Emperor on 15 August 1945. His voice had never before been heard by the Japanese public, and only after he made his announcement did the Japanese accept the enormity of their defeat.

RIGHT: The bombing of Osaka Castle on the last day of hostilities, 14 August 1945.

BELOW: The legacy of the Japanese War Machine: Hiroshima, 6 August 1945.

such time as the Allies showed some sign of being willing to accept something less than unconditional surrender. As this question was being debated in Tokyo, the Soviets entered the war.

On 8 August 1945 the Soviet Union declared war on Japan. One day later, on the day when the second atomic bomb was dropped on Nagasaki, Russian forces entered Manchuria, overrunning the Japanese protectorate within less than two weeks. Ironically, the Soviet intervention, which Roosevelt had sought so vigorously at Yalta, came when it was no longer necessary from the American point of view. Indeed, many Americans, President Truman among them, viewed Russia's belated declaration of war against Japan with alarm, fearing that the Soviets would gain a foothold in East Asia from which it would be difficult to dislodge them. This was one of the reasons why Truman and his advisors appeared so eager to use the atomic bomb against Japan, hoping to secure a Japanese surrender before Russia entered the war.

The coincidence of the bombing of Nagasaki and the Soviet intervention in Manchuria forced the hand of the Japanese, causing Emperor Hirohito to break the deadlock between those who called for continued resistance to the Allies and those who called for peace at any price. At his urging, the Imperial Government sent a note to the Allies on 10 August 1945 calling for a cease-fire and subsequent peace talks. This note stated:

> The Japanese Government is ready to accept the terms enumerated in the joint declaration which was issued at Potsdam on 26 July 1945 . . . with the understanding that this declaration does not comprise any demand which prejudices the right of His Majesty as sovereign.

On 11 August Allied leaders replied to the Japanese note, responding to their request that the Imperial institution be maintained as follows:

> The ultimate form of the government of Japan shall, in accordance with the Potsdam Declaration, be established by the freely expressed will of the Japanese people.

Clearly, the Allied response contained no promise that Imperial prerogatives would continue to be recognized in the postwar period. Such being the case, diehards within the Japanese government renewed their call for a fight to the finish, forcing Emperor Hirohito to intervene once again. At the risk of losing the very powers that made his intervention in the debate over acceptance of Allied terms for peace so important, Hirohito announced acceptance of an unconditional surrender to the Japanese people on 15 August:

> Despite the best that has been done by everyone, the war situation has developed not necessarily to Japan's advantage. . . . In order to avoid further bloodshed, perhaps even the total extinction of human civilization, we shall have to endure the unendurable, to suffer the insufferable.

On the following day, 16 August 1945, Japanese forces were instructed to lay down their arms and a new government, headed by an Imperial Prince, was formed in Tokyo to prepare for the formal surrender.

Japan formally surrendered to the Allies on 2 September 1945. After almost nine years of being at war, Japan was at peace but the legacies of war were to be found everywhere. The country had been devastated by Allied air raids. Japan's urban centers were in shambles. In Tokyo alone, over 700,000 buildings had been destroyed during the war and the population of the city had shrunk from 6.5 million at the start of the conflict in 1937 to approximately 3 million at the end of the war. Frightful as the physical destruction was, economic dislocation was even more alarming.

By 1945 the Japanese economy had totally broken down. Industrial pro-

FAR LEFT: General of the Army Douglas MacArthur signs the surrender of Japan aboard the USS *Missouri*, 2 September 1945. World War II was over.

BELOW LEFT: Japanese soldier comes home from the war.

ductivity had fallen to one-third of that recorded in 1930 and worse still, agricultural output had similarly declined. Food was in such short supply that desperate city dwellers literally invaded the countryside in search of rice or paid exhorbitant sums to black marketeers to provide sustenance for their families. Prized possessions and family heirlooms were regularly bartered for food, and once such possessions were gone many had to resort to theft. However, despite this growing chaos, there were still those who opposed surrender. Fortunately, such people were in the minority and their sense of honor which led them to *hara kiri* eliminated many of the reactionaries from political life. Thus, when the Allied occupation of Japan was initiated, it did not encounter serious resistance.

The majority of the Japanese people accepted defeat and enemy occupation with a resignation and stoic acceptance that surprised their enemies. Unlike the Germans, who sought at almost all levels to place the blame for their predicament on others, the Japanese, whether of high or low station, did not seek to evade responsibility for what had happened between 1937 and 1945. Accepting the inevitable, the Japanese were able to cooperate with occupation forces in a manner unique in the history of warfare.

When MacArthur's army of occupation arrived in Japan in the autumn of 1945, it encountered no overt resistance. To many of those in this occupation force, veterans of the bitter Pacific campaigns, the passivity with which the Japanese accepted the occupation seemed beyond belief. Conversely, the Japanese, who had been led to expect an orgy of carnage and rape in the wake of an Allied attack only weeks before the final surrender, were equally surprised at the discipline and order of occupation forces. Within weeks after the end of hostilities, both sides were cooperating to rebuild the country and reshape her institutions.

Despite the fact that the occupation of Japan was an Allied effort, it was, in fact, an American show. Unlike the situation in Germany after the war, the occupation of Japan was an orderly affair with only one of the powers, the United States, dictating and directing the recovery effort. In no small way, this fact contributed to a reasonably amicable and trouble-free period of postwar adjustment, during which Japan, like the proverbial phoenix, rose from her own ashes. History provides us with few similar phenomena.

# ACKNOWLEDGEMENTS

The editor would like to thank the following people for their help in preparing this book: first and foremost, Mr. Masami Tokoi, who helped collect the rare Japanese illustrations and photographs which are found throughout *The Japanese War Machine*. His translations of Japanese captions proved invaluable. Special thanks are due to Mr. Tadao Nakada for the use of material from his book *Imperial Japanese Army and Navy: Uniforms and Equipment*. I would like to thank Helen Downton for her technical illustrations, as well as Jinbo Terushi, who prepared some of the aircraft line drawings. Charles Haberlein helped collect material in Washington for the

illustrations and photographs. John Kirk prepared the aircraft charts to accompany his article. Col. A. J. Barker prepared additional charts for infantry weapons, artillery and tanks, for which I am grateful, and I would like to thank Ian Hogg for vetting some technical points on small arms and artillery. Richard Natkiel of *The Economist* prepared all the maps. Susan Piquemal prepared the index. Last, but by no means least, since his stalwart efforts turn Bison Books from assorted illustrations and galley proofs into cohesive volumes, David Eldred deserves my thanks and the congratulations of all contributors for designing *The Japanese War Machine*.    *S. L. Mayer*

## PICTURE CREDITS

**National Archive:** 4–5, 17 (top), 20–21, 21 (top), 95, 137, 141, 144–145, 146–147, 170–171, 171, 174, 175 (top), 178–179, 184, 186 (bottom), 198 (bottom), 201 (top), 202 (top), 202–203 (bottom), 204–205, 209 (center), 246–247 (bottom), 248–249.
**Robert Hunt Library:** 2–3, 6, 7, (bottom), 9 (bottom), 11, 14–15, 17, 18–19 (all 5), 20, 21, (bottom), 23 (bottom), 24 (both), 27 (center), 26, 27, 28, 30, 31 (top 2), 32 (below), 33 (top), 38, 40 (bottom), 42, 43, 43 (both), 44, 45 (below right), 46 (right), 48, 49 (bottom right), 50 (center), 59, 66–67, 67 (bottom), 68 (below left), 75 (top), 92, 93, 93 (both), 101 (bottom), 107, 108 (top), 110–111 (both), 116–117, 118–119 (bottom), 122–123, 124–125 (top), 132–133, 136, 136–137, 145, 152 (center), 152–153, 154–155, 155 (all 4), 156, 157 (both), 158 (all 3), 159 (both),

172, 172–173, 173 (center), 188, 192, 193, 194 (both), 199 (bottom), 206–207 (bottom), 212–213, 213, 215 (both), 216, 216–217, 218 (both), 219, 221 (all 4), 228 (top), 246, 250–251.
**US Navy:** 1, 4–5, 8, 9 (top 2), 10–11, 12–13 (both), 16, 21, 22, 22–23, 23 (top), 30–31, 40 (top), 72, 72–73, 74 (center), 79 (all 4), 80–81 (2), 83 (both), 86–87, 88–89 (2), 90, 90–91, 92 (both), 97, 104, 104–105, 114–115, 128–129, 129, 141 (top 2), 148–149, 149 (both), 150–151, 151, 152 (left), 160–161, 163 (both), 164–165 (both), 166–167, 175 (left and bottom), 177 (insets), 181 (top), 184, 185 (top), 191, 192 (both), 192, 194–195, 198 (top), 200, 201, 201 (below), 202–203 (top).
**US Army:** 58 (both), 58–59, 60, 60–61, 61, 62 (both), 62–63, 63 (both), 173, 209 (bottom), 218–219.

**US Marine Corps:** 175 (right).
**Novosti Press Agency:** 247.
**Mainichi Newspaper Company:** 25 (all 4), 27 (top 2), 29, 31, (left), 32 (top 2), 33 (bottom), 34, 34–35, 35 (both), 36–37 (both), 37, 38 (bottom), 39 (all 3), 41 (all 4), 47, 73, 74, (right), 94, 94–95, 96, 98 (both), 98–99, 101 (top 3), 102–103, 108 (bottom), 109 (top), 112, 115, 118, 119 (left), 147, 161 (2), 164, 170, 176, 177, 178, 179, 180, 181, 195, 195–196, 196 (all 3), 199 (top), 200, 202 (bottom), 204, 205, 206, 206–207, 207 (both), 208, 210–211, 214, 222–223, 223 (both), 229, 230, 232, 233 (both), 234 (bottom), 235, 236–237, 239, 240–241, 243 (all 3), 244–245, 246–247 (top), 248 (both), 249, 250, 251, 252–253.
**Courtesy of Masami Tokoi:** 38 (right), 45 (top 2 and bottom), 46 (top and bottom), 48 (top and bottom), 48–49, 49 (top left), 50–51

(7), 52–53 (6), 55 (both), 66, 68–69 (2), 71, 119 (right), 120–121, 122–123, 124 (2), 125 (3), 128 (all 6), 130 (all 3), 131 (all 5), 132, 133 (all 3), 134, 140, 161 (2), 225 (both), 229 (below), 234 (top).
**Courtesy of A. J. Barker:** 50 (top center), 51 (right), 54 (top).
**Courtesy of Mr. Tadao Nakada** from his book *Imperial Japanese Army and Navy: Uniforms and Equipment:* 7 (top 2), 49 (bottom left), 53 (center right), 57 (center), 60 (left), 64 (all 3), 65, 69.
**Courtesy of Jinbo Terushi:** 124 (2), 131 (2), 134 (2), 140 (2), 142 (4).
**Conway Picture Library:** 74–75, 85 (2).
**Bison Picture Library:** 81 (2), 85, 86, 89, 112–113, 168–169, 176–177, 180–181, 182 (both), 182–183, 183, 185 (bottom), 186 (top), 186–187, 187 (both), 188–189, 231, 242, 252.

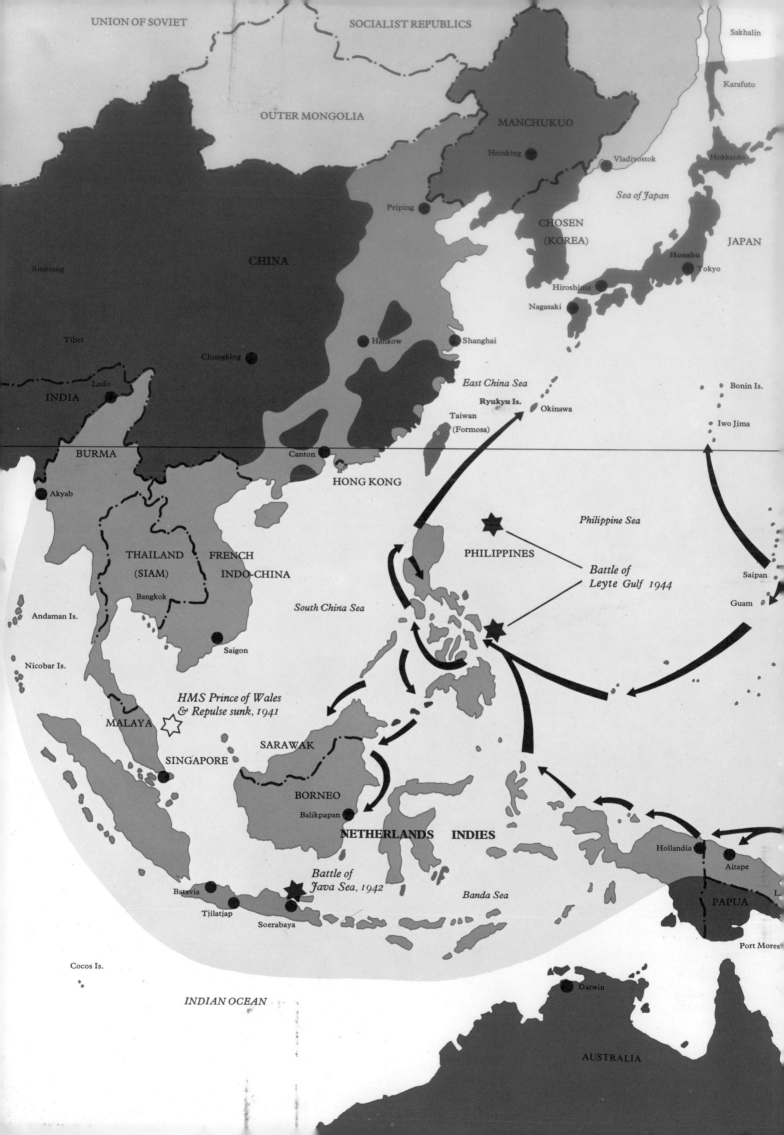